VOICES from EARLY AMERICA

T. N. Pollio

Mechanicsburg, PA USA

Published by Sunbury Press, Inc.
Mechanicsburg, Pennsylvania

www.sunburypress.com

Copyright © 2024 by T. N. Pollio.
Cover Copyright © 2024 by Sunbury Press, Inc.

Sunbury Press supports copyright. Copyright fuels creativity, encourages diverse voices, promotes free speech, and creates a vibrant culture. Thank you for buying an authorized edition of this book and for complying with copyright laws by not reproducing, scanning, or distributing any part of it in any form without permission. You are supporting writers and allowing Sunbury Press to continue to publish books for every reader. For information contact Sunbury Press, Inc., Subsidiary Rights Dept., PO Box 548, Boiling Springs, PA 17007 USA or legal@sunburypress.com.

For information about special discounts for bulk purchases, please contact Sunbury Press Orders Dept. at (855) 338-8359 or orders@sunburypress.com.

To request one of our authors for speaking engagements or book signings, please contact Sunbury Press Publicity Dept. at publicity@sunburypress.com.

FIRST SUNBURY PRESS EDITION: December 2024

Set in Adobe Garamond | Interior design by Crystal Devine | Cover by Lawrence Knorr | Edited by Lawrence Knorr.

Publisher's Cataloging-in-Publication Data
Names: Pollio, T. N., author.
Title: Voices from early America / T. N. Pollio.
Description: First trade paperback edition. | Mechanicsburg, PA : Sunbury Press, 2024.
Summary: This book preserves the words and experiences of Colonial and Victorian Era Americans, as preserved in their actual diaries, letters, journals and memorabilia. Our forebears certainly dressed and acted differently than us, their descendents. But their emotions and perspectives on life were virtually identical to our own. These are their stories.
Identifiers: ISBN 979-8-88819-253-5 (softcover).
Subjects: HISTORY / United States / 19th Century | BIOGRAPHY & AUTOBIOGRAPHY / Historical.

Designed in the USA
0 1 1 2 3 5 8 13 21 34 55

For the Love of Books!

Cover Art: New York Street Scene, c. 1893 by Frederick Childe Hassam

For Isabella Ann

CONTENTS

Acknowledgments *vii*
Prologue *ix*
Introduction *1*

PART I	THE VICTORIAN ERA	9
1.	Marital Relations in the Age of Unenlightenment	*19*
2.	Early American Technology	*22*
3.	Rural Life in the 18th and 19th Centuries	*27*
4.	Roadways and Transportation	*32*
5.	Closeness to the Food Chain	*38*
6.	Maple Sugaring	*41*
7.	Harvest Festivals and Husking Bees	*43*
8.	Agricultural Fairs	*46*
9.	A Victorian Family in New England	*50*
10.	Shaker Villages of New Hampshire	*62*

PART II	JEFFERSON COUNTY & THE NORTH COUNTRY	65
11.	Memories of the Old Homestead	*70*
12.	Diaries from the North Country	*75*
13.	The Story of Hattie and Frank	*81*
14.	Southern Pines and Hot Springs	*136*
15.	Thousand Island Park	*139*
16.	Evangelicalism and the Methodist Faith	*146*
17.	Temperance Movements	*153*

PART III	EVERYDAY LIFE IN THE VICTORIAN ERA	*159*
18.	The Chautauqua Movement	*162*
19.	Racial and Religious Intolerance	*165*
20.	Telephones, Radios and Phonographs	*172*

21.	Weather Readings	177
22.	Clothing and Laundry	180
23.	The Old Time General Store	187
24.	Health, Hygiene and Medicine	191
25.	The Scourge of Consumption	205
26.	Green's Diary, Almanac and Inimical Quackery	209
27.	Early Automobiles	212
28.	The Economy and Retail Sales	218
29.	Entertainment and Recreation	225
30.	The Farmer's Almanac	237
31.	Beckwith's Almanac in New Haven	245
32.	Death and Remembrance	254

Epilogue 264
Bibliography 268
About the Author 270

ACKNOWLEDGMENTS

IN recognition of the many people who provided invaluable information and material towards the completion of this study, I extend my heartfelt thanks. Without their assistance, the story of these Victorian Age people would not have been possible. Of course, without my inimical touch, all errors, omissions and *faux pas* contained herein would have been equally impossible.

I especially wish to thank David, Bilkey, and all the other descendants who gave permission to memorialize the life and times of their predecessors. David uncovered a number of period photographs for use in this publication and also provided invaluable data from his research into 19th century medical practices. Bilkey forwarded much historical and genealogical information regarding the North Country families to help flesh out the narrative. Judy in Adams dug up a treasure trove of material and supplied images of the memorial stained glass windows in the United Methodist Church. To the foresight of Lisa, the antique dealer is due the survival of much of the material that inspired these stories. Her simple trip down country roads unveiled a world of hidden wonders and rescued the burnt and tattered remains of Victorian Age people from certain oblivion.

Invaluable insights into genuine Americana were gleaned from the works of the late Eric Sloane, whose peerless watercolors and illustrations bring the world of old New England to life. His clear, concise explanations make otherwise inexplicable concepts like colonial engineering understandable to even the simplest minds, like mine. My gratitude goes out to Mrs. Charmaine Sloane-Thacker of the Eric Sloane Estate, as well as the staff of the Eric Sloane Museum in Kent, Connecticut.

Assistance was readily forthcoming from a number of other sources, including but not limited to The Hill Historical Society, Tilton Historical Society,

VOICES FROM EARLY AMERICA

Tilton School, New York Public Library, Canterbury Shaker Village, Enfield Shaker Museum, Thousand Island Park Association, Historical Association of Southern Jefferson County, and The Conference of Methodists in New York State. Thanks also to researchers in Hot Springs, Arkansas and Southern Pines, North Carolina, for information regarding the seasonal stays of New England and North Country "snow birds" during the 19th and early 20th centuries.

The fortunate thing about illustrations from this period is most are in the public domain. Unless otherwise specified, all remaining images are the property of the author. David accomplished the development of Frank's 125-year-old glass negatives at Clark Art USA. Phojoe.com provided image restoration and colorization services.

And lastly, much gratitude to Isabella, whose charming picture atop my desk provided endless inspiration through long, solitary months of study and scribbling. This book is dedicated to her.

PROLOGUE

To the antiquarian, even simple things from times past take on new meaning simply because they're so old. I have no special interest in cars or trucks and certainly couldn't care less about the keys people use to turn them on. But I remember finding a key to a 1929 DeSoto in the woods behind our house and feeling like I had stumbled upon Captain Kidd's fabled treasure. Maybe some guy way back then lost his shirt in the stock market crash, then his DeSoto to repossession, and simply flung the worthless key away in disgust. He certainly didn't drive the car that far out into the woods. Or then again, maybe someone did. This was the Prohibition era, and New Haven had its fair share of bootleggers. Maybe some guy and his fellow mobsters hid their still out in the trees and brush, and he carelessly dropped the thing on one of their runs. Sorry, old timer—no cell phone or tow truck services back then to help you out of your predicament and get your stash into town.

Whatever really happened, this silly key managed to conjure up a veritable mental playground precisely because it was so old and wholly disassociated from its original context. This tiny, insignificant strip of metal hinted at a world of historic possibilities, irrespective of the real owner or how it ended up where it did. By now, the moonshiner, his gang and his car are long gone. Never find out whether he dropped the thing in a drunken stupor or relegated that task to his ditzy gun moll girlfriend. Never know if he cussed like a sea cook when he realized he, his hooch and peroxide blonde were all stranded out in the woods. And, was he ever collared by Prohibition Agents like Elliot Ness and his merry men? These profound mysteries and so much more of day-to-day human history have been irretrievably lost to time.

VOICES FROM EARLY AMERICA

Not only DeSoto keys but almost anything old and lost seems to take on new meaning in the here and now. The Oxyrhynchus Papyri in Egypt are a stash of miscellaneous ancient documents, including personal letters, tax bills, wills, horoscopes, insults, sales receipts, etc. If this stuff were from last week, we'd just leave it where we found it or maybe have trashmen cart it away. But personal memoranda from twenty centuries ago suddenly become tangible links to vanished times and situations. The diaries and other personal effects detailed in this book have likewise acquired a fascination for precisely this same reason. These random vestiges of antique ephemera somehow managed to survive the intervening years and, in doing so, act as doorways into the lives of everyday Americans in centuries past. Lives that remain part of the collective human experience. Their stories and others are what life is made of.

INTRODUCTION

WHAT was life really like for most Americans in the 18th and 19th centuries? What is it that renders these generations so unique in the popular imagination? Seems unlikely these people began each morning with the thought, "Here we go again! Another day jam-packed and bursting at the seams with all the activities unique to our momentous age!" The fact is, their accidental time and place of birth never instilled a sense of playing a part in some clearly delineated epoch or set piece. What we expect to find when we conjure up images of life in these centuries is based almost entirely upon our frames of reference, with a healthy allotment of hindsight factored in for good measure. But most of our *a priori* assumptions are gross simplifications designed to make life in these centuries intelligible in the here and now. The people involved probably envisioned themselves quite differently from our modern portrayals.

Our historical reconstructions will always contain elements of artifice and arbitrary selection, as they are based upon episodic insights into times and situations that, for the most part, no longer exist. And when contextualized as such, understandability equates to believability. To reveal the actual thoughts and feelings of people from vastly different times and places, their stories need to be augmented by insights unattainable from most modern studies. Their narratives often lack the dramatic appeal of modern recreations. But their value is their authenticity and the glimpses provided into what life was really like in centuries past.

The first-person accounts in this narrative reveal what actually went through people's minds as they arose each day, opened the window in the bedchamber, and made their way to the fireplace to stave off the morning chill. How often did they shudder at the thought of hearing even more neighbors were lost overnight to some malignant fever making its way through town? Did their thoughts turn at once to pity or to alarm at the prospect their own family might be next? Or were people in these centuries so inured to rampant disease and early death they merely blocked out such morbid thoughts and went about their daily routines?

They say every person has a story, and every life is a story worth telling. While this is undoubtedly true, most people never have the opportunity to tell their story, let alone have it committed to writing. What follows is the story of ordinary Americans born into various communities during the 18th and 19th centuries. Their lives were not so noteworthy that when certain details go missing, it constitutes an egregious loss to posterity. But the details that remain are a remarkable illustration of the continuity of American life throughout multiple generations. These people could never have imagined their experiences would be researched and chronicled a century or two after their passing. This is the late Colonial and Victorian Eras as experienced by everyday people and recorded in their personal diaries, letters and memoirs. Rarely do such insightful, first-person narratives survive the years to speak to us so poignantly today.

These remarkable antique documents reflect not only the thoughts and activities of real Americans throughout multiple generations but also the changes these people experienced during the rapid industrialization and technological advancements occurring between the late 18th and early 20th centuries. These generations experienced dramatic increases in interconnectivity between the Atlantic and Pacific as railroads, automobiles, telegraphs, telephones and radios made the conveyance of people, material goods and ideas over long distances possible for the first time. The gradual introduction of electricity into homes and businesses vastly accelerated the process of modernization and the invention of many innovative and labor-saving devices. Indoor plumbing was available to most by the late century, and with it the many advantages that come from running water and flush toilets in domestic settings. Thus, the world that these generations inherited from their predecessors in no way resembled the world they later bequeathed to their children.

Their writings contain a rawness, immediacy and authenticity, which is often lacking in modern portrayals of life in previous centuries. Although most everything they experienced is eminently relatable to us today, much of it occurred under radically different circumstances and in archaic social environments. But through their recollections we enter into communion with individuals that were in most respects identical to ourselves and the people we meet each day. They certainly dressed and acted differently, but the antiquated constructs of their daily lives and society cannot efface the strong sense of shared humanity that is evident between them and us, their descendants.

Introduction

A degree of voyeurism is always a factor when delving through personal material that was never meant to be shared with others, aside from perhaps with immediate family or close personal friends. One wonders what future generations would think were they to chance upon our private thoughts in diaries and other records. The electronic format of today's musings may or may not survive the centuries and allow a degree of insight into our own lives. But we are all the richer from the chance survival of these tattered sheets of antique paper in their brittle and worn bindings. Life is an accrual of vestigial traces, and very little of substance hasn't already been experienced by those who came before. Their story is our story. And memories are what life is made of.

To some, delving through these types of writings might seem less than a genuine study of history. But such views are a fallacy. Pick up most "history" books, and what inevitably follows is a refresher course (or primer, if it's your first go-round) on all the "notable" people and events from before you arrived on the scene and helped instill some sanity into it all. The experiences of the vast majority of humankind throughout history are rarely, if ever, touched upon or considered important enough to record for posterity. The fact of the matter is, a hundred years from now (if not sooner), nobody is going to give a rat's rear what most of us did, what we dreamt about, who we fell in love with or what we had for breakfast. Once we are gone, society will forget all about us and turn its collective attention to newer generations.

They say history is written by the victorious, meaning whoever is left standing after all the latest and greatest adversaries have been duly vanquished. The losers rarely get to tell their side of the story. Of course, by then a lot of them are probably deceased. The survivors largely suppress the unpleasant memories and simply move on with their lives. Most will be too busy going about their business to jot down their feelings, thoughts or experiences. Thus, our historical narratives always betray a decided slant, e.g., schoolroom learning about *Manifest Destiny* was not about avarice, collateral damage and genocide but nation-building. History records the people and events worth remembering. What happened to the rest is superfluous and eventually forgotten.

They say life doesn't take place in a vacuum, and most have some inkling of events outside their parochial sphere. This includes whatever newfangled ridiculousness our neighbors and friends are up to, as well as the latest outrages and sordid details in the daily news. If the average person sat down and recorded their life's story, what would they write about? Most would have no inclination for profound statements or insightful commentaries on current events and other topics of general interest. They would write about the things that mattered to them as individuals—the details that impacted their wellbeing in the here and now. The stories of bygone generations like those in this narrative are noteworthy not because they accomplished great things or killed lots of people but because their experiences are readily relatable to us today, and some of them took the time to write it all down. Like us, they arose each morning, played their parts in society, and reflected on what, if anything, it was all about.

A goldmine of unanticipated knowledge is contained in personal material left moldering in some forgotten spot for over a century. What would people from the distant past think if we informed them distant descendants were scrutinizing their lives? In all likelihood, such revelations would evoke doubt and suspicion, as the natural inclination in times past was to ascribe anything fantastic or unusual to sorcery and black magic—the *devil's work*. Most of us would shrug off the suggestion our lives might one day be subject to similar scrutiny. But in today's world, personal privacy is all but nonexistent, and everything we say, do, write, think and feel stagnates within the virtual realm for the indefinite future.

Regardless of our modern conceptions of the Victorian Era, most of these years were hardly a time of elegance, simplicity, luxury and creature comforts. Rather, their lives were circumscribed by unrelenting hard work, drudgery and disease, with the occasional festivity thrown in to break up the monotony and make it all seem worthwhile. Many aspects occurred in situations utterly dissimilar to the normative in modern industrialized societies. Yet despite their hardscrabble existence, these people nevertheless carved out a life within their assigned spaces, raised their children, experienced their fair share of happiness and solace, and buried their dead in essentially the same manner as is done today. A fuller appreciation of the *sameness* of the human experience becomes evident through a study of their memoirs and personal effects. The stories that follow are amongst the rare, surviving examples from everyday Americans over the late 18th and 19th centuries.

The illustrations of everyday life in this narrative were extracted from the memoirs of four separate groups of people in New England and the North Country.[1] There was no intention of limiting the selection to these two geographical areas. It just so happens this is where they lived and where their writings were discovered in later years. And in no sense is this meant to be a comprehensive overview of the late Colonial and Victorian Eras, but rather a selection of episodic insights from specific individuals, and as recorded in their diaries, memoirs, letters and other material. Nor were these types of writings

---

1. The North Country refers to the northernmost Counties of New York State. This largely rural region is bordered by Canada in the north, Lake Champlain and Vermont in the east, the Adirondack Mountains in the south, and Lake Ontario and the St. Lawrence Seaway to the west.

INTRODUCTION

particularly unique during a time of rising literacy rates in this country. Similar first-person accounts have turned up in forgotten nooks and crannies, musty trunks, old storage boxes and stashed between the rafters in antique farmsteads and other structures. Their valuable is simply that, through an accident of history, their stories somehow survived to allow a conceptual resurrection of people long gone.[2]

If these antique pieces of paper hadn't survived, most of us would have no clue these people ever existed. None of them are renowned for great deeds which should elicit our attention. Nor were they infamous, scandalous, notorious or otherwise memorable for all the wrong reasons. They weren't obscenely wealthy robber barons, show business celebrities, or mass murderers like Jack the Ripper, nor did they possess other characteristics that earned them at least a footnote in our collective history. We know them because their writings were mercifully spared by Father Time. Nothing in creation remains dormant forever, and we are all the richer for their survival.

Included is a collection of diaries from a family of English immigrants arriving in North America in the early 18th century and whose writings help put a human face on the early settlers in the original Thirteen Colonies. Their American journey begins when husband Asa and wife Abigail arrive in central New Hampshire in the early 1700s and erect a homestead on acreage just south of the Winnipesaukee River in the town of Northfield. Early the next century, their granddaughter Amanda married a man from Sanbornton Bridge, and together they raised a family of multiple children. Their little girl Belle survived the usual childhood diseases and, as a young adult, married into a prominent farming family in neighboring Tilton. Sons John and Joseph enlisted in the Union Army during the War of the Rebellion and were fortunate to return home, marry their sweethearts, and begin families of their own. The progeny of these three children represent the fourth generation of this English family in New Hampshire, where their descendants are traceable to this day.

These early New England generations are typical of the vast majority of Americans over the 18th and 19th centuries. As was the case with most of their contemporaries, their primary pastimes included crop raising and animal

---

[2]. One noteworthy find from New England is the diary of Noah Blake, a Colonial-era farm boy born in Litchfield County, Connecticut, in 1790. His meticulously detailed account for the year 1805 survived by being hidden in the recesses of an 18th-century farmstead, where it laid dormant until discovered in the mid-20th century. His story was painstakingly brought to life by artist and historian Eric Sloane in Diary of an Early American Boy. Modern attempts to track down Noah Blake in period records have proved unsuccessful due to the commonality of his first and last names in Colonial America. Also unknown is whether he survived to adulthood and finally married Rachel, his neighbor and love interest. These people are examples of the many generations now largely forgotten and lost to time.

husbandry. All experienced the hardships endemic to life in the early countryside, including disruptive outbreaks of contagious disease and the inevitable litany of funeral services for family, friends and neighbors. Frequent trips by wagon are mentioned as they bring their products to market, including firewood, chickens, eggs, maple syrup in the spring and barrels of cider in the autumn. Trading was carried out with the Shaker Villages of New Hampshire, whose residents were renowned for a number of specialty products exported throughout the northeast. Agricultural fairs were common during harvest and were one of the few opportunities everyone had to get out and forget about all the drudgeries of antique life.

Further south in New England is New Haven, which, until 1873, was the co-capitol of Connecticut with the city of Hartford. The Elm City is notable for a number of features, including Yale University and, in the early 20th century, as the birthplace of a hallowed American institution—pizza. During the 19th century, it was also home to the redoubtable George Beckwith: polymath, social reformer, incorrigible eccentric and founder of *Beckwith's Almanac*, one of the most widely read periodicals in southern New England. The present narrative includes a fascinating overview of his life and activities, including time as an educator, social activist, abolitionist, author, and publisher. In his day Beckwith was well known as a rabble-rouser and iconoclast, but an individual of considerable talent and intellect, and certainly someone worth remembering.

In addition to these Yankees of old New England, the narrative contains two families from the North Country, specifically Jefferson County, New York, along the border with Canada. The memoirs of Henry H. Lyman illustrate that, despite his inauspicious beginnings, he had the wherewithal to raise himself up, serve with distinction as an officer during the Civil War, become successful in business and work his way up the political ladder in State government. His recollections of growing up in the antique countryside are both detailed and strangely evocative. When he passed in 1901, a former Confederate officer journeyed to upstate New York and presented his widow the sword he confiscated when Lyman had been captured and interned in a prisoner-of-war camp.

Also from the North Country is another family of English immigrants, beginning with a Colonial-era couple named Joel and Bethiah. Following their relocation from southern New England to upstate New York, they built a farmstead on land that would remain in the family for over two centuries. Like many local men of his generation, Joel served in the New York militia during the American War of Independence. Among their children was son Daniel, who served with distinction in the War of 1812. He returned home after the conflict and raised five children with his wife, Luna, including a son who became one of the most successful businessmen in southern Jefferson County. Daniel's granddaughter, Harriet Irene (Hattie), came of age and married a minister's son named Frank. The sheer volume of surviving material from this family allows a fairly clear picture to emerge regarding their activities throughout multiple generations. Harriet and Frank's daughter Laura and her descendants represent a lineal continuation of this family in the North Country from the mid-18th century to the 1900s.

Out of respect for their descendants' privacy, some last names have been omitted from this narrative. Seemingly insignificant details sometimes strike a discordant note when they happen to involve your distant relatives. But aside from this, everything is exactly as contained in the material they left to posterity. By now, the individuals in these stories are all long gone, along with the familiar scenes they awoke to each morning. Their world has largely vanished, including horse-drawn carriages clacking noisily over covered bridges, summertime gazebos and marching bands on the green, ladies with bonnets and parasols tending children in the park, hammers clanging in the blacksmith's shop - virtually every vestige of life as they knew it is no more. But the quintessential beauty of the American landscape remains and is experienced in much the same way as it was centuries ago.

Any endeavor to understand the rhythms and tenor of bygone times is hampered by the dissimilarities between today's world and virtually everything it has replaced. The world of yesterday can only be glimpsed through narrow insights from material that, through happenstance, managed to survive and speak to us today. Although of immense interest, these literary fragments are by nature episodic and incomplete and must be supplemented by material from a variety of sources. For a fuller appreciation of these people, some background information on America's past is included. Material which hopefully affords some needed context and insight into life in the late Colonial and Victorian Eras.

PART I

The Victorian Era

"Keep, ancient lands, your storied pomp . . . Give me your tired, your poor, Your huddled masses yearning to breathe free, The wretched refuse of your teeming shore. Send these, the homeless, tempest-tost to me; I lift my lamp beside the golden door!"

—Emma Lazarus, 1883

THE lives of the people in these memoirs occurred primarily during the Victorian Era, a period transcending the geographical and chronological confines of an English monarch who reigned thousands of miles from American shores. The age of Queen Victoria of England—from June 1837 to January 1901—gave name to an epoch that retains a unique fascination well over a century after her passing. In modern times, the expression *Victorian* has been conceptualized as an *esprit de l'époque*, encompassing social movements, mores, dress, decorum, speech, art, and architecture in America, England and the far-flung British Empire. Although most aspects of Victorian life appear antiquated, they have nonetheless become idealized as something fascinating and uniquely apart from anything in modern life.

How often have people looked back upon the ornate, romanticized relics of Victorian life and felt how lucky they were to have lived in such an age of elegance! This mental journey back through time is a hearkening to some illusory golden age that somehow appears more genteel—and more desirable—to anything in modern times. But in reality, their colorful lithographs and elaborately layered outfits were among the few things in their lives that *weren't* dirty, unhealthful and, for the most part, flat-out boring. Surely none of these people looked at their lacy parasols and satin hankies and thought to themselves: How lucky I am to be alive in the age of Queen Victoria! Such fanciful ideations are purely modern inventions gleaned through rose-tinted glasses.

VOICES FROM EARLY AMERICA

Because the reign of Queen Victoria involves so much more than a mere chronological period, a number of expressions have arisen to help describe what are believed to be its most quintessential aspects, including Victorian-ness, Victorianism, Victorianesque and so on. All of these are helpful in conjuring up images of an age that retains such a unique fascination in the modern mind. But as with all *de facto* labels assigned to help contextualize life in past periods, these terms conjure up a set of images with varying degrees of relevancy, as they are mere generalizations that fail to capture the actual conditions and tenor of life in this period. The 19th century in America, England and beyond encompasses a number of distinct trends and developments, including the Industrial Revolution, the abolition movement, labor reforms, women's suffrage, temperance, the Belle Époque in France, and such literary, musical, artistic and architectural movements as transcendentalism, Romanticism, Classicism, Neoclassicism, Impressionism and Art Nouveau. Simplistic terms may help us comprehend historical periods and events but can never accurately summarize life at any one moment in time.

The problem is most portrayals of the Victorian Era have become so idealized, romanticized, and sanitized they are more pieces of historical fiction than factual representations. As has happened with so many historical periods, a standardized set of icons supplants the people and events of an entire era. Through sheer repetition, these stock images have become the *summa totalis* of historical knowledge in the public's imagination. Ancient Egypt has been reduced to images of the Great Pyramid and Sphinx of Giza. Classical Greece is defined by the Acropolis, and of that, mostly the Parthenon. A thousand years of Roman civilization is distilled down to endless depictions of the coliseum, with perhaps a few battered and broken marble columns thrown in for added effect. Likewise, the Victorian Era consisted of horse-drawn carriages conveying elegantly dressed people to their gaily colored and ornately appointed Queen Anne mansions. Queen Victoria herself has become crystallized into an elderly and rather somber looking lady, like her portrait on labels of Bombay Gin. These force-fed images go only so far towards promoting any real understanding of or appreciation for these historical epochs and the people involved.

Most modern depictions rarely give a sense of the actual experiences and living conditions of most Americans in the 19th century. Something approaching ninety-five percent of the population never lived in showcase Gothic Revival homes with elegant spiral staircases, gas lighting, ornately crafted wooden furniture with loads of doilies, an army of maids scurrying about so homeowners could dress in elegance for tea parties on immaculately manicured lawns tended by a cadre of well-mannered groundskeepers. In most towns and rural areas, the best people could actually hope for were living arrangements analogous to the Amish population in present-day Pennsylvania.

Conditions were considerably worse in the eastern cities, which absorbed the initial impact of millions of emigrants arriving in this country between 1860 and 1910. In cities like New York, Boston and Philadelphia, the huddled masses were crammed into filthy tenements or ramshackle structures more suitable for lab animals than human beings. In post-Civil War Manhattan, one out of three people in a population of 1,500,000 became mired in tiny, slum-like tenements, with as many as a dozen people crammed into a 10 by 12-foot living room and adjacent 6 by 8-foot bedroom. The majority of these fetid fire traps contained little to no circulating air, heating, running water, indoor plumbing, or exterior fire escapes. Millions of immigrants expecting to find the streets of the New World paved with gold instead fell victim to predatory landlords, rampant vermin, contagious diseases and a myriad more miseries.

The cause for all this institutionalized poverty was the enormous wealth disparity between the upper classes and virtually everyone else in society. It was the age of Robber Barons and their obscene displays of conspicuous consumption, as satirized by Mark Twain in his 1873 novel *The Gilded Age: A Tale of Today*. In this work he deftly satirized the rampant greed and corruption of America's elite in a format readily digestible by most readers. But despite his insights the narrative still lacked the shocking, full frontal impact of Jacob Riis's 1890 exposé *How the Other Half Lives: Studies among the Tenements of New York*. Riis was a pioneering social reformer who capitalized on the invention of flash photography by roaming the streets of Manhattan's Lower East Side and capturing in stark detail all the dimly lit streets, saloons, and filthy tenements with their sickly, starving inhabitants. With over 1.5 million residents by 1890, New York was by far America's largest city and destination for most immigration from European ports.

The appallingly squalid and slum-like conditions he chronicled in these early pictures shocked most Americans and prompted New York Police Commissioner and future President Theodore Roosevelt to accompany Riis on his midnight ramblings and observe firsthand the appalling living conditions in the city. What he witnessed affected him so profoundly that he soon proposed the nation's first social welfare legislation to curb the most egregious abuses and assist people to live like human beings instead of sewer rats. The age of photojournalism had arrived and was put to good use in Riis's campaign for justice and social reform. But a full comprehension of these worsening urban conditions was slow in arriving to more distant areas largely insulated from the rampant problems of city squalor and unfettered immigration.

Although Riis was the first American to document living conditions amongst the urban poor, a photojournalist on the other side of the Atlantic had earlier published a book entitled *Street Life in London,* which also utilized the camera to illustrate the shocking conditions amongst lower-class people living and working in the metropolis. Textual exposes had previously appeared in Great Britain, notably Friedrich Engels' *The Conditions of the Working Class in England* in 1845. But Thompson's 1877 treatise was the first to add startling emphasis through "permanent photographic illustrations taken from life expressly for this publication." His work is imbued with much obvious empathy for the plight of London's destitute masses. On the other hand, Engels' earlier polemical diatribes had been directed against the *bourgeoisie* he considered responsible for the miserable plight of the working class during the Industrial Revolution.

Aside from radically different environmental conditions, the aspects that most clearly delineate modern conceptions of Victorian life are unique modes of dress, decorum, and behavior. Strict adherence to formality was expected in all spoken and written communication. Everyone was addressed as a Mr. or Mrs. or Miss. Under-aged males were addressed as Mister So-and-So's boy or son. And with the exception of common laborers and the very poor, everyone went about town in full head-to-toe dress, regardless of the season or situation. Our 20th-century notion of casual attire was virtually nonexistent in the public sphere. Any radical notions of shedding a few layers of clothing or exposing a little skin would have been scandalous. Even at the seashore or in tropical climates, men went fully dressed in suits and hats, with women decked out and dolled up as if on their way to a lawn party. A song satirizing these antiquated notions of dress was composed by Noël Coward:

> In tropical climes, there are certain times of day
> When all the citizens retire
> To tear their clothes off and perspire
> It's one of those rules that the greatest fools obey (but)
> Mad dogs and Englishmen
> Go out in the midday sun.

To his list of *Mad dogs and Englishmen* should be added most middle and upper class Americans during the 19th and early 20th centuries. A look at Victorian artwork or period photography of people by the seaside brings into sharp focus the enormous differences in leisure apparel for people at play in this period.

The quaintness of Victorian portrait photography is due to factors including differences in dress, artistic conventions, and all the limitations imposed by antique cameras and equipment. People were unaccustomed to having their pictures taken, and certainly, the majority of them never sat for the artist's brush. Most surviving daguerreotypes, ambrotypes and tintypes from the mid-century feature faded and blurry images of men with unkempt hair wearing giant bow ties and women in voluminous, homespun dresses with dark, greasy hair pulled back and parted in the middle. In early political life, Abe Lincoln once told a photographer to hold off while he tousled his hair to ensure voters he was a simple, unassuming frontiersman like the rest of them. Exposure times were long, and sitters had difficulty remaining motionless with Cheshire cat grins throughout the session. As a result, many photographs appear slightly out of focus, with expressionless zombies staring out vacuously into the lens.

Technological improvements by the late century shortened exposure times, and brought people into focus with an immediacy often lacking in earlier works. Some images from the 1890s look as clear and sharp as pictures taken in the mid-20th century. Regardless of how antiquated these photographs appear, their value remains the memorialization of past places and people long gone, in a manner undreamt of in earlier generations. It remains to be seen whether today's digital images and electronic formats match the longevity of these tattered, yellowed and creased mementos of Victorian life.

With the Colonial period mostly over, the Victorian years nonetheless ushered in yet more inhibitions and strict formality into people's lives. Reminiscent of 17th-century Puritanical restrictions, obsessive moralizing, prudish behavior and untoward *gravitas* remained the order of the day. People's notions of propriety were so radically different because the legacy of Puritanism included a belief that everything is as pre-ordained by the Creator, and any doubts or deviations are both deleterious and sinful. The evangelical fervor of the *Great Awakening* movements confirmed in religious minds the belief in the Bible as the perfect yardstick by which to judge human conduct. Any discussion of newfangled, radical notions like Darwin's theory of evolution was tantamount to blasphemy because it cast doubt upon Christian orthodoxy, including the biblical account of creation.

The renewed religious fervor of these 18th and 19th-century religious movements also affirmed the popular belief that, in Christian households, the husband was *pater familias* (head of household) and absolute master of his realm, to whom wife and children remained in total subservience. This *a priori* assumption of male dominance was summarized in these few lines by Tennyson:

> Man for the field and woman for the hearth;
> (He) for the sword, and for the needle she;
> Man with the head, and women with the heart;
> Man to command, and woman to obey;
> All else is confusion.

This simple stanza appeared in his 1847 poem "The Princess" and expressed a sentiment that resonated well within contemporary society. The public sphere was man's domain, including issues of commerce, politics and war. Swearing, drinking and striking your wife in public was considered sinful but often overlooked when limited to the privacy of one's home. The domestic sphere was the domain of women, the *custos domi* (guardian of the household), including childrearing, cooking and other domestic activities. In the latter half of the 19th century, women acquired somewhat more latitude outside the home for church-related activities such as teaching Sunday school, fundraising, missionary work and tending to poor or infirm neighbors. But participation was still subject to approval from her head of household and male Minister.

So many aspects of daily life were radically different back then. Anytime you left the house, it meant being subjected to your daily dose of crappy weather because most traveling was done while fully or at least partially exposed to the elements. Aside from enclosed spaces like railway carriages, people got about by walking, riding a horse, or sitting in open phaetons or wagons. Romantic conceptions of winter travel in a one-horse open sleigh belies the fact these fancy, uncovered sleds were the only way people could get about when road conditions made walking or wheeled transport impracticable. In Colonial and Victorian times, snow-laden roads weren't routinely cleared of snow, but rather, horse-drawn rollers packed down accumulated snowfall to facilitate travel by vehicles equipped with runners rather than wheels. Stretches of roadways containing bare spots—like beneath covered bridges—became hindrances that required remedial snow packing in order to keep traffic moving. The voluminous wraps worn by travelers who could afford them were the only way to shield skin from wind, bitter frost and chafing snow. In the late 19th century, commercial moisturizers began appearing on the market in response to women's chronic complaints of ruddy, ravaged complexions from chronic overexposure to the elements.

PART I : THE VICTORIAN ERA

The massive increase in the availability of consumer goods brought about through increased industrial activity and distribution networks changed virtually every aspect of life in this era. By the end of the 19th century, improvements in photographic technology resulted in black-and-white imagery comparable to pictures taken prior to the digital revolution of the 1980s. Kodak also released their wildly popular Brownie camera, which people snatched up and headed out to memorialize all their Victorian silliness. We may never know what compelled these ladies to grab their parasols and stand on the park fence. The goings-on so enchanted the guy in the modified stovepipe hat he choreographed a special dance for the occasion. (Wikimedia-public domain)

Children in the countryside fared no better, as most had to walk long distances to attend classes in substandard, poorly heated schoolrooms. Sometimes, their arduous journey was uphill—both ways—through torrential rains or blinding snowstorms. If snow drifts or mud accumulations made the route impassable, the lucky kids got a snow day. Being outside more often also meant people got sick more often, which in the 19th century often earned you a one-way trip by horse-drawn hearse to the local cemetery. The town doctor could be miles away, and treatment was limited to whatever he happened to carry in his little leather bag. Almost all communicable diseases became inadvertent forms of population control. When people came down with a sniffle or fever, they found their best chance for recovery was often rest, hope and prayer. In the good old days, making it to your next birthday party was never a sure bet.

One aspect of Colonial and Victorian life that was certainly superior was the relative *lack of noise* encountered wherever you went, especially when traveling from the countryside into towns and cities. Rural life constituted ninety percent of America in times past, and its peaceful tenor prevailed up to the introduction of gasoline powered tractors and other noisemakers in the first half of the 20th century. People might spend their entire lives without hearing anything louder or more intrusive than thunder, gunshots from nearby hunters, or fireworks on Independence Day. The silence was sometimes broken by the clamor of water wheels revolving through tons of water at the local mill. Or by the sudden report from a blacksmith's hammer or the piercing squeal of tools being sharpened on grindstones. Church bells sounded periodically to announce the times of day or the departure of a nearby resident from earthly suffering. The distant sound of a whistle from a steam locomotive was more akin to a dog whistle than the piercing shrieks emitted by modern trains.

But in previous centuries, towns and cities were still relatively noisy places, even before the advent of large factories with assembly lines and massed machinery. Farmers driving their wagons from the countryside to the market became unsettled by sudden increases in noise and commotion, even if it never reached the maddening crescendo of the modern metropolis. But the farmer nevertheless found his peace and complacency disrupted by crowds of people jostling about and the din of merchant's cries as they peddled their wares up and down city streets. But he never had to contend with trucks and automobiles clogging the roadways, emitting endless racket and choking exhaust fumes. Emergency vehicles weren't speeding by with sirens blaring and lights flashing like someone's life depended on it. Municipal workers weren't out clearing debris off walkways with industrial-sized leaf blowers strapped to their backs. Jackhammers weren't tearing through the pavement during endless construction projects. Low-flying airplanes and helicopters didn't shake buildings while zooming overhead. Yet still, these 18th and 19th-century farm folk complained about the unsettling racket, hustle and bustle encountered during their visits to town. And reflected on how anxious they were to return to the solitude and serenity of the antique countryside.

American society, from the death of Queen Victoria to the outbreak of the First World War, is often referred to as the Edwardian Era in reference to the reign of her son, King Edward of Great Britain. But such labeling of American society is a misnomer, because although the years were contemporary, the term more accurately applies to the sociopolitical and economic situation in England and the British Empire in this period. But the expression is nevertheless applied to the intermezzo between the gravitas of Victorian life and the spontaneity of the Jazz Age that followed. The Roaring Twenties are remembered not only as the years of gangsters, bathtub gin and the Charleston but also a time of innovation, unparalleled economic prosperity, an increased availability of consumer goods, and, in general, an added *joie de vivre* to many aspects of life.

At least in the cities, the social scene reflected an overall diminishment in inhibitions, something seen in hindsight as a backlash to all the moralizing and stifling restraints of the preceding years. The allied nations had endured four long years of agony and economic hardship during the Great War but emerged in decidedly better shape than the Dual Alliance of Germany and Austria-Hungary. Yet people in small-town America still became shell-shocked at all the post-war shenanigans and were reluctant to embrace this new culture with its blatant disregard for traditional mores. Many wondered with a growing sense of despair, "What will they think of next?" as if the worse was still to come.

One prominent aspect of the Edwardian years, which is readily noticeable in period photographs, is the easing of restrictions on both public behavior and clothing. Women's dress shops noted a precipitous drop in demand for voluminous, one-piece outfits as clothing became lighter and less restrictive. Fashion trends called for sporty, two-piece wardrobes consisting of a skirt and a separate shirtwaist (blouse). Upper and middle-class women increasingly took up the recreational activities that emerged during the 1890s, including lawn tennis and bicycling. All these pastimes required lighter, looser and less formal attire. The Edwardian Era would also be the last time corsets were considered an indispensable component of a lady's wardrobe. The times, they were a-changin'. And in the popular imagination, all six decades of the preceding Victorian Era gradually became relegated to a standardized set-piece replete with antiquated customs, clothing and behaviors—an utterly remote, alien and vanished world of yesterday.

The New Woman, circa 1900. Sodom and Gomorrah have nothing on us these days, my friends. Look at all the effronteries to stolid and stogy Victorian values encapsulated in this one advertisement! Is she home scouring the gentleman's smoking lounge with Sapolino? No! Is she out in the yard replenishing her family's supply of brown soap? Of course not! She is out and about on her bicycle, smoking a cigarette, fitted in baggy pantaloons molded indecently to hips and thighs. And just look at that haughty demeanor and obvious impertinence! One hand thrust rebelliously on the hip, and the other tucked scandalously inside her shirtwaist (reaching for a hidden flask, no doubt). Thank heavens flashing the bird hasn't been invented yet, or old Jezebel here would be guilty of that, too. (Wikimedia Commons-public domain)

CHAPTER 1

Marital Relations in the Age of Unenlightenment

OVERALL, people of the Victorian Era were more inhibited in their everyday speech and behavior, at least in the public sphere. Societal conventions and religious prohibitions led to much emotional and sexual frustration, providing no end of fodder for early psychopathologists like Sigmund Freud. All the stuffiness and prudishness inherent in 19th-century society, he reasoned, resulted in conflicting layers of repression and neurosis within the human psyche. And to a certain extent, he was correct in identifying a number of the causative factors for mental illness. For centuries, old fashioned notions and puritanical morality had governed nearly every aspect of daily life. Topics that routinely arise in modern discussions were positively *verboten* back then. Complaining openly about your sex life or some similar impropriety would trigger a visit from your Minister to ensure you hadn't strayed too far from the prescribed path. Open displays of kissing, hugging, swearing or similar forms of licentious or lewd behavior would warrant an intervention by the local constable.

It was anticipated that even the most intimate details of your private life conform to certain socially prescribed parameters. When uncertainties arose in the bedroom, people were expected to seek counsel from older family members or close friends. Common marital problems, especially during the early years, were *terra incognita* to older generations, who had been there and seen that in younger days. Awkwardness and mistakes were understandable and would elicit chuckles rather than any real sense of disapprobation. And besides, navigating through life's mysteries was never meant to be easy. One should accept certain awkwardness during intimacy with good grace and remain mindful that things always turn out as preordained by the Creator.

In centuries past, a person's intimate marital problems were never appropriate topics for discussion at dinner, tea time, or any other gathering for that matter. Conversation at family or neighborhood get-togethers might include the latest gossip, such as your randy neighbor's latest indiscretions or the fact unwed Cousin Beatrice was in a *family way*. But they were never appropriate forums for discussing conjugal difficulties or sexual hang-ups. The 19th century hasn't gone down in the popular imagination as Prudishness Central without some justification. The story is told of Queen Victoria's heartfelt advice to her daughter regarding wedding night jitters: "(just) keep your eyes closed and think of England." Such sage and heartfelt advice from the royal matriarch of 19th-century propriety! And after all, newlywed brides weren't supposed actually to enjoy the experience! Best to stop whining, lie quietly and do your duty to perpetuate the family line.

Printed material and other resources for advice on marital relations and birth control were virtually nonexistent in early America. Aside from observing the mating rituals of farm animals, there were few avenues toward enlightenment regarding the nitty gritty of procreation. How could young adults in these years have gotten their hands on useful printed material, even if they wanted to? Venues for advertising *any* new publications were extremely limited, even in cities with largely literate populations like Boston, New York and Philadelphia. At university, obtaining this type of material was still nearly impossible, as clergymen and other traditionally conservative sources largely determined the curriculum. Any professor endeavoring to educate students on sexual matters, family planning or other progressive subjects would have been summarily escorted off campus and railroaded out of town. Still, during the Victorian Era, a number of carefully worded publications quietly entered circulation to help enlighten the public on the amatory arts.

Albert Sidebottom got the ball rolling in 1865 with his scandalous *A Guide To Marriage,* in which he infamously suggested that newlyweds "explore" each other as a step towards developing a lasting, loving relationship. Religious censors were tied up in knots with such blasphemies as "All love between the sexes is based upon sexual passion . . . the sex instinct is in itself neither coarse nor degrading unless it exists in a coarse or degraded individual." Cotton Mather was undoubtedly spinning like a top in his grave. In 1877, Charles Knowlton, M.D. further outraged the righteous with *The Fruits of Philosophy*, essentially a rewrite of his anonymous 1832 pamphlet advocating such sinful practices as family planning and contraception. Both versions were promptly condemned as obscene and illegal under American and British statutes. Henry Granger Hanchett, M.D. fared little better in 1887 with his *Sexual Health: A Plain and Practical Guide for the People in All Matters Concerning the Organs of*

Reproduction in Both Sexes and All Ages. All this pseudo-scientific jargon, it was argued, dissuaded no one from recognizing it for what it was—a vulgar piece of pornographic garbage.

In response to the growing proliferation of this type of material, Congress passed the Comstock Law in 1873 as an "Act of the Suppression of Trade in, and Circulation of, Obscene Literature and Articles of Immoral Use." This empowered all duly authorized defenders of public decency to prosecute blasphemers and deposit their immoral rear ends where they belonged—in jail. By the closing decades of the 19th century, there remained strong legal and religious restrictions against any printed material of this sort. Victorian society was still firmly entrenched in the puritanical ethos of the early 17th century. As late as the 1920s, social reformers could still be prosecuted for offering simple advice on things like contraception and the avoidance of sexually transmitted diseases. The biblical admonition to be fruitful and multiply remained indelibly enshrined in the *ethos* of Western society. Aside from the occasional French postcard or other example of illicit erotica, the only allowable path towards the acquisition of carnal knowledge was old-fashioned trial and error.

CHAPTER 2

Early American Technology

FOR most of the 19th century, rapid industrialization and increasing access to advanced technology were viewed as embellishments to things that had endured for as long as anyone could remember. Prior to this time, few people had experienced any abrupt discontinuities in their workday routines or living arrangements. The skill sets learned from their parents were basically the same skill sets *their* parents found passed on from previous generations. The profit motive driving most modern innovations, improvements and upgrades never resulted in the discontinuation of things found useful in the past. The frugal and staunchly traditional folk of the Thirteen Colonies believed that if something worked, it would probably suffice for the foreseeable future. Things that weren't broken didn't require fixing or replacing simply because the latest and greatest thingamajig had once again come down the pike.

However, attitudes began to change later in the century. Things old and traditional no longer sufficed, and it became fashionable to acquire things for which there was no expectation of permanence. Rapid changes occurred at home and in the workplace when people started eschewing what was around yesterday for whatever would hopefully suffice until the morrow. In his comparison of early American life to conditions at the turn of the 20th century, Eric Sloane noted that "There was an insidious logic that men must adapt to machines instead of machines to men; that production, speed, novelty and progress at any price must come first, and people second." A paradigm shift had occurred in the public mindset: people no longer enhanced their lives through new products and services; they began basing their very identities upon such things. Instead of relying upon the tried and true, society was slowly becoming structured upon trends and chimeras, which, in reality, were precarious bases upon which to build for the future.

In the 21st century, living conditions for most Americans are far removed from those of our forbearers. The rapidly accelerating pace of modern life is a continuation of trends that began during the Industrial Revolution of the late 18th century. Not only are radical alterations continually occurring in products and services, but the very rhythm and tenor of life are now being structured upon whatever innovations were most recently force-fed into the public's consciousness. By 1920, most aspects of daily life would have seemed fantastical merely a century before. Trips by foot or horse that occupied a day or more could be made in under an hour by train or automobile. Projection of the human voice from rural towns to distant cities was accomplished by simply picking up the telephone. Distant events that took weeks to appear in the local papers were reported each morning by radio. Farm chores, which took several workers a number of days, were now accomplished in a single afternoon by gasoline-powered tractors. The birth of the modern, consumer-driven economy was well underway.

America's initial industrial capacity had developed along the rivers and streams required to turn the waterwheels supplying power to early mills and factories. Sections of the country with insufficient water resources relied upon windmills, which soon proliferated across the early landscape. Population centers grew adjacent to these sites to take advantage of products, services and employment opportunities. As the population grew, fewer choice sites remained available, and businesses were forced to seek alternative locations and sources of power. The answer came courtesy of perhaps the most important innovation of the Industrial Revolution—steam power—which generated many times the output of even the most efficient water and wind sources. Beginning in the mid-19th century, industry began gravitating away from the countryside and into the cities with their newly installed steam-powered machinery.

By the mid-1800s, newer and larger population centers grew adjacent to these industrial centers with their dedicated railway lines. Increasing investments gave rise to the massive industrial base, so characteristic of America's Gilded Age. These enormous factories and dark, satanic mills incentivized millions to migrate from the countryside to the city to take advantage of modern industrial techniques with assembly lines and interchangeable parts. Railway service was greatly expanded, including the terminals and distribution networks essential to speed goods from factories to consumers. Production and distribution rates soon eclipsed the old water and wind-based businesses, with their antiquated reliance upon horse-drawn transport and water barges. In just a few years, the steam engine had totally transformed the nature of American business and economy.

However, transformation in the urbanized industrial sector was slow in effecting most aspects of life in rural areas. The small communities into which

PART I : THE VICTORIAN ERA

the people in this narrative were born were as technologically distant from New York City and other metropolises as the imagination can conjure. Up to the late 19th century, no one in their sections of the country was equipped with services now taken for granted, including electricity, running water, central heating, telephone connections, effective public transportation, and reliable refuse removal. In the North Country, the installation of their first *water closet* (flushable toilet) in 1889 went down as a notable event in Hattie's diary.

Indoor plumbing was undoubtedly a godsend to people accustomed to chamber pots and outdoor privies. But even into the 1930s, not everyone in rural areas had indoor plumbing. The story is told of one farmer in Lorraine, New York, who purchased but steadfastly refused to install his new indoor toilet. After he passed, his neighbors found it out in the barn, still unpacked in the original crate.[3] The old timer was too accustomed to his bracing walks out to the privy—even in blizzards and minus twenty-degree weather. People were not more eccentric in former times; it's just their circumstances were so radically different that it makes any peculiarities that much more pronounced.

Prior to mid-century, it would have seemed unfathomable to live in a world where people and materials could be transported across the continent *ad libitum*. Roadways were poorly constructed and haphazardly maintained and rarely extended beyond the local area. Their miserable condition was a considerable impediment to long-distance travel. The best one would encounter were 18th-century postal roads constituting the principal routes between larger population centers. Even after the extension of roadways into more distant areas and widespread paving projects, the appearance of interstate highways was still decades away. The introduction of railway service after 1850 greatly accelerated public mobility across much of the nation. In later years, the automobile would further enhance one's ability to travel.

The accelerating pace of technology in the early 20th century was greatly facilitated by the transition from steam power to electricity. However, the ability to turn on a radio or run electrical equipment was hampered by the slow arrival of electrical service in more distant areas. But by the 1930s, widespread access had largely been accomplished, initiating profound changes in the public and private spheres. Although people loved their new electrical devices, their maintenance and repairs required the acquisition of entirely new skill sets. In the past, if a repairman was unfamiliar with your particular gadget, he could still figure it out by disassembling and examining the mechanical components. But traditional methods were unavailing with electrical motors, which were

---

3. This anecdote is related on page 114 of *The Huddle-The Way It Was* by Donald Moore.

beyond anything he had encountered. New knowledge was required to keep the modern world running.

Relative to conditions in the 21st century, the lack of technological sophistication becomes evident throughout these antique diaries, memoirs and correspondence. Winters in northern New England and along the Canadian border were long, dark and exceedingly cold, with northern winds gusting through the house—regardless of how well constructed. The most up-to-date methods of central heating were beyond the reach of most, and families still relied upon fireplaces and stoves to heat their homes. In Jefferson County, Hattie and Frank were fortunate to have installed a coal and wood burning furnace in the basement around 1900. This upgrade to steam heating made a huge difference, and once the cast iron radiators kicked in, considerably more heat was generated throughout the interior than by previous methods. But in extreme conditions, even with radiators and fireplaces at full tilt, it was nearly impossible to stay warm. Frank purchased a portable oil-burning stove in 1913 to move about between the parlor and sitting room. For hot running water, Hattie mentions that in the fall of 1925, they finally connected an electrical water heater to the basement furnace. How it was configured and what, if anything, it replaced is unknown.

Most businesses in the late 19th and early 20th centuries still lacked essential services like electricity, running water, central heating and telephones. Although the North Country businesses in this narrative had telephone service by the late1880s, electricity was still slow in arriving. The dry goods store in Adams, New York, where Frank worked, was one of the first shops in town to have both telephone and electrical service, albeit on a limited basis. The Adams Electric Light Company began operating in 1889, providing part-time service for streetlights, shops and offices along the business district. Full 24-hour service was unavailable prior to early 1913. A new generating station began supplying power to additional areas of southern Jefferson County in 1912. But the small community of Worth and more remote sections of Lorraine were not fully wired until as late as the 1940s.

Like most Americans at the beginning of the 20th century, Hattie and Frank were pleased as punch to welcome all these newfangled innovations and gadgets into their lives. The ability to flip a switch and let electricity light up the room and do loads of other things was one of the blessings of modern technology. Frank felt a real sense of pride over his ability to drive about town on business in their first automobile instead of walking, borrowing Laura's bicycle, or bumming rides on fertilizer wagons. Their home was among the first on their block to install electrical wiring. Although an electric doorbell had been installed in 1912, a full upgrade with electric lighting fixtures didn't occur until the following year. Prior to this, family expenditures on wood, coal, gas, oil and kerosene took up a significant portion of the monthly budget. Considering that the average Victorian gas fixture generated merely the equivalent of 20-25 watts of illumination, their electrically lit home must have seemed a dazzling wonderland by comparison. Their diaries record a steady influx of neighbors and family stopping by to marvel at all the brilliant new lighting. Surprisingly, Frank never charged admission.

In addition to interior lighting, electrical service in residential neighborhoods became the impetus for the gradual transition to new appliances and gadgets, including refrigerators, toasters, ovens, vacuum cleaners, clothes irons, doorbells, alarm clocks, phonographs and eventually radios. One neighbor cheerfully relegated her old cast iron encumbrance to the basement and brought over her new electric iron for Hattie to marvel at. Hattie and Frank's complete transition to electrical appliances was still a slow and incremental process, and it wasn't until the mid-1920s that the coal stove in the kitchen was finally replaced with an electric oven. Hattie was happy to note their Thanksgiving turkey "cooked just fine" that first year in the new appliance.

The family retained their old icebox up to the purchase of a Kelvinator in the mid-1920s. The national austerity of the 1930s forced many homes and businesses to forego the transition to electrical refrigeration, and the ice wagon remained a familiar feature across American towns well into the 1940s. Aside from the initial expenditure, these new electrically powered units were a vast improvement over old-fashioned iceboxes. One New Englander tells of his sudden disenchantment with the old appliance after taking delivery of a less-than-pristine block of ice from the local lake. Once the block had sufficiently melted down, the kitchen became befouled by the stench of defrosting horse manure, which, unbeknownst to anyone, lay frozen at the center. Teams of horses were used during ice harvesting on the lake, and apparently, some of their droppings went unnoticed by the crew.

CHAPTER 3

Rural Life in the 18th and 19th Centuries

For everything, there is a season and a time for every purpose under heaven:

a time to be born and a time to die;
a time to plant and a time to pluck up what is planted;
a time to kill and a time to heal;
a time to break down and a time to build up;
a time to weep and a time to laugh;
a time to mourn and a time to dance;
a time to cast away stones and a time to gather stones together;
a time to embrace and a time to refrain from embracing;
a time to seek and a time to lose;
a time to keep and a time to cast away;
a time to rend and a time to sew;
a time to keep silent and a time to speak;
a time to love and a time to hate;
a time for war and a time for peace.

—ECCLESIASTES 3:1-8

CONTRARY to popular belief, life in the past was never simpler in the sense of being easier. It was certainly less complicated, if for no other reason than the near-total absence of electronic gadgets and other technological complications. Like most men in the North Country, Frank in Adams had a number of chores to tend to before journeying downtown on business. This included going out to the wood house and fetching fuel for the stove and furnace, lighting the fires, feeding the chickens and collecting their new eggs. The family derived some income from their sales, as well as ensuring a steady supply for the kitchen table. Life in farm country also subjected people to a number of peculiar problems. In February of 1889, newlywed Hattie in Adams described a bone-chilling night out back tending to a sick hen: "The day twenty-eight degrees below zero. Tremendous wind and storm at night. Took oil stove out to warm henhouse and stayed with it (the sick hen) all the time." On the whole, not only was 19th century life more physically demanding, people had more pressing problems to deal with than lousy Wi-Fi connectivity.

The people in these memoirs were all born sometime between the Colonial period and the late 19th century. These years encompassed the period of Manifest Destiny, an imperialistic doctrine of the inherent right of Americans to expand beyond the original Thirteen Colonies to the Pacific coast and establish dominion over everything in between. The pioneers who embarked upon these westward migrations referred to this experience as going west to see the elephant, a metaphor for all the strange and wonderful things they expected to encounter en route. Beginning around 1820, millions of Americans and recently arrived immigrants made the journey to the promising new territories of the mid-western and Pacific regions. The European notion of America as a nation confined to the Atlantic seaboard was utterly and irrevocably dispelled.

Of course, the western territories were hardly unexplored, and these early pioneers were not the first to see it. The indigenous tribes of North America had lived there for something like the last 15,000 years. But to the early settlers, they were the first Europeans on the scene, and that's what mattered. The effects of Manifest Destiny upon the native populations from Appalachia to Oregon and California were catastrophic, as entire nations were forcibly uprooted from ancestral lands and succumbed to disease, starvation and neglect. The total number of Indigenous deaths in this period is estimated at somewhere between 100,000 and 200,000 souls. Although these tragedies have been duly enshrined in the oral traditions of Native Americans, in most school texts, they are routinely glossed over as collateral damage during the period of nation-building.

By the early 16th century, European colonization of the "New World" was well underway. The Age of Discovery was driven mostly by the desire of European monarchs to find shorter and cheaper trade routes to Oriental markets. In 1492, Christopher Columbus disembarked from his flagship, *Santa Maria*, and informed the native population he was empowered to claim this land on behalf of the King and Queen of Spain. Columbus referred to these people as *Indians* because, for all his highly touted navigational skills, he was under the impression they had landed somewhere near India. For reasons still unclear, the silly name stuck. What *didn't* stick were the "Indians" to their native lands, as efforts to summarily dispel them were soon rigorously underway. Of course, the aboriginal nations of the Americas were hardly pristine, peaceable lots in their own right. Being of the human persuasion, they were subject to the same inconsistencies, insecurities, and aggressive behaviors that resulted in genocidal competition for land and other precious resources. But, by the late 16th century, the increasing influx of Europeans forced many tribes to set aside their differences and enter into an alliance to thwart this mutual threat. The arrival of thousands more Europeans during the 17th century only increased their problems and anxieties.

In 1620, a small band of English Puritans arrived at Cape Cod, disembarked from the Mayflower, and informed the native population of their right to settle these territories by the grace of God. Within a decade, more Puritans had arrived, resulting in the displacement of more and more people from their ancestral lands. Before long, nearly every Native American who had originally greeted these arrivals had died from a combination of superior European weaponry and an arsenal of Old World diseases for which they had no natural immunity. The settling of Plymouth Colony has been memorialized in the American mythos as the holiday of Thanksgiving. By the 18th century, expansion beyond the original colonies was well underway. It was a time fraught with hardships and bloodshed, not only for the pioneers but also for Native and African Americans who became caught up in the process, only to find themselves disenfranchised from any resulting benefits. The fact is, not everyone was happy to see Daniel Boone and his merry band of pioneers traversing the wilderness in search of adventure. The westward expansion might have made perfect socioeconomic sense back east, but it resulted in appalling levels of collateral damage to millions along the way.

As per the initial federal census in 1790, almost ninety-five percent of the population resided in rural areas, including the numerous farms and homesteads spread out across arable sections of New England and the North Country. By the end of the Civil War in 1865, the general migration from farms to population centers was well underway, with only an estimated eighty percent remaining in the countryside. The demographics of upstate New York, New England, and northern Pennsylvania between 1790 and 1860 were still predominantly Anglo-Saxon, with a minority of German, French Canadian, Scotch, Dutch, and Native American inhabitants. By the 1920 census, there occurred a phenomenal growth in smaller, rural communities, and the

PART I : THE VICTORIAN ERA

population ratio between town and country became almost evenly divided. Most new settlements were given English, Native American or French names. Places with names of eastern or southern European derivation were almost nonexistent.[4]

The undeveloped and thinly populated Midwestern and Great Plains regions not only attracted millions of newly arrived immigrants and unemployed Americans, but they also presented a golden opportunity for unscrupulous corporations and land developers to fleece the rubes endeavoring to escape from the depressed economic conditions of the 1870s. To encourage emigration and economic growth, the federal government transferred 129 million acres of public land to privately owned corporations eager to expand railway service into these areas and over to the West Coast. Railroad monopolies embarked upon a massive advertising campaign promoting unlimited business and agricultural opportunities in these territories. Newspapers and periodicals were flooded with offers to sell individual lots on extremely attractive terms, opportunities which proved irresistible to countless people back east.

But such enticements were merely a ploy to snare the unwary into economic dependence once the contracts had been signed. Landowners charged exorbitant rates to deliver supplies and ship products, produce and livestock to market. Prices for goods dropped dramatically, and many homesteaders found themselves worse off than before heading west. A sustained drought in the summer of 1887 led to widespread crop failures and plunging land values. In record numbers, mortgage holders began foreclosing on anyone unable to make payments due to circumstances beyond their control. Public disenchantment grew as farmers and businessmen became fed up with evictions, falling prices, and deceptive marketing practices. In many areas, these settlers began to mobilize, and for the first time in the nation's history, populist movements and farmer's alliances began appearing in severely impacted areas.

The wild frontier nature of early American society also proved a colossal disappointment to more cultured European observers. A scathing assessment of life in this period appeared in Charles Dickens's *American Notes for General Circulation* in 1842. He recalls his great expectations prior to embarking upon the tour, believing the New World a living embodiment of Rousseau's *Liberté, Egalité, Fraternité* egalitarianism. But what he encountered fell far short, as he later spells out in a letter to a friend: "This is not the republic I came to see; this is not

---

4. An obvious exception is the Village of Pulaski in Oswego County, which was named after Count Kazimierz Puławski, a Polish nobleman and cavalry general in the Continental Army during the American War of Independence. If an Italian general had served under George Washington, Oswego County might have ended up with a village named after the Marquis of Mozzarella.

the republic of my imagination." The continuous assaults upon his upper-crust English sensibilities became increasingly grating, as indicated in his memoirs:

> All that is loathsome, drooping, or decayed is here . . . "It is a nation of self-interested grubbers who cared only for politics and money, pretending at liberty and equality while condoning slavery . . . Despicable trickery at elections; under-handed tamperings with public officers; and cowardly attacks upon opponents . . . As Washington may be called the headquarters of tobacco-tinctured saliva, the time is come when I must confess, without any disguise, that the prevalence of those two odious practices of chewing and expectorating began about this time to be anything but agreeable, and soon became most offensive and sickening.

Although the disagreeable habit of expectorating tobacco-tinctured saliva has mostly fallen by the wayside, the case could be made that not much else has changed in Washington since Dickens's day.[5]

---

5. Excerpted from Charles Dickens's *American Notes for General Circulation* and later memoirs.

CHAPTER 4

Roadways and Transportation

THE asphalt highways and byways of modern America are the result of 20th-century projects to improve the nation's transportation infrastructure so as to facilitate trade and commercial development. Prior to then, most roadways were unpaved, consisting of packed dirt, gravel, bricks, cobblestones, wooden planks, logs (*corduroy*), and even crushed oyster shells in coastal sections of New England. During his 1842 tour of America, Charles Dickens recalls a most disagreeable ride by stagecoach along a corduroy road in Ohio:

"At one time, we were all flung together in a heap at the bottom of the coach, and at another, we were crushing our heads against the roof. Now, one side was down deep in the mire, and we were holding on to the other . . . A great portion of the way was over what is called a corduroy road, which is made by throwing trunks of trees into a marsh and leaving them to settle there. The very slightest of the jolts with which the ponderous carriage fell from log to log was enough, it seemed, to have dislocated all the bones in the human body . . . Never, never once, that day, was the coach in any position, attitude, or kind of motion to which we are accustomed in coaches. Never did it make the smallest approach to one's experience of the proceedings of any sort of vehicle that goes on wheels."[6]

Even in New York City, some roads remained unpaved up to the end of the 19th century. A trip by stagecoach from Manhattan to Boston still took six days over ostensibly superior postal routes. In rural areas, anything approaching safe, reliable and passable roads simply didn't exist, rendering travel an altogether dangerous, uncomfortable and time-consuming experience. Icy and snow laden roads made wheeled transport impracticable, requiring a seasonal changeover from wheeled carriages and wagons to the open sleighs and sleds most kept ready in the barn. And, of course, there was always some danger from renegade "Indians" who were less than tickled pink to see more and more strangers traipsing across their ancestral lands.

---

6. Dickens, *American Notes*, Chapter XIV.

In cities and towns, the reliance on animal power for the conveyance of people and materials was fraught with its own environmental and health-related horrors. Horses poop a lot, and they're not good at holding it in until they're back at the stable. In 1900, there were an estimated 150,000 horses plying the roadways of New York City alone, with each animal generating approximately 20-25 pounds of manure every day. Historically, this equine malfeasance had been somewhat mitigated by the hoards of pigs that were permitted to roam about *ad libitum* and for whom this nastiness constituted a readily available snack. But even this municipal army of porcine street sweepers was insufficient to eradicate the chronic mess from the metropolis. Manure was inevitably caked onto carriage wheels and people's footwear and, from there, into domestic and commercial interiors. Equally insidious was when the desiccated dung dried into a fine powder and became windborne through open doors and windows onto people, furniture, bedding and dining room tables.

In more distant sections, travel by foot, horse, cart or wagon occurred over primordial dirt trails winding precariously through thick forests, meadows and swamps. For centuries, these pathways had been the domain of wild animals and the occasional Native American. But they were ill-suited for heavily laden traffic by stagecoaches, wagons and prairie schooners. Long-distance land travel was so precarious that, whenever possible, people opted for watercraft across lakes, rivers and coastline sections of the ocean. Around 1800, considerable investment went into building a network of canals as a cheaper, safer and quicker alternative to road travel. Despite the high expectations, the era of canal boats was short-lived due to a rapid rise in railway service by mid-century. Within a few decades, thousands of miles of railways crisscrossed the country, with the steam locomotive the conveyor of choice for passengers and freight. One spring day in 1877, Reverend Gordon brought the children to a railroad crossing in Verona, New York, to watch what he described as the nonstop "fast mail train" flying by at an astounding 30 miles per hour.

Another contributing factor towards abysmal traveling conditions was that large sections of the country were much wetter than at present. The early pioneers didn't so much walk across the land as they did *slosh* their way through. In later years, bog meadows, swamps, marshes, ditches and ponds had been largely filled in and replaced with farmland and real estate development. But before then, most areas were comprised of wet, squishy grassland over a layer of mossy compost. Below this was a layer of moist humus atop a foot or more of topsoil. No frontiersman would have cleared the land and built a homestead until fitted with a stout pair of waterproof boots. By the late 20th century, large swaths of American wetlands had vanished to be replaced by buildings and asphalt,

PART I : THE VICTORIAN ERA

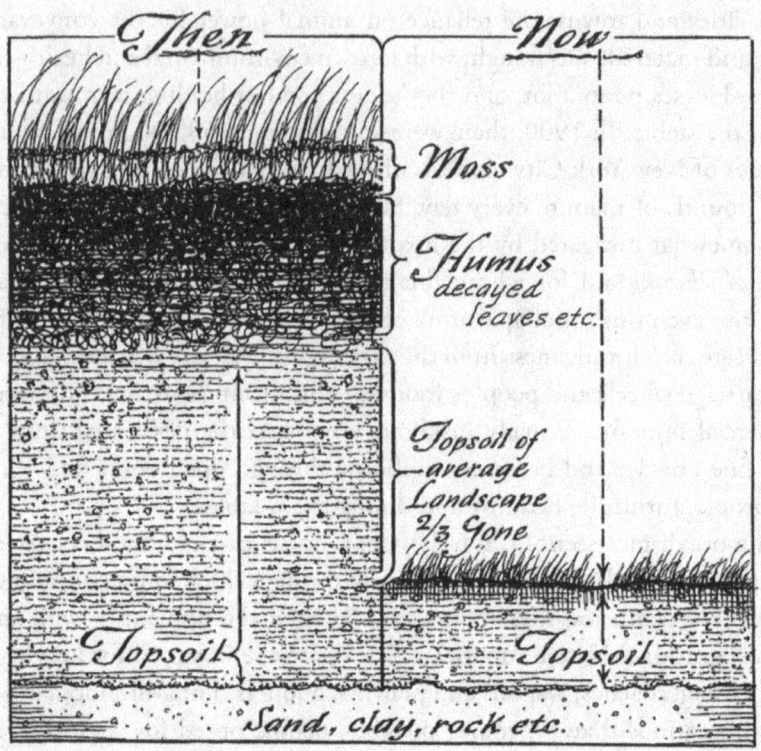

An illustration by Eric Sloane, renowned historian and artist of early America. This sketch contrasts modern soil conditions to those found by early settlers between the 17th and 19th centuries. Much of the countryside was wet grasslands atop deep levels of humus and topsoil. By the 21st century, these same ecosystems have been largely denuded of their original layers of healthy soil (The Eric Sloane Estate)

leaving only a thin layer of healthy topsoil in place. The early settlers would have scoffed at modern soil conditions in the Northeast Corridor.

Original environmental conditions created no end of problems for early travel across landscapes riddled with rivers, streams, brooks and ponds. Although early roadways were often built adjacent to these waterways, in some places, crossing the water barrier was essential if you endeavored to reach the other side. Shallow sections provided adequate fording spots, but deeper waters required some degree of human intervention. In the 18th century, the solution was an alignment of stepping stones, sometimes with ropes strewn at shoulder height as handrails. In more densely populated areas, wooden and stone bridges eventually replaced many of these early stepping stones and fording spots.

During the 19th century, covered bridges became a popular way to cross rivers and streams. Over time, improvements in structural details like truss designs led to the construction of much longer spans. Their similarity in appearance to barns is hardly coincidental. They were built by many of the same people, utilizing the same materials, tools and techniques. In essence, all they were doing was erecting another barn across a waterway rather than dry farmland. If one of these structures were to be hoisted up and moved inland, only a few modifications would be required to make them practical for farm use. An advantage to the roofing was the protection these overhangs afforded to the underlying wooden roadways, effectively delaying any weather-related deterioration and collapse. By the mid-19th century, an estimated 12,000 covered bridges had been constructed across New England, New York, Pennsylvania, Ohio, Oregon and Indiana.

A sense of romance and mystery has long been associated with these antique structures, something attributable to the privacy afforded during a few fleeting moments of darkness and seclusion. Nicknames abounded, including Kissing Bridge and Wishing Bridge; the former alluding to brief, intimate encounters and the latter to the belief that wishes made while underneath were sure to come true. If the underpass was long enough, or if you stopped to linger a bit, the experience must have seemed tantamount to the Tunnel of Love at amusement parks. Generations of people undoubtedly looked back fondly upon moments spent in these musty, liminal spaces. Thousands of covered bridges provide memories for as long as they remain standing. Sadly, most have now vanished, along with their secret promises and trysts.

An early incentive towards roadway improvements was the implementation of privately funded toll roads equipped with turnpikes (turnstiles) at each end, requiring travelers to stop and pay for passage. Toll money helped defray construction and maintenance costs and provided landowners with varying degrees of profit. Rates were based upon the nature of each passerby, e.g., one or more individuals on foot, one or more on horseback, one or more onboard a cart, carriage or wagon, and the composition of each load. Most tolls were reasonably priced and in the range of one cent per foot passenger and several cents for wagons. Some rates became so arbitrary they led to complaints about overcharging and unnecessary regulations. No doubt toll takers were persuaded to let people pass in exchange for things like kisses or a jug of hard cider (I'd like one of each, please). There were no counters on these wooden turnstiles, so owners had no way of knowing if receipts were a bit light on any given day. And gate operators were rarely sitting idly by, waiting for passersby. Rather, a

PART I : THE VICTORIAN ERA

The Allendale covered bridge, which once spanned Towles Gulf on the road from Adams to Lorraine in Jefferson County. The North Country families in this narrative all crossed here often, as had countless others during its years of operation. The original bridge at this site was erected in years prior to the Civil War and replaced by this roofed structure in 1898. This photograph dates to 1910, shortly before it was torn down and replaced with a more modern structure. Prior to demolition, it had been the last remaining covered bridge in Jefferson County. By the mid-19th century, an estimated 12,000 covered bridges were in operation across the country. At present, very few remain standing. Perhaps more than anything, these picturesque relics evoke images of horse-drawn carriages strolling down country roads in rural America. (author's collection)

bell was hung by the gatehouse and sounded by travelers upon their arrival. The agent would then have to cease work at a mill or farm and make his way over to collect the toll. If he was lying abed sick or had a hangover, his wife or other family member was obliged to head over and complete the transaction.

Rapid land acquisition in the central and western territories created living and business opportunities for residents of the original Thirteen Colonies. Throughout the 19th and early 20th centuries, more and more Americans and recently arrived immigrants made their way out west in search of land and employment. But the dangers inherent in such long journeys forced many to opt for water travel across rivers and coastlines. Either way, there was no quick and sure way to get to your destination rapidly and in one piece. The risks by land included deprivation, disease, and attacks by hostile Native Americans who didn't want them there in the first place. The risks by ocean included shipwrecks during voyages, which averaged six months and 18,000 nautical miles around the Horn of South America. Six of one and half a dozen of the other—naming your poison became a popular pastime.

A major factor in the rapid population growth in the Pacific region was the California Gold Rush from 1848 to 1855. In these years over half a million people made the long, arduous journey in search of personal fortune. Many elected to settle down after finding no more gold than it takes to fill a cavity. Their memoirs vividly convey the hardships of both getting there and the primitive living conditions encountered in squalid, overcrowded mining camps. One band of eager New Englanders boarded a *barque* at New Haven harbor in March of 1849. After nine harrowing, death-defying months at sea, they arrived at San Francisco Bay in late November. The only news they received *en route* was a three-month-old American newspaper during a stop at Concepción, Chile. By the standards of the day, three-month-old news was still relatively recent, and the voyagers became alarmed over accounts of the cholera epidemic raging across the States. Their first letters back home arrived almost a year after their departure; by which time their families had abandoned all hope and presumed them lost at sea.[7]

---

7. Details extracted from the *Diary of Nelson Kingsley: A California Argonaut of 1849*, first published in 1914.

CHAPTER 5

Closeness to the Food Chain

SINCE the Neolithic period, foremost among humankind's preoccupations has been tilling the fields and animal husbandry. These were the predominant pastimes in New England and the North Country between the 17th and 19th centuries. Every farmer's toolkit included the standard repertoire of plows, pitchforks, thrashing machines, exhausted farmhands, sickles, scythes, shovels, rakes and hoes. The availability of gasoline-powered tractors in the first decades of the 20th century greatly eased the burden and time required for many common tasks. The farms and dairies in Jefferson County have always turned out an impressive array of products, including horses, cows, pigs, sheep, chickens, turkeys, fruits and vegetables, grains, hay, eggs, milk, butter and cheese. Most farmsteads also had a surplus of manure for sale as fertilizer. Hattie in Jefferson County records that when the deliverymen at the family's milk company went on strike, their contingency plan was converting all the milk into cheese so nothing went to waste. Very little farm output went to waste in years past.

In prior centuries, people were more intimately involved with their sources of food. Our sanitized conception of purchasing clean, USDA-inspected wrapped meats and fish at the local supermarket would have seemed like science fiction in centuries past. Dinner was prepared from whatever produce the family grew or the animals they raised or purchased at nearby farmsteads. The slaughterhouse was a familiar outbuilding in everyone's yard and was where future main courses were brought to be slaughtered, gutted and cut up so the lady of the house could dress and cook everything in the coal or wood-fired stove. The butchering process left very little behind as waste. Every edible portion was retained: blood for puddings and other uses, fat for lard, intestines for sausage (people were presumably diligent about removing the contents first), hearts, livers and other delectable organs for savory side dishes at the table. In Colonial times, even hides and sinews were recycled into clothing, threading and various other utilitarian materials.

Closeness to the Food Chain

Much of the stuff our forbearers enjoyed at the dinner table has long since vanished from the average family menu. An example of recipe tips in 19th-century periodicals includes these mouthwatering suggestions from an 1879 edition of the *American Agriculturist For The Farm, Garden & Household*:

When the beef carcass (has been) properly slaughtered and dressed, it must hang 12 to 24 hours that it may cook and set . . . The head and tail are skinned and should by no means be thrown away. The head is split into two cheeks, which makes excellent soup, or boiled with the feet and then cut into small squares and put away in molds to jelly for eating cold. The tail makes a savory, highly gelatinous soup, Ox-tail Soup, being in great demand at the restaurants in cold weather.

In general, food cultivation and preparation procedures remained fairly consistent throughout the northeast in the Colonial and Victorian periods. The Northfield family records their numbingly redundant routine on the farmstead, the only variation being the differing tasks specific to changing months and seasons. In the North Country, Hattie contracted with an on-site manager to oversee daily operations on the family farm, including planting and harvesting, tending the animals, and dairy procedures. The manager and staff were expected to maintain a steady supply of fresh produce, meat and dairy for the family and designated shops in town. The pigs and cattle were butchered on site and transported by team to Adams. Husband Frank would then take possession of an entire pig or side of beef, which he finished carving up into smaller sections in the barn. Chickens and turkeys were brought over alive and slaughtered in the backyard. It took Hattie several days to carve up pig portions into roasts, ribs, bacon, lard and other consumables. This setup was certainly cheaper than purchasing everything at the butcher shop, but also a whole lot messier.

As did the folks in New Hampshire, Hattie and Frank cultivated a large selection of crops in the backyard in Adams, an assemblage they referred to as their "*garden*." It was significantly larger than our modern conception and, over the years, was used to cultivate not only decorative plants but also cash crops, including corn, tomatoes, beans, cabbage, asparagus, celery, beets, turnips, potatoes, squash, melons, grapes, and assorted berries. The vegetables and fruits were tended, harvested and gathered for local sale and personal consumption. A significant portion of their basement was used as storage space for potatoes, apples, fruit preserves, maple sugar, syrup and molasses, as well as various other products. This was in addition to the many crops grown on the farm and transported for sale to various destinations. Hattie makes frequent mention of preparing mass quantities of succotash in the kitchen after each year's corn harvest.

PART I : THE VICTORIAN ERA

Don't know how much the family enjoyed succotash, but it was certainly one of their best sellers.

Although the family's farming and dairy operations in Jefferson County were the property manager's concern, maintenance of their backyard "garden" on Main Street was their responsibility. One summer, Hattie mentions coming back from the cottage at Thousand Island Park and finding their backyard fruits and veggies all parched and riddled with weeds. The winters may have been long and snowy up north, but the thermometer could still top off at 90 degrees during the Dog Days. They rectified the problem by hiring local help to stop in daily and tend to planting, plowing and watering during their absences.

CHAPTER 6

Maple Sugaring

IN the early years, the largest industries in the northeast had been logging, tanneries, agriculture, and dairy operations, with milk, cheese and egg production remaining prominent into the 21st century. Another longstanding industry is maple grove or "sugar bush" operations, involved with harvesting raw sap from maple trees which was then processed into various products for local use and exportation. Sweeteners in early American recipes were limited to honey and the various maple products, and demand for the latter gave rise to an entire industry across the North Country and New England. In the maple groves of central New Hampshire, sugar bush operations occurred between March and April, when the transition from colder to warmer weather causes the sap to flow freely inside the tree, thus allowing it to be tapped into a sap bucket affixed to each maple. Temperature fluctuations above 40 degrees or below 24 degrees brought the sap flow to a standstill, making further efforts impossible until the temperature had returned within the optimal range.

By 1860, annual sap production in the northern States had risen to many millions of gallons, with the yield from each healthy maple tree averaging between five to fifteen pounds each season. It was a long and laborious process, from tapping to the production of saleable products. As recorded by Henry Lyman in upstate New York, mistakes along the way would easily ruin an entire batch, involving a significant loss of income. The initial sap from each tree was the purest and most refined of the season and resulted in a delightfully pure white sugar for the table. Subsequent tappings resulted in progressively darker flows, which were refined into syrup, molasses and more sugar. In 1886, the American naturalist John Burroughs penned this whimsical recollection of sugar bush operations in the Catskill Mountains:

> A sap-run is the sweet good-bye of winter. It is the fruit of the equal marriage of the sun and frost . . . Maple syrup, in its perfection, is

rarely seen, perhaps never seen in the market. When made in large quantities and indifferently, it is dark and coarse, but when made in small quantities—that is, quickly from the first run of sap and properly treated—it has a wild delicacy of flavor that no other sweet can match. What you smell in freshly cut maple wood or taste in the blossom of the tree is in it. It is, then, indeed, the distilled essence of the tree. Made into syrup, it is white and clear as clover honey and crystallized into sugar; it is (completely) pure . . . The way to attain this result is to evaporate the sap undercover in an enameled kettle; when reduced about twelve times, allow it to settle half a day or more . . . The result is virgin syrup or sugar worthy of the table of the gods.

Maple Sugaring, Early Spring in the Northern Woods, a Currier and Ives lithograph from 1872 with an idealized depiction of sugar bush operations. In reality, harvesting and processing were arduous and time-consuming processes. Similar setups were in operation each spring alongside maple groves in the northern states and became home to family and hired help for the duration of the season. The Northfield family from central New Hampshire spent several weeks each March and April in similar settings. The resulting sale of maple products was a significant source of family income. The exact location of the "Northern Woods" pictured here is not specified, but undoubtedly somewhere in northern New England. This same scenery was commonplace each springtime in maple groves across the North Country and southern Canada. (Public Domain)

CHAPTER 7

Harvest Festivals and Husking Bees

Husking bee (noun): a gathering of farm families or friends to husk corn, usually as part of a celebration or party.

CELEBRATION of a successful harvest is an ancient tradition, and was widely practiced in colonial New England and the North Country. The Methodist Church was intimately involved with corn cultivation and harvest festivals, including the annual Corn Festival in Adams, which began by the Church in the autumn of 1877. Corn was such an essential component of the local diet it was serious business across the northeast. The 1863 edition of the Methodist Almanac for New York featured an article entitled "Use More Corn For Food," followed by these health and recipe tips: "A tablespoonful of coarse Indian corn meal stirred in a glass of cold water and drank quickly on rising in the morning has an excellent effect in keeping the system healthful and free. Living for a week wholly on sweet, fresh pure milk and corn meal mush has a most wholesome effect where there is headache, dullness, cold feet and an indifferent appetite." The article continues with a dozen recipes for preparation, including cornbread, griddle cakes, muffins, pudding, samp, whitpot and maize gruel for invalids.

Each autumn, freshly harvested corn needs to be husked and cleaned before being carted over to the gristmill for grinding into meal. Harvest celebrations typically included a husking bee, in which family and friends gathered and competed to see who would be the first to finish an entire basket. Husking and shucking were essential components because if the corn didn't dry sufficiently, it would spoil in storage over the winter months. Men, young adults and children would gather and husk their brains out while the women stayed in the house preparing the communal feast. The diaries from Northfield illustrate how important these events were in everyone's autumnal schedule. It is remarkable how efficient rural families became in turning these monotonous, time-consuming chores into an eagerly awaited social tradition in early America.

Despite the fluctuating anti-alcohol movement common to these periods, fermented beverages of all varieties flowed freely at these events. The men would partake of homemade beer or hard cider—or sometimes both. The barnyard joviality included the hallowed tradition of allowing whichever fellow found an ear of red corn to kiss the girl he fancied before dinner. One wonders how often he chose to smooch the sweetheart of another celebrant. After the husking was completed, young adults would slip away for more clandestine canoodling and finish whatever booze the men hadn't gotten to. The Puritan ministers of Colonial times hadn't frowned upon these seasonal festivities for no good reason.

A mid-19th century engraving of autumnal corn husking in New England, a ritual known colloquially as a husking bee. It illustrates the moment a lucky fellow finds an ear of red corn, thus earning the right to kiss the pretty girl of his choosing. Seems unlikely he'd opt for the wife or sweetheart of another attendee unless he were fixing to get smacked back into the 18th century. Freshly cut corn needed to be husked and dried if it was to survive the winter season. Much of it was transported to the local grist mill and processed into corn flour. Turning this annual task into a communal event instilled an element of fun into an otherwise monotonous and time-consuming chore. People routinely made the rounds at neighboring farms and were rewarded for their labor with camaraderie, food, and plenty of hard cider. (Public Domain)

WAR IS UPON US

Food is High, Hoover says "Eat Corn"
If You Can Can, Can Corn, Yes, Can the Kaiser,

But Come to the
THIRTY NINTH ANNUAL

CORN FESTIVAL

at the

METHODIST CHURCH

TO-NIGHT OCT. 30

and get your fill of the
Old Time Corn Dainties at the Old Time Price

Here's the Bill of Fare

Corn (Fed) Chicken Pie

Corn Hasty Pudding and Milk	Samp and Milk
Hulled Corn and Milk	Fried Corn Pudding
Corn Griddle Cakes	Corn Gems
Corn and Beans	Corn(ed) Beef Hash
Corn Starch Pie	Good Old Pumpkin Pie
Cabbage Salad	Corn Coffee

Ice Cream and Cake

All Things Ready at Five O'Clock

WELL - - - - COMB
WELCOME

Flyer for the annual Corn Festival at the Methodist Church in Adams, New York. This seasonal event was a major money maker for both church and town and is typical of the harvest celebrations held each autumn throughout the northeastern States. Note how all entries on the Bill of Fare include corn, including Corn Coffee (major yuck!). This notice dates to 1917 or 1918. The suggestion to Can the Kaiser reflects the war spirit sweeping America after it entered into WWI. The need to economize on groceries is indicated by the first two lines on the flyer. Future president Herbert Hoover was the country's Food Administrator during the war years. (author's collection)

CHAPTER 8

Agricultural Fairs

HUSKING bees and harvest festivals were local events that brought neighbors and towns together for a day or two of camaraderie and celebration. Agricultural fairs, on the other hand, were on a different order of magnitude and attracted merchants, participants and curiosity seekers from across the vicinity. All eagerly anticipated county fairs remain staple attractions in most places each summer and autumn. State fairs arrived later and developed into major regional events, attracting crowds from throughout the neighboring States. What began in the early 19th century as promotional gatherings for the display of livestock, produce, farm equipment and new agricultural technology soon evolved into sophisticated social gatherings containing any number of displays, food vendors, special attractions, entertainments, local produce and handicrafts put up for sale. The enduring popularity of these festivals is obviated by the vast number remaining in operation after almost two centuries.

When and where the first markets and fairs appeared is impossible to determine, although these types of gatherings certainly predate the span of recorded history. Hunger has always been a prime motivator behind many human endeavors, and the first markets likely arose after the development of agriculture and husbandry in the early Neolithic Period. The food surpluses generated within these small prehistoric communities likely gave impetus to trade with outside groups unable to obtain such essentials for sustaining life. Certainly, people were also motivated by the need to obtain commodities, raw materials and luxury goods unavailable in the immediate vicinity. Personal mobility has always been hindered by a number of factors, including the impracticality of long-distance travel and the risks inherent in venturing into remote and unfamiliar sections. And in ancient times few could afford the animal power required to move carts and wagons to their intended destinations. At some remote point in time, a solution was devised to bring these needed goods directly to the consumer. The first marketplaces and fairs were soon open for business.

Regularly scheduled market days had traditionally appeared in most communities to provide essentials such as fresh produce, meats, fish and other perishable goods. These larger fairs usually appeared only once each year and provided locals with a much wider variety of goods, including livestock, plants, seeds, spices, fabrics, medicine, tools, furniture, housewares, and various luxury goods. To promote foot traffic, most began offering incentives such as curiosities, cooked food and entertainment, including musical presentations and dances. Unlike the charter fairs of medieval Europe, which were scheduled around Christian holy days, county and regional fairs in early America appeared either in the summertime or during the harvest during early autumn.

Certainly, the street markets and traditional fairs of Europe provided a ready template for these later events in North America. Most émigrés were of English, French, Spanish, Dutch or German descent, and immigrants brought along their Old World traditions of regularly scheduled markets and fairs. The charter markets and fairs of England are of particular relevance, as the evolution of social life in the Thirteen Colonies was largely predicated upon Anglo-Saxon designs. A number of celebrated English fairs trace their origins to the Middle Ages and became increasingly larger and more raucous in later years. For 500 years, the Bartholomew Fair in the Smithfield section of the City of London remained one of the country's preeminent summer attractions.

Tracing its origins to a humble three-day cloth fair in the 12th century, the Bartholomew Fair had, by the 17th century, expanded into a two-week extravaganza of trading, eating, drinking, bawdy entertainment, pickpocketing, prostitution, and near-unbridled revelry. Massive crowds made their way to Smithfield from all over England and virtually all classes of society—royalty, tradesmen, paupers, and everyone in between. Young aristocrats regarded the yearly attraction as the perfect opportunity to engage in *slumming* amongst the anonymity of the crowds. By the late 18th century, the event had degenerated into several days of frightful debauchery and general disorder. In 1855, the storied history of Bartholomew Fair came to an abrupt end when City authorities were compelled to close the whole thing down for good.[8]

The first agricultural fair in America is a little easier to pin down than its prehistoric predecessors. Most records accede the honor to merchant, traveler and agriculturalist Elkanah Watson, who, in 1807, came up with the notion of organizing a sheep-shearing demonstration in Pittsfield, Massachusetts. There

---

[8]. The increasingly odious nature of this annual event was brilliantly satirized by 17th-century English playwright Benjamin Johnson in his five-act comedy Bartholomew Fair. Arguably the greatest Jacobean literary figure after William Shakespeare, Johnson's insightful characterizations have kept this comedic work in circulation since its premiere in October of 1614.

PART I : THE VICTORIAN ERA

is not much family-oriented excitement there. But in 1811, Watson upped the intensity a notch by rebranding the event as a Cattle Show, which in turn became known as the Berkshire County Fair. Although still somewhat short on rides, concessions and assorted titillating amusements, the expanded format nevertheless combined animal exhibits with various competitions and prizes, displays of farm equipment, domestic goods and artisan's crafts, and—as an incentive towards female participation—musical entertainment and dancing. In short order, this fledgling New England event was soon duplicated in numerous sections of the country. The original, modest agrarian gatherings soon evolved into major enterprises reminiscent of the fairs and markets of old Europe. An American tradition was born.

A view of Sanbornton Fair in central New Hampshire sometime in the late 19th century. Everyone in the community eagerly anticipated these annual events. Anyone not laid up sick in bed made an effort to get out and join in the festivities. Agricultural fairs began to proliferate across America, beginning with sheep-shearing demonstrations in New England during the early 1800s. County fairs were held at various locations in New Hampshire, including Sanbornton, Tilton, Laconia and Manchester. All were scheduled during harvest from early September through the middle of October. Awards were presented for best of show in numerous categories, including animals, produce, baked goods, arts and crafts, etc. Then as now, these annual events generated much sorely needed income for rural towns and residents. In the modern era, county and state fairs remain a cherished tradition in most sections of the country. (Public Domain)

AGRICULTURAL FAIRS

Over the years agricultural fairs continued to proliferate, and local societies and governments soon recognized the vast revenue potential and opportunity for attracting new settlement and business development. Funds were allocated for the construction of permanent fairgrounds, and railway lines expanded service to accommodate the increasing activity at fair times. Regional variations in format reflected the varying needs and interests of different communities. In 1841, New York took the step of establishing the nation's first State Fair in the city of Syracuse. Other States followed suit in tandem with the increased public optimism and prosperity of the post-Civil War years. The appearance of increasingly more sophisticated entertainment, gaming, carnival rides, food concessions and other amusements eventuated into annual events far removed from the sheep shearing, cow mooing agricultural displays of the early 1800s. Over 2,000 county and state fairs remain active across America in the 21st century.

CHAPTER 9

A Victorian Family in New England

PRESERVED for posterity is a collection of diaries penned between 1861 and 1888 by several generations of a New Hampshire family just south of the White Mountains in Belknap and Merrimack Counties. The surviving material affords precious insights into the lifestyles of people in the years prior to, during and just after the Civil War. Diary entries mostly revolve around everyday life amongst the farms and countryside of northern New England. Due to the period and location, their experiences of urban life were few and far between, consisting mostly of periodic trips to nearby towns and cities for business or pleasure. Their livelihood was entirely within the agrarian sector, including farming, dairy production, sugar bush operations and the sale of firewood gathered and chopped from surrounding forests. Unlike the North Country people described later in this narrative, no one in the years covered by these diaries made the transition from farm to town life. Whenever a female member married, she simply packed up her stuff and moved away over to her husband's farmstead. Everyone in these memoirs was born, lived and passed into eternity in basically the same isolated section of 19th century New Hampshire.

The small communities in which these generations moved about were remarkably similar to those detailed further on in upstate New York; and especially Northfield to Lorraine and Tilton to Adams in Jefferson County. At the time of the 1870 census, the largest of the four was Adams, with 3348 residents spread out over 42.5 square miles. Neighboring Lorraine was similarly sized at 39 square miles but counted only 1377 residents. At 29 square miles, Tilton was the smallest town in Belknap County, containing a population of only 1147. Northfield was somewhat larger at 29 square miles but, like Lorraine, was relatively underpopulated, with only 833 residents.

But it is the cities in these two northern States that display the real disparities in population density in these years. As a destination for most European immigration, by 1870, New York City alone contained almost 1.5 million

Antique postcard of Main Street in Tilton during the first decade of the 20th century. Imagery is similar to the commercial district on Main Street in Adams in these years. The building on the left is the Town Hall. Official business was conducted on the second floor, with street-level set aside for various purposes over the years, including the local post office. This impressive structure dates to 1879, and was financed by the town's chief benefactor, Charles E. Tilton. The gift came with a major caveat: the town would never change its name from Tilton back to Sanbornton, nor any other name for that matter. (Public Domain)

inhabitants. By contrast, the county seat of Watertown in Jefferson County was home to only 9,400. At the State level, New York reported 4,400,000 residents, while all of New Hampshire was able to muster a scant 318,300 at the time of the census. Most of New Hampshire remained sparsely populated and underdeveloped throughout this period, while the rapid pace of industrialization and new immigration turned New York into the premier population center of North America.

Geographically, these towns were all about the same distance from Santa's workshop at the North Pole: Adams at latitude 43.8092° N and Sanbornton Bridge at 43.4426° N. Similar to seasons in the North Country, northern New Hampshire could be beautiful in summer and fall but brutal once the snow season rolled in. Winters were long and cold, with ice and snowstorms compounded by blowing and drifting snow, which greatly hindered visibility and travel. Long winters translated into shorter growing seasons, with optimal times limited to the beginning of May until the middle of October. Although lake effect weather was less pronounced in New Hampshire, their climate was still affected by pressure systems arriving from the White Mountains and Atlantic Ocean.

Like many small communities in the Victorian Era, most residents were engaged in the agricultural, dairy, logging and milling industries. And as was seen in Adams, Tilton possessed more commercial development; something encouraging migration from the countryside to take advantage of consumer goods and greater business opportunities.[9] Tilton and Adams also benefited from the introduction of railway service in the mid-19th century, which further stimulated population and commercial growth. The topography of Northfield was similar to Lorraine in that both were comprised almost entirely of farms and woodlands. But while Lorraine had "the Huddle" as a modest town center, nothing comparable ever developed in Northfield. Residents had to travel north to Sanbornton Bridge or Tilton Center or over to Belmont and Canterbury whenever they needed anything they couldn't produce at home.

The inland topography of New England has always been noted for its excellent scenery, and in particular the expansive forests and mountain ranges so characteristic of the northernmost States. The Green Mountains of Vermont and the White Mountains of New Hampshire are both part of the northern Appalachian Range and constitute the most rugged landscape in the American northeast. Until just recently, the Peak at Cannon Mountain included the Old Man in the Mountain, an iconic rock formation at an elevation of 1200 feet. This well-known feature functioned as a muse to generations of artists and authors, including novelist and short story writer Nathaniel Hawthorne. Sadly, in 2003, the Old Man had deteriorated to the point he succumbed to gravity and collapsed into Franconia Notch.

At the foothills of the White Mountains is the Lakes Region, a picturesque section of waterfalls and waterways, including the majestic Lake Winnipesaukee. This freshwater giant of 264 lakes and 178 miles of shoreline was gifted by the glaciers that receded from North America at the end of the last Ice Age. Issuing off the lake is the Winnipesaukee River, which flows southwestward through the State until it merges with the Pemigewasset to form the Merrimack River. About midway through this watercourse are the towns of Tilton and Northfield, which straddle the border between Belknap and Merrimack Counties. In the mid to late 19th century, these Colonial era settlements were home to the family which memorialized their lives and experiences within the rolling countryside of New England.

---

9. The most well-known figure from these parts is undoubtedly Mary Baker Eddy, author, religious leader and founder of the Church of Christ, Scientist. Eddy had been born in Bow, New Hampshire, in 1821, and as a teenager relocated with her family to Sanbornton Bridge.

The old covered bridge spanning the Pemigewasset River between the towns of Hill and Sanbornton in central New Hampshire. When built in 1824, it was an impressive 150 feet long and 30 feet wide. In 1913, an ice storm lifted the wooden structure off its abutments and carried it downstream to its doom. At the time, and electrician was in the process of installing electric lighting to the interior. The hapless fellow was fortunately able to yank off the wiring and leap to safety. Visible above the entranceway is a sign with the posted speed limit: travelers must go no faster than a man can walk—or be subject to a $5 fine. (Hill Historical Society)

Since Colonial times, a bridge has spanned the Winnipesaukee River, connecting the towns of Northfield and Sanbornton. The settlement that grew adjacent to the bridge has been referred to under various names, including Sanbornton Bridge, Bridge Village and simply The Bridge. In 1869, the land on the north side of the river was carved out and renamed Tilton in honor of Nathaniel Tilton (1726–1814), whose great-grandson Charles (1827–1901) was the town's wealthiest citizen and chief benefactor. Although Charles' money, fame and nearly inexhaustible largesse enticed the town fathers into the name change, the locals continued referring to their village under its original designation. For the remainder of the century, anyone journeying up from Northfield or down from Tilton Center would state they were on their way to "the bridge." Old habits die hard, and a steadfast adherence to tradition has always been a hallmark of New England life.

PART I : THE VICTORIAN ERA

A woodcut of the village at Sanbornton Bridge in the mid-19th century. Although the area just north of the Winnipesaukee River was officially renamed Tilton in 1869, the locals continued to refer to this settlement as Sanbornton Bridge, Bridge Village or simply The Bridge. This picturesque and heavily wooded community is situated south of the White Mountains in central New Hampshire. Like much of northern New England, it remains a popular destination for foliage viewers during the autumn months. (Public Domain)

Like most in early New England and the North Country, the majority of settlers in Belknap and Merrimack Counties could trace their roots back to 17th and 18th century England. For the most part, these immigrants settled first in Massachusetts, Connecticut or Rhode Island prior to migration into northern New England and upstate New York. With regard to the diaries, the earliest family members for whom records survive are Asa and his wife, Abigail, who relocated from England to Merrimack County in the early 18th century. Daughter Sarah was born around 1740 and eventually married a local farmer named Jonathan. This second generation was roughly contemporary to Hattie's great grandparents Joel and Bethiah in Jefferson County. The couple established their homestead on a 50-acre allotment of land outside the village at Sanbornton Bridge. Like their contemporaries in New York, the land was to remain in the family for the next two centuries. In the course of their long marriage, Sarah gave birth to 10 children, although not all survived to adulthood. Similar to other men of his generation, Jonathan took up arms during the French and Indian Wars and later served with the New Hampshire militia during the American Revolution.

The following generation included their son Thomas and wife Rachel, who were contemporary to Hattie's grandparents Daniel and Luna. This is the first generation to appear in these surviving diaries. The couple proved almost as prolific as Sarah and Jonathan and raised a house full of children in the ensuing decades. This included daughter Amanda, who lived to adulthood and married a man named Clyde from Northfield. After marriage, the couple relocated to his family's farm, where they gave birth to six children, including a daughter, Belle, and sons, John and Joseph. Clyde died suddenly from unknown causes, forcing Amanda to raise the family while overseeing the farm.

During the Civil War, both surviving sons enlisted in the 12th Regiment of the New Hampshire Infantry and were fortunate to return unscathed after their tours of duty. Joseph married a local woman named Arline, while John managed to hold on to his bachelorhood another ten years before getting hitched to a Northfield girl named Betsey. Oddly enough, Sister Belle married a man named Frank (!), with whom she raised a family in Tilton in the years after the diaries. These three siblings were thus contemporary to Hattie and Frank in Jefferson County, although it is certain none of them ever met. Belle and Frank also represent the last generation of this New England family to be chronicled in the extant material.

One of the endearing characteristics of personal memoranda from Colonial and Victorian New England is the Yankee dialect you often encounter. Most of these people were simple rural folk from the hills and farms, and their writings display the same colloquialisms undoubtedly expressed in their everyday speech. Although most in the North Country had their regional dialects, it is rarely encountered in their written material. But the diaries of this family in New Hampshire are an entirely different matter, where the idiom of Olde New England is everywhere on display. For instance, the transitive verb to carry was employed in the sense of giving someone a ride/lift on their horse, buggy, wagon or cart, e.g., "Stanley carried the girls to school on the milk wagon." Walking to your destination meant going afoot, e.g., "Samantha and Etta went to the bridge afoot in the forenoon." In addition, most verbs were preceded by the preposition "a," as in "Etta and I went a berrying," meaning "we picked berries." "Belle is a going to an entertainment at the grange," as well as the all too frequent "Nobody is a going to church today."

Between planting and harvests, everyone from Amanda's generation and after that was afforded some degree of formal education, something evident from the level of literacy encountered in their diaries. Their classes were mostly at Tilton Seminary, and mention is frequently made of one family member or another boarding at the school for the term. Their classroom experiences are rarely mentioned, aside from the retention of a few completed school assignments

PART I : THE VICTORIAN ERA

Woodcut from 1859 with a view of New Hampshire Conference Seminary and Female College. The school was founded in 1845 by members of the Methodist Episcopal Church and had an initial student body of 74 males and 56 females. In 1862, the original classroom and boarding house in Northfield were destroyed by fire. The school soon reopened on the opposite side of the Winnipesaukee River as Tilton Seminary. In the early 20th century, this facility also served as the public high school for several neighboring communities (Tilton Historical Society).

stashed in the back of their diaries. Entries for each class day read simply "at school," with no further notation prior to the indication "back home" at the end of the term. That these small Victorian communities were diligent in ensuring all male and female children had some formal education is noteworthy. Prior to the enactment of educational mandates in the 1870s, school attendance had always been optional in most of early America. A student's responsibilities at home, at work or in the field took precedence over time spent in the classroom.

The curriculum at most public schools in the 19th century was limited to aggressively drilling basic reading, writing and arithmetic into student's heads through the repetition of monotonous exercises (the three R's). One-room schoolhouse education was a mechanical regimen more akin to Pavlovian conditioning than genuine teaching. Conspicuous by its absence is any cultivation of true understanding, creativity or independent thought in young minds. But the levels of literacy nonetheless attained are evident in these diaries. Of course, their educative experiences never prevented anyone from lapsing back into their traditional New England idiom whenever school was out of session.

Relative to their contemporaries in Jefferson County, none of these people were overly religious. Their ancestry might have some Puritan blood, but that "gotta go to Church six times a week, even if it kills you" spirit from Adams and Lorraine is nowhere apparent in Northfield. Their religious observance was limited to attending services at the meeting house two or three Sundays a month—health, weather and other responsibilities permitting. Based upon prevailing demographics, their denomination was most likely Congregationalist. But in the early 1860s, several of them began attending services at the Methodist Episcopal Church at Sanbornton Bridge. Around this same time, some also attended a camp meeting held in the vicinity, either a Methodist service or a Second Great Awakening revivalist event. However, this exposure to fire and brimstone theology didn't result in any sort of epiphany, nor did anyone feel compelled to ride about the countryside spreading the gospel like Methodist circuit riders. The following day, everyone was back out in the pasture for a little haying. The day after that, several of them skipped their farm chores and went fishing.

Their degree of civic involvement also fell far short of Hattie and Frank's bewildering responsibilities. Mention is made of attendance at town meetings, "railroad meetings," and local political events near election time. But mostly, their free time was spent visiting with friends and family, attending bake sales and quilting bees, barn raisings, auctions, fairs and other area events. The adults all belonged to the Winnipesaukee Grange of Tilton and, in 1885, became charter members of the Friendship Grange, Patrons of Husbandry. Both grange halls were, of course, without electricity during the 19th century. Meetings occurred in dark, unheated halls illuminated by a few kerosene lamps, lanterns and wood stoves. Records show how the dim lighting reflected eerily on the faces of everyone gathered therein. A twilight experience that continued up to the installation of electrical wiring around 1900.[10]

The family was mostly engaged in raising crops and livestock, in addition to a significant dairy component of milk, cheese and eggs. It is remarkable how closely their routines parallel the descriptions in Henry Lyman's *Memories of the Old Homestead*. This is hardly surprising, as their experiences occurred during approximately the same years and in similar agrarian settings. The farm in Northfield raised mostly horses, pigs, cattle and chickens, the sales of which

---

10. In 1885, the New Hampshire Grange Fair Association was formed "under the auspices of the Patrons of Husbandry for the encouragement of agriculture and its kindred branches of domestic industry."

added significantly to the family's income. Mention is made of the men delivering milk and other dairy products around Northfield and Tilton in horse-drawn wagons. In winter, this required clearing a path from the farm to the packed dirt street, an activity referred to as "breaking the roads."

Tending livestock was everyone's responsibility. In late spring, cattle and other grazing animals would be set out in the adjacent pasture. For some reason, this property was either unenclosed or inadequately fenced because the animals frequently wandered off, triggering extensive search and recovery efforts in the surrounding countryside. Except during snowstorms, someone was always out at work at the woodpile, chopping up whatever had been gathered from the nearby forest. The logs were then loaded onto the wagon and transported to various destinations for sale as firewood.

These Victorian-age people were certainly not as mobile as their descendants undoubtedly became in the years to follow. Mention is made of business and social trips to the Bridge and Tilton center, as well as more distant destinations like Franklin, Salisbury, Hill, New London, Laconia and Concord. The arrival of railway service in Tilton by mid-century no doubt enhanced everyone's traveling opportunities. The family also made periodic trips to the Shaker Village in Canterbury, where they traded syrup, sugar, eggs, cheese, milk and firewood for specialty products, including housewares, knitted garments, medicines, herbs and seeds.[11] Although entries in surviving diaries are ambiguous, it is likely they also traded from time to time with the Shaker Village in Enfield.

In the modern age of mass transit, automobile ownership and global interconnectivity, it is difficult to appreciate the importance of agricultural fairs to the livelihood of these small communities in Colonial and Victorian America. Most towns had markets and greengrocers, but they featured a limited variety of goods, and the foot traffic was decidedly on the lighter side. Regional fairs were larger and offered a greater variety of goods. As a result, they inevitably attracted a considerable number of merchants, customers and curiosity seekers from throughout the surrounding region. Although the early fairs of medieval Europe appeared around holy days on the Christian calendar, the agricultural fairs of early America were almost entirely during the harvest in late summer and early autumn.[12]

---

11. In addition to the Village in Canterbury, there was a second Shaker community some ways off in Enfield. The United Society of Believers in Christ's Second Appearing—more commonly known as Shakers—supported themselves through the manufacture and sale of various goods, including furniture, housewares, medicines and seeds.

12. The largest medieval fairs in Great Britain were at Stourbridge Village in Cambridge and Bartholomew Fair in the West Smithfield district of London. The former was the inspiration for *Vanity Fair*, a Victorian novel by William Makepeace Thackeray. The latter had already been satirized by playwright Ben Johnson in his 1614 comedy Bartholomew Fair, as previously noted.

The family in Northfield attended a number of these events each September and October, including the fairs at Sanbornton, Manchester and Laconia. The sights to see and the variety of goods offered always made the trip worthwhile, as they found an array of fresh produce, seeds, livestock, cloth and furs, housewares, tools, patent medicines, exotic spices and other luxury goods unobtainable at local markets. A new fair began operating in Tilton in September of 1886, as described by local archivist Lucy Cross:

The series of 14 successful fairs held on the Franklin and Tilton Driving Park grounds under its auspices of the late Charles E. Tilton. The first fair was held in September of 1886. In the evening, the fairgrounds and village were brilliant with illumination; cannon boomed, red lights burned. The displays of cattle, horses, sheep, swine, poultry and farm crops were marvels in quantity and quality. These were a succession of splendid festivals, the discontinuance of which in 1900 was greatly regretted.[13]

Sugarbush activities occupied much time each spring and involved most family members on a rotating basis. Tapping of maple trees commenced around the second week of March and continued until the middle of April. The men had to first "break the road" (remove the snow, mud and accumulated debris) from the farm over to the sap house in the groves prior to setting up operations. Once tapping had started, it was subject to periodic interruptions from the snow squalls that plagued northern New England until the end of April. Within a few weeks, sufficient buckets of raw sap were collected, and boiling operations occupied their time up to the third or fourth week of April. The processed sap was further refined into various maple products and then transported by wagon to the Bridge and Tilton Center for sale.

Corn gathering commenced around the end of September, followed by husking activities the first three weeks in October. Much anticipation preceded these seasonal activities. Although they involved much work, it was one of the few opportunities people had to gather and socialize with others who often lived miles away on unpaved country roads. Neighbors and family would regularly make the rounds at various homes and farmsteads. A notation appears for the 9th of October regarding an unusually large husking bee at Sanbornton Bridge. Two weeks later, they attended another in Salisbury: "Have had a husking this evening. About 25 present. Husked 125 bushels."

Apple picking also began around this time and lasted until the middle to end of October. Most everyone would be out gathering from nearby trees, followed by both preservation for the winter season and processing into cider.

---

13. Lucy Cross, *History of Northfield New Hampshire, 1780-1905*.

PART I : THE VICTORIAN ERA

The volume of barrels they generated was impressive, and cider sales added significantly to the family's income. Most in New England had a real affinity for hard and sweet cider. Although unspecified in the diaries, a portion of what they produced was undoubtedly fermented. Everyone also became extra thirsty around holiday times because an entry in mid-November tells of a trip by wagon to stock up on more empty barrels.

With regard to the family's health, it is startling how often mention is made of someone being "about sick" or "*some sick*" from one condition or another. Most times, the illness is relatively minor, including respiratory infections, digestive disorders, lacerations to the extremities, and skin eruptions/rashes. Recovery was usually within a few days, and we read the person was now "some better." But occasionally, these afflictions were a bit more serious. As a youngster, Belle became bedridden for several weeks with an inflammation of the auditory canal. Whatever the causative agent, it resulted in a great deal of pain and sleepless nights. As a teenager, her brother Joseph suffered from chronic oral swelling and pain from rotten teeth and inflamed gums. Amanda writes of taking him to Laconia to have most or all of his teeth extracted (the wording is unclear). A few weeks later, they ventured back to the city to "get his new teeth." Seems odd for someone his age to require dentures. Maybe the family was just cursed with crummy teeth.

One empathizes with people who were born too soon to take advantage of modern medical treatments and pharmaceuticals to alleviate much of their suffering. As in all times and places, people learned to make do with whatever treatments were available and however much they could afford. A family's predispositions towards certain illnesses no doubt played a factor. Everyone in 19th century New Hampshire experienced their fair share of contagious diseases and illnesses related to inadequate diet, unsanitary environmental conditions, occupational hazards and other factors. In 1886, the Board of Health of the city of Manchester published its first annual report detailing conditions for the year just ended. Although antiquated and limited in scope, their findings are nonetheless revealing of the prevalence of common diseases, and the overall health of city residents. Of course, their statistics would have varied somewhat had the study been conducted in the countryside rather than in the city.

Out of a total population of almost 40,000, the study recorded 771 deaths during 1885, of which an unbelievable 325 were attributed to contagious diseases—over 42 percent of the total. The number of deaths for children under age 5 was 312—another staggering figure by modern standards. The clinicians in Manchester recorded the following fatalities from contagious diseases:

tuberculosis-related (93), cholera (89), pneumonia (42), measles (36), scarlet fever (24), typhoid fever (20), diphtheria (18) and smallpox (3). The city was fortunately not in the midst of another smallpox epidemic, or this last figure would have been considerably higher. Amongst the overall fatalities, people diagnosed with influenza often succumbed to such complicating factors as pleurisy or pneumonia. Water-borne diseases from contaminated sources are also cited as a significant health risk. Mortality statistics for today's common conditions, such as heart disease and cancer, were barely touched upon in the study.

Overall, the people in these diaries come across as conscientious, hard-working lot who endeavored to make the most out of the few resources available to them in the 19th-century countryside. Most everything they owned was produced locally, either by themselves, family or neighbors. Their frugality is everywhere apparent, with no inclination towards lavish living or frivolous expenditures. Although their existence was hardly hand-to-mouth, the impression is very little was left over for spending on luxury goods, entertainment or other caprices. Whatever surplus cash they did generate was undoubtedly stashed away for future contingencies. They purchased only the essentials, including livestock, a new wagon, or farm equipment, at auction. The birth of calves, chicks, horses and other animals always elicits mention. The stereotype of stolid, conservative New England Yankees in days of yore may be more legend than anything. But it acknowledges their legitimate need for economy and modest living to ensure the family's survival within these relatively isolated farms and homesteads.

It is questionable how many of them would recognize their old homesteads if suddenly transported through time into 21st-century New Hampshire. In later years much farmland was lost to developmental projects to accommodate the burgeoning tourist industry of northern New England. What were once rustic villages, woodlands, crops and pasturage has morphed into roads, motels, restaurants and parking lots for vacationers destined for the Lakes Region and the White Mountains. Possibly, a row of tourist cabins now occupies the land where they once fed their chickens, husked their corn and prepared barrels of cider for the holiday season. These makeovers may be more profitable, but whether modernization constitutes a qualitative improvement over the simple, bucolic beauty of the antique countryside is a matter of debate.

CHAPTER 10

Shaker Villages of New Hampshire

THE Shakers of New Hampshire were another prominent feature of the New Hampshire countryside in this period. Known officially as the United Society of Believers in Christ's Second Coming, this religious group had its inception in the First and Second Great Awakening movements of the 18th and 19th centuries. The common designation *Shakers* was bestowed in reference to their ecstatic dancing and other animated expressions of the divine presence during religious services. Due to the climate of religious intolerance in 16th and 17th century Britain, groups of disaffected individuals left the Church of England and formed new Protestant denominations, including the Puritans and Quakers. Similar to John Wesley and the Methodists, the Shakers could trace their origins back to England during the 18th century.

Shortly after its inception, the Shakers left Great Britain and immigrated to the English colonies of North America in search of greater independence and religious freedom. In ensuing years they formed a number of large and small communities, including twelve in New England and three in New York. Many were self-sufficient or nearly so, and by the Civil War years, an estimated 3000 to 4000 people were working and residing in these communities from Maine to Kentucky. The village in Canterbury was established in 1792 and, by the mid-19th century, included 300 residents and 100 buildings on a 3,000-acre site.

Their egalitarian beliefs were similar to Methodism and a number of other Great Awakening movements. As a society, they practiced gender and racial equality, pacifism, communal living and ownership of property. Although they initially brewed hard cider and other spirits, enactment of rather draconian *Millennial Laws* in 1845 resulted in a society of teetotalers—at least officially. One difference between the Shakers and most other Great Awakening movements was their strict vows of celibacy, an esthetic that led to depleted church membership in later years. As more and more elderly members passed away, they found fewer converts willing to take their place in these small, tightly knit, celibate and alcohol-free communities. The last remaining resident at Canterbury Village—Sister Ethel Hudson—passed away in 1992 at the age of 96. In the 21st century, the United Society of Believers is mostly remembered for its distinctive Shaker furniture, a style characterized by its functionality and simple, unornamented design.

A view of Enfield Shaker Village around 1880. Founded in 1793, it was one of two Shaker communities in New Hampshire. The building with a steeple at the center is the Great Stone Dwelling. Constructed between 1837 and 1841, it was the largest Shaker edifice ever built in North America. The Shakers were renowned in the 19th century for a number of specialty products, including their distinctive style of furniture. Visible between the Village and the background hills is Lake Mascoma. The complex is now a public museum and situated several miles southeast of Dartmouth College in Grafton County (Shaker Village Museum)

PART II

Jefferson County & the North Country

JEFFERSON County is situated in the northwesternmost corner of New York State, at the junction of Lake Ontario and the Saint Lawrence River. It is bordered in the north by Canada, to the west by Lake Ontario, and to the south and east by Oswego and Lewis Counties, respectively. The total land mass is approximately 1,253 square miles, of which over half was devoted to farming and grazing in the 19th century. The remainder of the land is comprised of rolling hills, woodland, rocky gorges, clay plains and other physiographic features common to southern Canada and the northeastern United States. The aboriginal population along Lake Ontario and the St. Lawrence River was the Iroquois League (later the Iroquois Confederacy), comprised of the Five Nations: the Oneida, Onondaga, Mohawk, Cayuga and Seneca tribes. In 1788, the Oneida Nation signed a treaty giving the territory that became Jefferson County to the State of New York. To French and English explorers in the 17th century, this land was found to be teeming with woodlands, pelts and many other promising resources.

In the early years of exploration, this land became known as the *North Country* because it constituted the northernmost frontiers of European settlement. Jefferson County was named after Thomas Jefferson, the founding father and third president of the newly incorporated United States. The principal city is Watertown, situated in the central region along the Black River. This waterway empties into Lake Ontario and essentially divides the County into northern and southern sections. During the 18th and 19th centuries, settlers steadily made their way over from Pennsylvania, New England and other sections of New York. They soon commenced with the logging, fishing, farming and dairy operations that remained mainstays for most of its history.

The Puritan settlers arriving from New England encountered soil and climatic conditions no better than what they left back home. Spring and summer

VOICES FROM EARLY AMERICA

seasons could be hot but lasted less than four months. The winters were longer and colder, with temperatures dipping into the double digits below zero. Killing frosts set in from September through the end of April. Lake effect weather from proximity to Lake Ontario resulted in an average snowfall of over 100 inches. The land is primarily glacial till, with topsoil comprised of a sandy loam mixed with clay, rocks and gravel. Overall, soil conditions were hardly conducive to farming or grazing. Early journals record the hardship of clearing the land of

Map of Jefferson County. This northwesternmost section of New York State is bordered by Canada in the north, Lake Ontario in the west, Oswego and Lewis Counties to the south and Saint Lawrence County to the east. Henry Lyman was born and raised in the town of Lorraine in the southernmost section. Hattie and Frank spent the majority of their time in the lower half of the County, with seasonal trips to Thousand Island Park on Wellesley Island. (Wikimedia Commons with revisions)

trees, scrub, boulders, rocks and other impediments prior to the commencement of building and cultivating. After much toil, soil conditions gradually became acceptable for certain crops, but on the whole, more adaptable to pasture land and dairy farming than large-scale agriculture.

The primeval forests encountered by these early settlers were comprised of first-growth woodland, which, when felled, provided them with strong, durable lumber for building farmhouses, barns, and outbuildings. These trees were age-old giants, which matured within the enriching peat and humus-laden ecosystem of the virgin woodland. Their number and stature also left more moisture in the air because these first-growth trees intercepted rainfall before they seeped into the ground, resulting in more evaporation and higher levels of humidity. The second and third-growth trees arising in later years were of altogether inferior stock and possessed neither the strength nor endurance of the original wood. The longevity of many 18th and early 19th-century wooden buildings is a testament to the quality of the timber from which they were constructed.

Woodworking traditions brought over by European settlers were augmented by knowledge from Native Americans who were well acquainted with these woodlands, as well as the practical applications of each wood type. The heavily forested land was a mixture of cedar, chestnut, hickory, pine, ash, birch, oak, spruce, butternut and maple. It wasn't unusual for builders and craftsmen to incorporate several types of wood into buildings, furniture, tools and housewares. Cedar was especially valued as fencing material and construction of insect resistant cedar chests. Chestnut was altogether more abundant in these years and prized for shingles and flooring. Hickory was used for homes, barns and other buildings. Pine was an all-purpose wood, good for furniture, flooring and general construction. Coopers utilized ash for barrels, buckets and similar containers. The sap from birch trees was traditionally processed into a beverage by Native Americans, who introduced *birch beer* to the early settlers. Oak was the heaviest of the hardwoods and was valued as a building material and long-burning fuel for stoves and fireplaces. Spruce was abundant and utilized for bridges and barns. The use of treenails (trunnels) was common in the construction of colonial buildings, bridges and watercraft. These wooden nails were non-corrosive and found to be more resilient than their metal counterparts. Very little timber was wasted after the clearing of the virgin forests for farms and towns.[14]

---

14. Much of this information is derived from the writings of the late Eric Sloane, Americana expert par excellence and a veritable walking encyclopedia of Colonial architecture and engineering.

VOICES FROM EARLY AMERICA

While clearing the land, settlers were suddenly confronted with tons of rocks and boulders that had been mixed in with the soil. Rather than wasting considerable time and labor in carting them all away, the larger ones were set aside and used in the construction of farmer's walls as property markers and livestock enclosures. For added height, many were then topped with one or more rails of lumber. Most of this wooden component was later stripped off for firewood or left to rot away in the fields. The frequencies with which these curious stone relics are encountered across the New England, Pennsylvanian and New York countryside are really quite remarkable. Like silent sentinels, they snake incongruously through the woodlands with no apparent purpose or justification for the obvious effort that went into putting them up in the first place. But early farmers were far too busy to waste time by capriciously hauling huge stones into the woods and erecting useless imitations of Hadrian's Wall or the Great Wall of China. These relics once served a worthwhile purpose and, when found, mark the location of a vanished farm or homestead. The buildings may be gone, but the stone walls remain as a mute testament to their former presence in the countryside.

By the mid-19th century, logging operations and sawmills became commonplace alongside tributaries of Lake Ontario, including in the Stony Creek

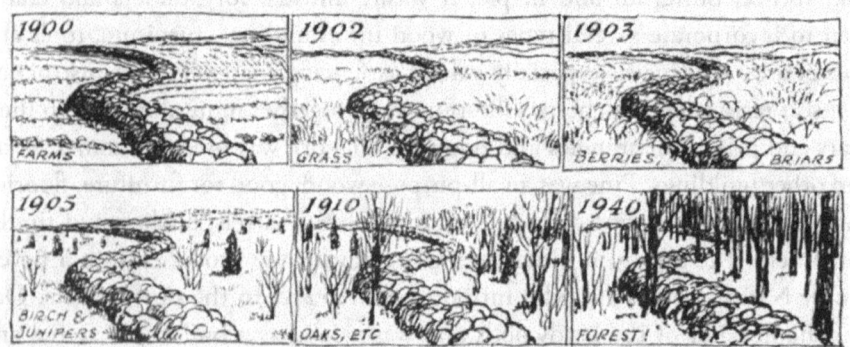

Different stages in the life of a "farmer's wall" by Eric Sloane. This illustration shows the rapidity with which unattended farmland invariably reverts to woodland. These enigmatic structures are frequently encountered in woodlands throughout New England and the North Country. Most of these stone fences were erected in the 18th and early 19th centuries for use as property markers and livestock enclosures. Once the land is abandoned, the surrounding property reverts to woodland in as little as half a century. The farmsteads may be gone, but the stone monoliths remain as silent sentinels of days gone by (The Eric Sloane Estate)

and Sandy Creek sections of southern Jefferson County. A number of tanneries were also in operation during this period. By the second half of the century, these industries underwent a sharp decline after years of systemic land clearance and deforestation. By the time of the 1900 census, the population of Jefferson County was listed as 76,748, with a total of approximately 7000 farms spread out across 745,000 acres of arable cropland and pasture. The output from the farming industry included livestock, hay, grains, vegetables and fruits. The 80,000 cows maintained by the dairy industry generated an income of almost $2,000,000 from products like milk, cream, butter and cheese. This figure didn't include the poultry sector, which contributed revenue from the production of eggs and meat.

Migration from New England and Pennsylvania into the North Country increased rapidly in the early 19th century. By 1802, the town of Adams had been established, deriving its name from John Adams, the second president of the newly formed republic. In 1804, the eastern section was carved out to form the town of Rodman. Around this same time, the westernmost part of Lorraine was separated off and designated the town of Worth. In 1813, another settlement arose about three and a half miles north of Adams around the intersection of five country roads. Originally called Adams Five Corners, in 1848, the name was changed to Adams Center.

By 1870, Lorraine's population had increased to approximately 1400 souls. With 3300 residents, Adams was considerably larger, with a well-developed commercial center, including a railroad station, town hall, post office, telegraph office, sheriff's office and jail, fire department, and a number of public schools, including the impressive Hungerford Collegiate Institute and athletic field. The town also featured a public library, three banks, an electric light company, a newspaper and printing office, surveyor's office, opera house, Masonic Hall, several hotels, several physicians and dentists, druggists, lawyers, grocers, bakeries, butcher shops, tailors, dressmakers, millinery shops, a book and stationery store, several insurance agents, undertakers and coffin manufacturers, photographic studios, piano & musical instrument sales and instruction, florists, jewelers and watchmakers, hardware stores, a reservoir and pumping station, a creamery, butter and cheese processing plant, furniture manufacturer and sales, blacksmiths, livery stable, feed store, carriage factory, foundry and machine shop, coal dealers, ice dealers, lumber yard, woodworking shops, a cooper, paint factory, sash, door & blind factory, canning facility, truss factory, and a manufacturing plant for medical equipment. Quite an impressive resume for a small, rural community in upstate New York.

CHAPTER 11

Memories of the Old Homestead

A GRITTY portrayal of 19th-century life in Jefferson County is contained in the memoirs of Lorraine native Henry Harrison Lyman, compiled late in life and eventually published in 1900. Lyman was born in 1841, the youngest of nine children to a family descended from New England Puritan stock. Along with so many others in the late 18th and early 19th centuries, his grandparents migrated from Vermont to the North Country around 1802. Lyman never achieved lasting fame for his innovative work in the social or natural sciences, or any other field for that matter. He didn't invent the internal combustion engine nor isolate the causative factor of some major illness. What makes his life so remarkable is the simple fact that, in later life, he took the time to reflect upon everything and commit his memories to paper.

Lyman's evocative descriptions of growing up were undoubtedly typical of many rural youths in the Victorian Era. He vividly conveys the family's initial, hardscrabble existence after settling into the countryside at the turn of the 19th century. The land was in dismal shape and required much filling in of marshes, chopping down of trees and scrubbing soil of rocks and other impediments before their initial crops could be planted. Due to inferior soil conditions, yields in the first few years were barely sufficient to feed the family. Although conditions had improved by the time his father came of age, the days were still filled with the same repetitive, labor-intensive tasks common to country life. But the most compelling part of the story is Lyman's vivid recollections of everyday life while growing up on the farmstead.

Regardless of the month or season, he relates the drudgery of their daily schedule, which involved endless chores that left scant time for diversions like fishing or meeting up with friends. Workdays began no later than daybreak and sometimes lasted well into the night. Even his sleep was preempted whenever his father roused him to hold a burning taper for illumination during nighttime work in the barn. The two managed to stay awake by singing songs together until daybreak. Their crop variety was considerable but typical for small landowners in Jefferson County. Potatoes and corn were staples, but acreage was also set aside for pumpkins, peas and assorted other vegetables. He states, "The farm was in no sense a grain farm, yet we always raised considerable grain for our own use and some to sell." These included oats, barley, wheat and hay for the animals.

Lyman relates how work always left him a filthy, sweaty, smelly, disagreeable mess. Frequent mention is made of being covered head to toe with muck, mud and whatever else they were working on at the time. There was so much manure his father made him pile it into refuse heaps for sale as fertilizer. The pace of activities accelerated around harvest time, with all available hands out in the fields, cutting grains and gathering everything for storage or sale. He especially dreaded all the laborious tasks associated with the horse-driven thrashing machine:

> It took four span of horses, hitched to the long arms of the sweep . . . A man stood on a platform laid at the center of revolving arms . . . It was a position much to be envied, even more than that of a stage driver . . . as the grain accumulated, it was raked back and thrown into a corner of the barn to be cleaned up later. It was nasty, choking, disagreeable work. One's face would soon look like that of a negro, and his eyes and nose were fairly closed with dust, dirt and sweat, but there was no letup . . . Everyone had to do his part and keep up.[15]

He recalled with much amusement how the cattle manure accumulated in the fields during winter months. Each spring, those interminable "dry, flat cakes" had to be broken up and scattered about so they would "dissolve and make a nice, even top-dressing" or fertilizer. The cow pies were smashed into top-dressing with a tool called the dung knocker, a square, hardwood mallet with beveled edges and a handle four feet long. The boys and men would compete to see who could whack them the hardest, causing fragments to fly around in a "wide scatter." Of course, the person wielding the mallet usually got the worst of it from all the flying crap, which only added to the overall merriment. Lyman writes, "It was a farm sport of great utility," and one which induced the "retired farmer" to take up croquet, a sport "which it particularly resembles."

---

15. Excerpted from Henry Lyman, *Memories of the Old Homestead*, pp. 84-85.

PART II : JEFFERSON COUNTY & THE NORTH COUNTRY

One of the few things that eased their summertime misery was his mother mixing up a pail of homemade switchel ("haymaker's punch") for everyone out in the fields. In modern times, this antique concoction is sometimes referred to as "nature's Gatorade" for its ability to replenish fluids lost after sweating like a pig in the hot sun. Although the recipe varies, the basic ingredients were basically the same: cold water, ground ginger, spice, vinegar and one or more sweeteners, typically molasses, maple sugar or honey. Old-time sailormen also favored this summertime treat. Being mushy traditionalists, they often added a cup or two of rum for good measure. Recipes for a decent switchel are sometimes encountered in antique almanacs, and reportedly, the drink is still favored by some in Amish country.

Like many northern farmsteads, springtime found the family heavily engaged with sugar bush operations. This activity not only provided sweets for the table but also generated much sorely needed income. He recalls a disaster of his own making, which occurred at the age of thirteen or fourteen. Not really mature or responsible enough to sit up all night with kettles of boiling sap, he and his cousin ended up doing just that. While scampering off to spy on neighboring operations, they completely lost track of time.

As a consequence, the sap boiled down into a worthless, blackened paste at the bottom of the kettle. They were alerted to the disaster by the bellows of sickly, pungent smoke permeating the forest in all directions. Running to survey the damage, they discovered the contents were almost completely gone, leaving only "a lot of shelly, scaly charcoal refuse at the bottom of the pan." The incinerated kettle was itself badly warped and beyond repair.

The loss of income was bad enough, but there was also the matter of the ruined kettle. With no way of covering everything up, they summoned the courage to return home with an elaborate cock and bull story about being victimized by a batch of "sour sap," which somehow might account for the disaster. For two days, Lyman deftly parlayed a series of increasingly pointed inquiries from his parents and was finally relieved when they decided to cut their losses and let the matter drop. It wasn't until years later he finally "'fessed up" and admitted to his guilt.

On the whole, farmers in past centuries had fewer amenities with which to freshen up after a hard day's labor. It is unknown whether the family was fortunate enough to own a portable wash tub that could be filled with water from the outdoor pump. In warmer weather, everyone probably utilized the time-tested method of jumping into a local pond or stream to soak off all the accumulated crud. But assiduous removal of sweat and filth and changing into clean clothing were hardly everyday occurrences on antique farmsteads. Although similar problems still plague modern farmers, at least nowadays, people have some readily available options to mitigate the unseemliness prior to donning diner jackets or pajamas.

In early adulthood, Lyman moved off the farm and relocated to Oswego County, and graduated from Pulaski Academy before continuing his studies in surveying and civil engineering. Despite his humble origins, he rose to considerable prominence in the business and political structures of upstate New York.

Portrait of Henry H. Lyman in later life. Despite having started life on a family farm in small-town America, he took pains to acquire a good education and managed to become successful in both business and State government. When he passed in May of 1901, his obituary read in part, "Although born into humble surroundings, (he) achieved respect, esteem, and high honors on account of his honesty, integrity, and hard work." A former officer in the Army of the Confederacy traveled to upstate New York to present his widow the sword he confiscated when Lyman was captured during the Battle of the Wilderness in 1864. (Public Domain)

PART II : JEFFERSON COUNTY & THE NORTH COUNTRY

Having enlisted in the Union Army during the Civil War, he rose to the rank of lieutenant colonel before being captured during the Battle of the Wilderness in May of 1864. After discharge from a Confederate POW camp, he reentered civilian life in a variety of guises, including directorship of several banks in Oswego. A momentous decision to join the Republican Party eventuated in his election as sheriff and ultimately to the position of administrator for the newly organized Fisheries, Game, and Forests Commission for the State of New York.

In his memoirs, Lyman looked back upon his youth and recalled the day the teacher informed his class that, one day, one of them might grow up to be President. This was far from his goal at that point in life. "I would gladly have swapped my chances for president," he mused, "for the dead certainly I would someday be a stagecoach driver." His later rise to prominence in business and political life was such that, after his passing on the 4th of May in 1901, his widow received letters of condolence from the governor and numerous other state officials. She also records an unexpected visit from former Lieutenant F. S. Johnson, CSA, who journeyed up north to return the sword he confiscated after her husband's capture in the war. The memoirs of H.H. Lyman are an engaging account of a remarkable man who started life as the son of a farmer in a small town in the North Country.

CHAPTER 12

Diaries from the North Country

PRESENTED for examination is a collection of various and sundry material, including three large boxes of letters, diaries, photographs and miscellaneous ephemera collected over two centuries by the owners of an early 19th-century home in upstate New York. The oldest is dateable to the American Colonial Period—the late 1700s—with the most recent from around 1930. The contents are of little historical importance nor possessed of high monetary value. Mostly found are diaries, letters, church journals, shopping lists, newspaper clippings, trade cards, tickets to events, receipts, memorabilia and other material which, being of such age, were deemed of no immediate relevance and relegated to storage in the attic.

On the whole, this collection was in pretty rough shape, with perhaps twenty-five percent so badly damaged it had to be discarded without attempting to unravel its secrets. Of the remaining material, a significant portion was assigned to oblivion after repeated attempts to decipher its burnt and brittle contents either partly or completely failed, leaving the examining table and examiner a blackened, sooty mess. The little that was gleaned from these tattered remains, along with information from less damaged material, has been summarized in this story, along with photographs and information from their descendants in various parts of the country.

The content of these boxes is mostly mundane, day-to-day stuff that may appear trivial and unremarkable to some. But to the antiquarian, they reveal priceless details on vanished aspects of everyday life a century or more ago. Shopping and to-do lists with entries barely explicable or simply obsolete in the modern world: Mended mother's bustle for the coterie. Rode stage with the new blacksmith. Attended a tureen at the Grange then returned team to livery.[16] Pick up new collars for Frank's shirts. Get kerosene for the reading lamps and

---

16. Although the difference is unclear, the terms coterie and tureen were used by this family for generations in reference to certain types of social gatherings. A tureen is, of course, a large service dish. In this context, the term may signify an event where dinner was being served.

hen feed for the coop. Ordered more ice for the icebox and two tons of chestnut coal for the stove. A hastily scribbled reminder to stop at the barber shop for a shave while downtown (the price of a shave: ten cents). Oleomargarine began to appear on Hattie's shopping lists around 1920 as an alternative to freshly churned butter and lard from locally slaughtered pigs—to the utter dismay of the livestock industry. All these entries reflect simple, day-to-day articles and activities that have long since disappeared from our domestic memoranda.

The collected letters of Hattie, Frank and family reflect the largely abandoned tradition of regular written correspondence, which had long been a hallmark of American life. Every thought, word and nuance transmitted in the modern world by text, telephone or in person was painstakingly committed to writing and dispatched by post. People were not as mobile in times past, and simple details of everyday life might go unreported if not memorialized at the moment of conception. They felt if they didn't commit it to writing, they may never have the opportunity to notify so and so of the laced handkerchief gifted by Aunt Nora, or the postcard from Cousin Wilbur out west. The immediate impression upon reading through stacks of such mundane matters is why people feel compelled to spend so much time writing about such trivia. We might mention such things in casual conversation, but that's as far as most would take it. We wouldn't grab pen and paper, write it all down, stuff it in an envelope and walk it to the post office. Our modern modes of interpersonal communication differ markedly from those of our forbearers.

Prior to the fire, there must have been mountains of correspondence and other ephemera up in the attic on Main Street. In keeping with custom, Hattie and Frank wrote letters on a daily basis to friends and relatives not within their immediate midst. If a family member was visiting at some distant location, regular correspondence was promptly initiated with the folks back home. If they didn't write daily, a letter would be dispatched weekly, or at minimum once a month. For some reason, these people also felt compelled to retain this paper for posterity. Hattie and Frank's daily ramblings to daughter Laura at school in Syracuse are a case in point. After graduation, Laura brought all these letters back home for safekeeping. We know their back and forth occurred daily because if a letter went missing on a certain date, the following day's post would contain the query: Are you alright? Was the mail train delayed yesterday? Did you not write because Herbert is sick? Please write back and tell us how you are doing. No real panic but genuine concern the daily cycle had been interrupted.

The poignancy of this material is not just the biographical detail but casual references to arcane topics and events, which are so enlightening to the modern reader. The necessity of postponing a trip because the horse is lying lame in the stable. An advertisement for Buffalo Bill's Wild West Show at the fairgrounds. Cleaning the dusty mess off faces and clothing after traveling in open carriages over muddy, unpaved roads. Deliveries of heating and cooking coal kick up a smelly, sooty cloud over house and furnishings. The dread of contracting summer fevers as the new season of communicable diseases races inexorably across town. These writings invariably capture details and sensations of everyday life that have, for the most part, vanished from the American landscape.

These diaries were written in the longstanding tradition of recording everyday thoughts and activities for their benefit, a sort of literary keepsake rarely meant for public viewing. This is in contrast to other types of journals, which were penned specifically for later publication. This latter type invariably contains the author's lofty, indispensable thoughts on contemporary events and social topics. As such, they are liberally peppered with polemics and commentaries on all the important activities of the day. Although Hattie, Frank and family were undoubtedly aware of important events, this is not what we encounter in this material. The unprecedented Big Burn of 1910 that decimated millions of acres in the western States is overlooked, but a fire at some downtown shop always merits notice. The 1903 debut of Enrico Caruso at the Metropolitan Opera House escapes notice, but we read an account of Laura's school recital later that year. Their thoughts, feelings and interpersonal experiences are what mattered and what is consistently reflected in this material.

Another marked characteristic of their writing is the rigid sense of Victorian decorum and propriety maintained throughout. Scandalous or embarrassing details are given but brief notice and with a vagueness which signifies that, although they knew exactly what occurred, modesty prevents them from relating any specific or sordid details. Disagreements with family or neighbors are recorded but without vitriol or any strong sense of disapprobation. The modern predilection for lacing messages with diatribes and gratuitous F-bombs is far removed from the literary conventions of Hattie and Frank's day.

Another noticeable difference is their strict adherence to formality in modes of address. Prefixes abound whenever a name appears. Every adult male is a Mr. So-and-so. The name of a married lady is unfailingly preceded with Mrs.; that of an unmarried lady or girl by Miss. This rigid adherence is maintained for all but family members and close friends. If a lengthy list of names is encountered, everyone is listed with their appropriate designation: "Those present at the tureen were Mr. Oren Jones and his spouse Mrs. Jones, their daughter Miss Annie Jones, Mrs. Agnes Flugelhorn and her daughter Miss

PART II : JEFFERSON COUNTY & THE NORTH COUNTRY

Gladys Flugelhorn, Dr. Hackenbush and his nephew Mr. Ernest Hackenbush along with his daughter, Miss Emily Hackenbush," etc. The redundancy is striking because such adherence to antiquated modes of address has largely fallen by the wayside.

The material that escaped the flames is also noteworthy for poignancy and emotive appeal, as it captures their fleeting thoughts and impressions at specific moments in time. These people didn't scour newspapers and periodicals for things to write about. But what they did include becomes all the more precious because of casual references to arcane places and events of long ago. The Chicago World's Fair in 1893 goes unreported, but we read of an unexpected encounter with Uncle George at the State Fair. The 1901 assassination of President McKinley in Buffalo escapes notice, but mention is made of the tragic death of the neighbor's kitten. The sinking of the Titanic in April of 1912 is completely overlooked, but we learn about the lightning strike at a nearby barn. If wars and conflicts are referenced, it is only in passing, but they vividly describe their walk to the train station in 1913 to send off town veterans to the 40th anniversary of Gettysburg in Pennsylvania.[17] Nightly sightings of Halley's Comet in 1910 *are* recorded because the family personally witnessed the phenomena. The kind of stuff that makes it into history books is rarely, if ever, encountered. But the simple, mundane aspects of everyday life always are.

The world in which Hattie and Frank grew up was a time of rising exuberance and optimism, as advances in technology and industrialization promised to usher in a milieu of happiness and prosperity for all Americans. Frank's father, the Reverend Gordon, believed fervently in an upcoming religious awakening as widely prophesized by fire and brimstone orators of the *Great Awakening* Movements. But, unseen by most, there was a dark side to all this progress. The complacency engendered by decades of unfettered advancement was shattered by the guns of August in 1914, as the conflagration suddenly eclipsing all of Europe utterly dispelled Victorian notions of unhindered achievement. The same spirit of innovation that put people into automobiles and electric lighting into homes and businesses was responsible for mechanized warfare that brought death and misery on a scale hitherto unimaginable. Daughter Laura came of age after her parent's belief in spiritual and material progress had been altered by the

---

17. In 1883, the DeAlton Cooper Post No. 281 of the Grand Army of the Republic was formed in Adams. At one time, 200 area residents were active, including 37 from Adams. The Post was named after a local soldier who died of Typhoid Fever in 1865 while serving with the 10th New York Heavy Artillery at the siege of Petersburg. The Post disbanded in January of 1929 because, by then, only five veterans were still alive. A notice in the local newspaper included this verse: On Fame's eternal camping ground their tents are spread, while Glory keeps in solemn round the bivouac of the dead.

exigency of millions of deaths and the desultory toppling of ancient dynasties in Europe and beyond.

> In Flanders fields, the poppies blow
> Between the crosses, row on row,
> That mark our place, and in the sky
> The larks, still bravely singing, fly
> Scarce heard amid the guns below.
>
> We are the Dead. Short days ago
> We lived, felt dawn, saw sunset glow,
> Loved and were loved, and now we lie,
> In Flanders fields.
>
> Take up our quarrel with the foe:
> To you, from failing hands, we throw
> The torch be yours to hold it high.
> If ye break faith with us who die
> We shall not sleep, though poppies grow
> In Flanders fields.
>
> —John McCrae, 1915

The optimism of generations evaporated in short order, and the halcyon days were assuredly over. As one commentator noted a century ago: "So the old life slipped away, never to return again, and wise men sensed it almost at once."

In more subtle ways, everyday life just before and after the Civil War had become stagnated by the dogged insistence on maintaining everything exactly the way it is. In this view, the world is pre-ordained by the creator, and any difficulties are the result of clumsy human intervention. In retrospect, certain aspects of their lives do appear simpler and more congenial, as they were largely bereft of the decadence, pollution and frenzy of modern society. But such superficial perceptions are grossly misleading, and fail to reflect actual social and world conditions. Many aspects of Victorian life would seem disagreeable to modern sensitivities, with others downright abhorrent. Their personal hygiene and cleanliness practices were primitive. Conditions at work and on the street were equally dirty and unsanitary. People were less comfortable and secure in their living arrangements, with domestic conditions more akin to camping out than the safe, comfy, everyday home life now taken for granted. The good old days weren't always so good.[18]

The complacency many experienced in their daily situations is at least partially attributable to their unfamiliarity with anything different or 'better.' People couldn't want anything they didn't know existed. In the countryside, things changed at a much slower pace than in the city. A family could live their entire lives without experiencing anything more innovative than a new type of plow or the sudden ability to communicate with distant relatives through telegraphy. Up to the second half of the 19th century, life continued as it had for generations amongst farms and the countryside. But continuous scientific advances and the lure of all this new technology inevitably affected the *zeitgeist* of almost all Americans, even in rural areas.

What is remarkable is the degree to which life in our modern cities and suburbs has become disassociated with the ebbs and flows of nature and changing seasons, observations so essential to our forebears. In times past, the tenor of everyday life had always been driven by an observance of and adherence to climatic conditions and the rhythmic cycles of nature. People wholly dependent upon their home-raised crops and livestock could literally starve without careful adherence to the activities specific to each season. Reverend Gordon began his mornings by making careful note of weather conditions, including temperature and barometer readings from his front porch. The habit of recording daily weather is a tradition dating back to the Colonial Period. In a society where people spent a greater part of their day out of doors, they needed to know when they would get rained on, snowed in or blown over by gale-force winds coming off the water. A simple walk into town could be problematic in the North Country and northernmost New England.

Contrary to popular misconception, rural people in time past didn't routinely satiate their desire for luxury goods by ordering from a Sears catalog. In most cases, such caprices were outside their economic reach anyway. The items they did purchase in town or by mail order were the bare essentials that couldn't be produced at home. Almost all food, clothing, household goods and tools were products of their industry. The raising of homes, barns and other structures requiring more help were accomplished by a communal effort with family and neighbors. Out of necessity, the isolated homesteads of a century or more ago maintained a level of self-sufficiency that has all but vanished in American society.

---

18. Otto Bettman's *The Good Old Days—They Were Terrible!* This humorous study strips away much of the sanitizing and idealizing that characterizes our modern perceptions of Victorian life. It illustrates the many aspects that, to modern sensitivities, appear downright abhorrent.

CHAPTER 13

The Story of Hattie and Frank

BY far, the most substantial assemblage of antique material used for this manuscript is from an extended family from the North Country, specifically the towns of Adams, Lorraine and Worth in Jefferson County, New York. The vast assortment of diaries, letters, photographs and memorabilia these people kept in storage is a veritable gold mine of first-person accounts for the years between the late 18th century and about 1930. Most of this material consists of personal diaries from a Methodist minister, the Reverend Gordon, his son Frank and his wife Hattie. These people were lineal descendants of Mayflower passengers, as well as owners of a historic New York home where most of this material was found. Their story hardly terminates in the distant past, as descendants remain alive and well in places like the North Country, New England and other sections of the country.

Around 1903, Hattie began researching her genealogy back to England in the late 16th century. Some years later, her relatives brought everything up to about the mid-20th century and began a fairly detailed family tree. Thankfully, several portions of these records managed to survive a fire up in the attic. Hattie originally limited her research to her paternal and maternal sides, but in 1927 added a few details regarding her late husband's family. Both Hattie and Frank traced their lineages back to the Puritan exodus from England to North America in the early 17th century. Hattie already knew she was a lineal descendent of Richard Warren, a passenger on the Mayflower in 1620. From Plymouth Colony in Massachusetts, these initial settlers spread out across New England and all adjacent territories. In late colonial times, Frank's family relocated from northern New England to Madison and Oneida Counties in New York, while Hattie's family moved from Connecticut to the sparsely populated land near the Saint Lawrence River in Jefferson County.

Here, their forebearers would settle down, clear the land, and build the homesteads and farms that were to remain in the family for the next 200

PART II : JEFFERSON COUNTY & THE NORTH COUNTRY

years. In early America, even people with occupations had crops, livestock and other responsibilities at home before heading off to work. As young adults, Hattie and Frank moved from the countryside into town but remained close to their agrarian roots. Their families were people of the soil and authentic sons and daughters of the American Revolution. Both sides of the family cited participants in all major conflicts up to that time, including the French and

One of the few surviving images of this North Country family together. The picture dates to 1905 or 1906 and includes Frank, Laura, Flora (seated) and Hattie. Flora's husband, the Reverend Gordon, had passed in April of 1905. The setting is possibly the backyard of their home on Main Street in Adams. Frank had his suits tailored in town, but the lady's outfits were all made at home from commercially bought patterns. After the Reverend died, his widow Flora wore mostly dark-colored clothing up to her passing in 1926. Frank finally broke down and shaved off that Victorian mustache in 1912, possibly at Hattie's insistence. (author's collection)

Indian Wars, the American Revolution, the War of 1812, the Civil War, and the Spanish-American War.

Due to the fortunate survival of much relevant material, a fairly detailed picture emerges regarding the men on both sides of the family, including Hattie's grandfather and great-grandfather. Most information regarding their mother's sides, assuming any was stored in the attic, went up in flames. Likewise, most records pertaining to Frank and his family prior to relocating from Madison to Jefferson County are now lost. What follows are brief biographical sketches derived from Hattie's records and a variety of other sources.

THEIR FAMILIES IN AMERICA

HATTIE'S GREAT GRANDFATHER JOEL

Hattie's great-grandfather Joel was born on the 7th of February in 1757. His family lived in the Connecticut town of Sharon, in Litchfield County. His parents may have been Baptist or, like so many others in colonial times, of the Congregational faith. Joel served in the 7th Connecticut Infantry Regiment during the American War of Independence, a service that earned him an annual pension of twenty dollars in later years. In 1783, he married another Sharon resident by the name of Bethiah, and together they raised a total of eleven children. At the beginning of the 19th century, the family packed up and embarked upon the laborious task of moving everything by oxen cart from Sharon to Franklin County, New York. Their stay there was only temporary, and by 1805, they were again on the move to the town of Worth in Jefferson County. They were among the first New England families to settle into this section of the North Country.[19]

Upon arrival, they realized, to their horror the man hired to build their new home pocketed the money and skipped out of town without completing the job. The house was without windows or doors and had only packed dirt for flooring. Joel was forced to finish construction with timber garnered from trees felled on the property. Land clearing then commenced in earnest, with the removal of trees, boulders, rocks and other impediments towards grazing and crop cultivation. In later years, son Daniel replaced this original structure with the large, two-storied house familiar to Harriet Irene. At the age of 91, Joel suffered a stroke at the home of his son John and died on his 91st birthday in 1848. He lies interred at Stears Corner Cemetery in Worth.

---

19. When Joel and family arrived in 1805, the land now comprising the towns of Lorraine and Worth was named Malta

PART II : JEFFERSON COUNTY & THE NORTH COUNTRY

Her Grandfather Daniel

Daniel was born at his parent's home in Sharon on the 10th of August in 1792. Along with father Joel, he served with distinction during the War of 1812, most notably with the 55th Infantry Regiment of the New York State Militia during the battles of Sackets Harbor. Daniel was one of approximately 100 North Country men forced to drag a four-ton nautical cable (actually, a 600-foot long, 18-inch thick hemp rope) the twenty miles from Sandy Creek to the naval station at Sackets Harbor. This mother of all ropes was destined to become either an anchor line or rigging for their new frigate, the USS Superior. The swift and successful launching of this warship was essential for the strategy of blockading the British Navy at port and establishing American dominance over Lake Ontario.

This herculean effort required each man to support around 100 pounds of weight over a distance of more than twenty miles. Their arrival two days later triggered a joyous celebration amongst the sailors, militiamen and families at the naval base. But the ordeal of carrying four tons of hemp for 48 straight hours left most of the men injured and scarred for the remainder of their days. In commemoration of their success, the State of New York and the State Chapter of the Daughters of 1812 erected three granite monuments along the route of The Cable Trail. One monument contains a bronze plaque with the following inscription:

> ROUTE TRAVELED BY THE MEN
> WHO CARRIED THE FOUR-TON CABLE
> FOR THE SHIP "SUPERIOR" TWENTY MILES
> FROM SANDY CREEK BATTLEFIELD
> TO SACKETS HARBOR IN JUNE 1814

Daniel married a Lorraine resident named Luna, and together, they raised five children on the family farm. Their date of marriage is uncertain, as for unknown reasons, this notation is consistently missing in surviving records. Hattie recorded her mother's recollections of grandmother Luna: "She was possessed of a vigorous constitution. She accomplished a large amount of labor and naturally assisted in making provision for the family."

In other words, she was the family workhorse. Luna died of unknown causes in 1866, and two years later, widower Daniel married another local by the name of Priscilla.

In later life, Hattie's grandfather converted to the Methodist faith and was elected a trustee of the Methodist Episcopal Church in 1853. During his lifetime, family income was derived from their 1000 acres of farmland and woodland. The property was later passed on to his son Lafayette and by succession to Hattie in the late 19th century. Uncertainty abounds regarding the precise boundaries of this property. When originally settled, it was entirely within the town of Malta. But in April of 1848, the westernmost section of town—including a portion of their land—was carved out to form the town of Worth. The remainder of the property became part of the town of Lorraine. We know the land straddled town lines because, in later years, Hattie would send property taxes to both Worth and Lorraine. Daniel died on the 23rd of September in 1887 and lies interred in Lorraine Rural Cemetery.

Her Father Lafayette

Lorraine has always been one of many small farming communities in upstate New York. Nothing really remarkable is recorded during its two century history. But records indicate a number of men and women who loomed large in their lifetimes; and among whom is Hattie's father, Lafayette.[20] Like many newborn males of his generation, he was named after the Marquis de La Fayette, the French aristocrat and cavalry commander in the Continental Army during the American Revolution. He entered this world on the 3rd of March in 1832, the son of Daniel and Luna in the newly formed town of Worth.

Despite having attended only a few years of common school, Lafayette became possessed of considerable business acumen and negotiating skills, which were put to good use throughout his business career. He was full or part-owner of a number of successful ventures, including a two-story grist mill in Allendale,[21] the Lorraine Central Cheese Factory (reorganized in 1909 as the Lorraine Milk Company), and in 1889 founding partner and long-time vice president of Citizens National Bank of Lorraine. Between 1867 and 1915, he was a copartner in a Lorraine egg pickling and packing firm, which, by 1881, became one of the largest egg distributors in the State. Operations were carried out on the basement level of the building on Main Street he co-owned with E.H. Moore, who ran his general store on ground level.

When old enough to assume control over the family's business affairs, their land in Worth and Lorraine became extremely productive and used for a variety of functions, including crop cultivation, dairy production, and pasture for a large number of cows, horses, sheep, goats and chickens they bred and sold at various times of the year. His cash crops were considerable, including corn and

---

20. His name is alternately rendered le plus français La Fayette.
21. A grist mill is where the local community brought their cereal grains to be ground into flour.

numerous other vegetables. They also derived significant income from summertime haying operations. Once the grassland had been cut and baled, it became valuable fodder for sale to other farmers. Lafayette's dairy operations included the standard repertoire of milk, butter, cheese and eggs. His property also featured a maple grove, which they utilized for seasonal harvesting of sap. Each spring, this valuable commodity was carefully tapped from each tree and then processed into the various maple products for sale both locally and by shipment to various destinations. These sugar bush operations were commonplace across the abundant maple groves dotting northern New York, New England and southern Canada.

Lafayette's unique egg pickling process ensured the product didn't spoil from lack of refrigeration during long trips by wagons and trains. The procedure involved purchasing eggs from local farms, followed by immersion for a specified time in a solution of water, lime and salt. This resulted in a preservative coating over the shell, which retarded spoilage and allowed shipment to businesses and restaurants in New York and southern Canada. By 1882, the firm was processing over 20,000 eggs per week at its headquarters on Main Street in Lorraine.[22]

Because of Lafayette's prominent standing in the community, a detailed account of his life and ventures appeared in the 1890 edition of *Child's Business Directory for Jefferson County*. Compared to the wealth of industrialists and robber barons in the big cities, Hattie's father was far from filthy rich. But by local standards, he was certainly well off. After he and his wife, Julia, had passed, Hattie retained half ownership of these businesses, which provided the family with a continuing source of income. After Hattie's passing, daughter Laura sold the family's share in the property on Main Street in Lorraine to descendants of E.H. Moore.

Like his parents before him, Lafayette held strong religious convictions and remained an active member and benefactor of the Methodist Episcopal group for many years. In the mid-century, the congregation lacked both a dedicated church and minister; and relied on the services of a circuit preacher for services at a neighboring church. To rectify these deficiencies, Lafayette sponsored the construction of the town's first Methodist church in 1857, where he served as principal officer and financier. He also held political offices in Lorraine and maintained membership in a number of civic and religious organizations. As noted in Harriet's diary, her father passed on the 4th of February in 1898. He lies interred in the family plot at Adams Rural Cemetery.

---

22. An excellent description of this process is contained in Debbie Quick's *History of the Town of Lorraine*.

THE STORY OF HATTIE AND FRANK

HER MOTHER, JULIA

Relative to information on their paternal sides, information for Hattie and Frank's moms unfortunately comes up a bit light. Hattie's mother, Julia Maria, was born in June 1828 in the town of Hopkinton in St. Lawrence County. Her parents, Norman and Laura, married in Vermont prior to migrating to Jefferson County in the early 1800s. While growing up, the family moved about the area quite extensively, residing in North Adams, Ellisburg and Rodman before finally settling into Lorraine. Julia was well educated for the time, having graduated from district Seminaries in Rodman and Adams. Of course, career paths for women two centuries ago were extremely limited. She taught at a number of district schools, during which time she became acquainted with her future husband through mutual affiliation with the Methodist Church. The couple was married in 1856 at her parent's home in Lorraine. Hattie was told of an incident where several wedding guests were capsized into Stony Creek while on their way during a snowstorm. The luckless attendees, fortunately, survived the ordeal and arrived at the ceremony both exceedingly cold and miserably wet.

Hattie's parents, Julia and Lafayette, in later life. Her father was a successful businessman, involved with a number of ventures in Lorraine and beyond. His egg preservation and distribution business was the largest such venture in New York. Julia was well-educated and extremely literate for the era. Prior to marriage, she held teaching positions at several district schools in southern Jefferson County. Both of Hattie's parents were devout Methodists and extremely involved with the church in Lorraine. When Lafayette died in 1898, Julia moved in with Hattie on Main Street in Adams, where she remained until her passing in 1903. (author's collection)

PART II : JEFFERSON COUNTY & THE NORTH COUNTRY

Three children were born to this marriage: Everett in 1859, Frankie—who died in infancy in 1866—and Harriet Irene in 1868. The combination of her husband's finances and the convenience of local railway service permitted them time to travel, including to the 1876 Centennial Exhibition in Philadelphia and the 1893 World's Fair in Chicago. They also spent time at their seasonal cottage at the recently opened Thousand Island Park on Wellesley Island. Throughout her life Julia remained active in several civic and religious organizations, including the Lorraine Grange and various women's committees of the Methodist Church. Julia's health started failing shortly after her husband died in 1898. Hattie records her frequent trips to the old Lorraine homestead to care for her ailing mother. In her final months, Julia relocated to the house on Main Street in Adams, where she continued to reside up to her passing in May of 1903. She lies interred alongside her husband, Lafayette, in Adams Rural Cemetery.

Hattie's parent's homestead in 1893. The house had been built by her paternal grandfather, Daniel, on farmland purchased by his father, Joel, in 1805. After a number of relocations during her childhood years, Hattie's parents settled here in 1876 when Hattie was eight years of age. The homestead was a gathering place for their large extended family throughout the region. From left to right: unknown boy, father Lafayette, brother Everett, mother Julia, Everett's wife Martha with daughter Ethel in a carriage and son Ross under the small tree. The name of Everett's dog is unknown, but possibly Pickles after the family business in Lorraine. Hattie is missing in this photograph and likely at home in Adams with Frank. (author's collection)

Frank's Father, the Reverend Gordon

Gordon James was born to parents Caroline and Dr. James in the year 1837 at Bennetts Corners in Madison County. He spent time during his formative years at family farms in Madison and Oneida Counties. Throughout his ministry, he and his wife, Flora, made frequent trips back home to visit relatives and see what the Reverend referred to as "the old farm." Based upon a few cryptic references, his physician father may have had a drinking problem, which would account for the lifelong anti-alcohol sentiments of himself and his mother. Gordon's mom was a devout Methodist, and her religious predilections rubbed off on her impressionable young son. From an early age, Gordon arose before daybreak to study the scriptures, a habit he maintained throughout his life. He notes how, at the age of 16, he "heard the Lord's calling" and joined the Methodist Church as an Exhorter. Four years later, he became licensed to preach at the Oneida Conference. He obtained Elder's Orders in 1884, followed by ordination as *Deacon* in 1888. A notable tribute to his long ministry was his appointment in 1892 as regional delegate to the General Conference, the highest governing body in the Methodist faith.

> By all accounts, he was a man of deep religious and moral convictions; as well as a dedicated minister and counselor to all who approached him for comfort and advice. Despite limited schooling, he possessed above-average intelligence, which he cultivated through voracious reading and a keen sense of perception. Although he was plagued his entire life with depression and feelings of self-doubt, most of his contemporaries would have disagreed with such low self-esteem. People made a point of attending services to hear his sermons, which consisted of substantive, expository discourses rather than the simple, fire and brimstone rhetoric of many Great Awakening preachers. One congregant noted how people were aware they were listening to a person "of unquestionable Christian character, in whom there was neither shame nor hypocrisy."
>
> Gordon married Florilla Fidelia in Madison County on January 10, 1860. During their marriage, they had two children, Frank in 1861 and Charles in 1864. The brief tenure of church assignments required the family to pack up and move about the State every few years. Assignments averaged only two to three years, a vigorous rotational schedule which was one of the hallmarks of early Methodism. Constant changes in scenery presented numerous challenges to his professional and personal life. A testament to his

devotion to family is the support given to Flora with the hardships of relocating every couple of years. He always lent a hand with domestic chores, including shopping, cleaning, mending clothes and assisting the children with homework. Darkness descended over the household with the death of son Charley in 1884. The reason for his passing is not recorded but likely due to one of many infectious diseases afflicting these communities in the 18th and 19th centuries.

Between 1860 and 1899, the Reverend was assigned to various churches in northern and central New York, including Warren, Knoxboro, Brookfield, Jordonville, West Winfield, Cherry Valley, Hamilton, Verona, New Hartford, Adams, Utica, First Church, and Little Falls. He then returned to Adams after he was appointed District Presiding Elder, an assignment which lasted for the next six years. As a senior member of the clergy, he was also a regular delegate to state and regional Church conferences. He also acted as a mentor and assistant to junior pastors during their assignments in southern Jefferson County. From 1900 up to his passing five years later, declining health severely limited his church and personal responsibilities, but he retained his status as Presiding Elder up until his death. Right up to the final months, he continued to teach Sunday school and somehow summoned the wherewithal to officiate at area weddings and funerals.

Throughout his forty-year career, the Reverend belonged to a number of civic and religious organizations, including the local Temperance League. His religious affiliations included appointment as Chaplain of the Independent Order of Odd Fellows (IOOF Lodge 806), the Masonic Rising Sun Lodge (No. 234 F. & A. M.) and the local Grange (Pomona No. 391). The latter was significantly the first national advocacy group for the agricultural, dairy and animal husbandry industries. Founded in 1867 by employees of the U.S. Dept. of Agriculture, The National Grange of the Order of Patrons of Husbandry was organized at the state level, with the Pomona Grange servicing Jefferson County with 34 chapters by 1905. The membership offered social, legislative and educational programs hitherto unavailable to most within these underserved sectors.

He came from a generation thoroughly versed in the literary conventions of late Colonial and early Victorian society, and this rigid adherence to formality is everywhere apparent in his writings. His diaries are imbued with near mechanical redundancy, with the same details and syntax appearing day after day after day. If you skipped all the repetitive stuff, some days would contain next to nothing. The family subscribed to a number of yearly almanacs, which supported his lifelong obsession with observing the weather and recording conditions throughout the day. He begins each entry with the inevitable weather report, including careful notation of morning temperature, barometric pressure and wind direction, with updates on overall conditions throughout the day: "Mostly fair this afternoon, with some clouds in the forenoon," or "somewhat colder this morning but becoming warmer by midday" or "weather pretty fair for this time of year," etc. If the temperature changed significantly over the day, a second reading is recorded for dramatic effect.

His entries continue with the obligatory "I have read" or "Have read considerable this morning," indicating he sat at bedside and studied the scriptures before doing much else that day. Then comes the unfailing "When down to check books at the store" or "Posted some books in the forenoon," referring to Bibles and other religious material he stocked and sold at some local bookstore. If illness or inclement weather prevents him from making his daily rounds or fulfilling other obligations, an explanation is invariably noted, along with a prayer for help in doing better next time. A rubber stamp would have made a useful stocking stuffer with all this repetition.

Reverend Gordon kept meticulous records of all ministerial duties in his church journals.[23] This includes every Sunday service and sermon, along with the biblical chapter and verse from which they derived; every prayer gathering, counseling session, temperance lecture, baptism, wedding ceremony, funeral service, minister's meeting and church conference. Daily ministerial calls, bereavement visits and private prayer sessions about town are all duly noted, along with the names of everyone present. He was struck by the early deaths of so many congregants and the staggering infant mortality rate so endemic to the period. Whether for official reports or just his records, he carefully tallied all his ministerial duties and totaled everything by month and year.

A curious feature of his written material is the minuscule size of his handwriting. His cursive and printed penmanship was impeccable, especially in comparison to his son Frank—the scribbler from hell. But the near-microscopic size of everything makes it difficult to decipher. No doubt this diminutive form of writing was common at the time due to the paucity of writing paper. A feature of most 18th and 19th-century correspondence is the continuation of

---

23. To ensure their preservation, Reverend Gordon's church journals and diaries have been donated to the archives of The Upper New York Conference of the United Methodist Church.

sentences into the margins and onto unused spaces on the reverse side. The number of pages mailed originally determined postal rates, so people utilized every inch of space and crammed in whatever would fit.

His spiritual beliefs were strongly influenced by his mother's Methodist convictions, including the belief in an upcoming *"great awakening"* through worldwide efforts by the church and other religious organizations. These strongly evangelical and revivalist aspects were products of religious thought arising from the Great Awakening Movements in Great Britain and early America. His mom assured him his life's mission is to devote himself to God and take an active part in this glorious transformation. However, throughout his ministry, the Reverend's youthful idealism gradually gave way to disillusionment and despair as he realized there would be no profound religious transformation in society. Despite years of fire and brimstone rhetoric, there was no discernable improvement in people's attitudes or behavior. All their sinful practices, debauchery and intemperance continued unabated and may actually have increased a bit.

He began to seriously doubt his ability to win over hearts and minds through his ministry and berated himself as an abject failure to his mother, the church and God. He was overcome by sadness and self-doubt, which led to prolonged bouts of depression in later years. All this doom and gloom brought on insomnia as he lay awake at night praying fervently for some sign of his worthiness and purpose in life. The following entries from various years help illustrate this despair:

> I am a poor, discouraged creature of suffering. How much I desire to know my calling and my true place.
> Am very depressed in my poor ministry. Desire more of Diving grace to help me and to guide me.
> I am feeling miserably, finding little encouragement in the work of the ministry.
> I seem to be of little use except as a burden on others and as a poor drudge in the midst of this world's activities.
> I am feeling quite miserable. My discouragements are not inclined to diminish. Oh God, if thou hast a work for me, show me what it is.
> I am conscious of suffering nearly always. Am feeling quite miserable in mind and body.
> Have passed a night of great mental agony with some physical suffering. My burden is my unfaithfulness and lack of success.

I am feeling my worthlessness and helplessness. Oh when shall I be
    able to win souls to Jesus?
I had a suffering time last night and a turn of palpitation(s). Have
    concluded I ought not to be a Pastor in the church

The Reverend apparently changed his mind about leaving the ministry and continued preaching for the next quarter of a century. In retrospect, one wonders whether this incessant daily mantra of angst and self-depreciation was actually a form of catharsis rather than genuine misery and discontent. In October of 1876, he noted with some facetiousness, "Have pared apples this forenoon. Have done some reading and some suffering and groaning this afternoon." His contemporaries never shared this self-perception as an abject failure. He probably could have benefited from counseling and an antidepressant, but neither option was available in his lifetime.

At the end of August 1875, he attended a weeklong camp meeting and Love Feast in Oneida County. Upon arrival, he pitched his homemade tent and assisted with putting up the temporary outdoor tabernacle. For days, he sat and listened to a succession of sermons from the other assembled ministers. When it was his turn to address the assembly, he flat-out declined to leave the tent and step up to the lectern. He later noted "I was asked to preach tonight but refused to do so," in the belief his oratorical skills were embarrassingly inferior to all the others. At the close of the camp meeting, he wrote "Am feeling miserable and disgusted with myself. The days have been busy and sad. What is life but a scene of meetings and partings, with some of them being final?"

With declining memory, eyesight and overall health in later years, he makes frequent mention of his inability to attend to responsibilities at home and church. He writes how "miserable in body, mind and spirit" he became, and questioned why "His Divine Wisdom and Mercy permits me to endure so far on in life." He notes how all this frustration and irritability had begun to affect relationships with family and friends. On the evening of December 31st in the year before his death, he penned this elegiac entry: "Thus another year has passed and I, a pilgrim stranger, still linger on these mortal shores looking toward the end."

The following spring, he was "seized with a chill" after returning from a church conference, a condition which developed into pneumonia. Depleted in body and spirit, he passed away at age 68 on Eastern Sunday in April of 1905. A lengthy obituary appeared in the *Northern Christian Advocate* on June 22, 1905. At his funeral, one of many eulogists remarked, "It was worth one's while

PART II: JEFFERSON COUNTY & THE NORTH COUNTRY

Reverend Gordon and fellow Methodist ministers during a Church conference in the 1870s. He is pictured seated at left. His melancholy expression perhaps betrays some of the despondency he experienced during most of his lifetime. Despite lifelong struggles with depression and feelings of self-doubt, he was nonetheless a devout Methodist and effective orator over the long course of his ministry. In 1892, he was appointed regional delegate to the Methodist General Conference, the Church's highest governing body. (author's collection)

to seek the friendship of such a man." Reverend Gordon was interred in the family plot at Adams Rural Cemetery. His widow, Flora, continued to live at the family home on Main Street for the remainder of her days.

HIS MOTHER FLORILLA
Florilla Fidelia (Flora) was born to Thomas and Fidelia in 1835 at Stockbridge in Madison County. Her first name was common to the family, and her middle name was obviously in honor of her mother. At some point in the Colonial

Period, her family relocated to New York from the town of Union in Tolland County, Connecticut. As occurred with Hattie's parents, Flora and Gordon met through their mutual affiliation with the Methodist Episcopal Church. Aside from church and town functions, there were few opportunities for young men and women to become acquainted in centuries past. The couple was married in January of 1860 at a local Methodist Church in Madison County. Their marriage certificate lists his hometown as Lenox and hers as Smithfield, both in Madison County. During their marriage, Flora gave birth to two children, Frank in 1861 and Charles in 1864. Although Frank lived to his 61st year, Charles died of unknown causes in 1884.

It is known that, throughout her adult life, Flora taught Sunday school at the various churches to which her husband was assigned. She was still actively teaching every week at age 90 in Adams. Her husband's continuous reassignments were a burden, as they involved reenrolling the children every few years into new school districts. She would always accompany the boys on their walks to and from class over muddy, unpaved roads that became treacherous to navigate in North Country winters. She made most of the children's clothes at home on her trusty old sewing machine. To ease the burden, she taught her husband how to mend his shirts and trousers. In his diaries, the Reverend took pride in mentioning his willingness to help Flora with this and other chores around the house, an attribute he passed on to their son Frank.

Hattie makes frequent mention of Flora's participation in church and town events; obligations to which she became accustomed as wife of a minister. Whether she maintained a personal diary is unknown, as none have survived. As was customary, she engaged in regular written correspondence with family and friends back in Madison County. Unfortunately, her only surviving letter was penned to granddaughter Laura while at school in Syracuse during the winter of 1917. Flora's religious convictions are evident throughout, including her admonition for Laura to "put your trust not in mammon, but remain true to God, Church and family."

Aside from these details, not much else is known about her or her parents. How she felt living in the shadow of her well-known husband is unclear. In his diaries, the Reverend rarely refers to her by name but as "Mrs. Gordon" or "mother." These forms of address probably reflect how she perceived herself as the wife of a minister raising two children. She died in 1926 at age 91 while at home in Adams. By then, almost everyone she knew in earlier years had passed, including her husband and two sons. Her tombstone is adjacent to Reverend Gordon's in the family plot at Adams Rural Cemetery.

PART II: JEFFERSON COUNTY & THE NORTH COUNTRY

Frank's parents shortly after their wedding in January of 1860. Both married relatively young: Reverend Gordon at 23 and Flora at 24. The brief tenure of his church assignments forced them to frequently pack up and move the family to new locations in northern and central New York. Despite these continuous disruptions in their home life, Flora remained a dedicated wife and mother throughout their marriage. Unknown is whether Flora maintained a personal diary like the rest of the family. Aside from a brief letter to granddaughter Laura, no other personal writings survived the attic fire on Main Street. Gordon shaved off his signature beard in later years. (author's collection)

HARRIET IRENE

Due to the chance survival of much material in the attic on Main Street, a fuller picture emerges regarding both Hattie and Frank, and the years they spent together. Hattie (Harriet Irene) was born at her parent's home in Lorraine in March of 1868. The source of her first name is unknown, but her middle name was given in honor of a great aunt on her father's side. In her formative years, the family moved back and forth between neighboring towns before settling into her grandfather Daniel's hilltop home in Lorraine. She was educated at regional schools in both Lorraine and Adams, with a focus in High School on musical curriculum. Her parents owned a piano, which she brought with her after marriage. Hattie developed into an accomplished singer and keyboardist and, over the years, was a tutor to many others in their musical studies. She sang in the school choir, as well as at church, where she was the organist. Her lifelong affiliation with the Methodist faith eventuated in an introduction to Frank, with whom she soon married and settled down.

Hattie's family was well-to-do by local standards, with her father owning a number of businesses, as well as a thousand acres of farming and woodland between Worth and Lorraine. Most of this land was devoted to crops and dairy production, including profitable sugar bush operations in the maple groves. In April of 1910, Hattie reports the farm manager tapped 44 gallons of sap for processing into maple syrup, etc. Mother Julia also taught Hattie her recipe for molasses cookies, a tradition she later passed on to daughter Laura. The family derived significant income from sales by the barrel to local businesses and by railway to Thousand Island Park and Southern Pines, North Carolina.[24] Her father had always invested his income into additional stocks, bonds and properties, a practice which added significantly to Hattie's income in later years.

A remarkable feature of her early diaries is the meticulous care taken in recording all income and expenditures, a habit no doubt picked up from her businessman father. This includes all proceeds from piano lessons, her job at the store, and hours spent at the family's egg-packing operation in Lorraine. Every penny earned or spent was carefully noted by date and then tallied both weekly and monthly. After marriage, she mostly abandoned this ledger, although income and expenses were still tracked to the penny by her husband, Frank. A charming feature of seven-year-old daughter Laura's 1904 diary is the record kept of her allowance, which was duly deposited into account at a local bank—a practice inherited from her parents and grandfather.

It was only a profound physical and emotional tragedy at age seventeen that gave Frank the opportunity to enter into Hattie's life. In September of 1885, the young man she had gone with for almost four years—and was fully expecting to marry—died suddenly from one of the diseases that periodically decimated these Victorian communities. Willard was approximately four years older than Hattie, and from a Methodist family of long familiarity to her mother and father. His unexpected departure shook her to the core. Month after month, her diaries are filled with unrelenting grief, anguish and thoughts of joining him in death. Her diary for 1886 includes two locks of his auburn hair obtained from his mother, a common *memento mori* in this period.

For four weeks following his death, his mother permitted Hattie to move into his room and sleep in his bed, an interlude during which she became intimately acquainted with his thoughts, as recorded in his diaries and letters at

---

24. In November of 1920, Hattie sold her 50 percent interest in the family's sugar bush business to her brother Everett for $500 in U.S. Bonds, an amount equivalent to around $6,000 today. Everett still provided her and Frank with an ample supply of maple products for domestic use and shipment to Southern Pines.

the bedside. In her diary for 1886, she inserted a poem laden with Victorian sentimentality:

> "Under The Daisies"
> They'll never miss me when I am dead,
> The world will swing on and on.
> The cows will come browsing above my head
> When I am dead and gone.
> Over my grave, the wind will sweep,
> The snow and the rain will drift and weep
> In the long grass, the goat will sleep,
> But I will rest quietly on . . .
> In the chill November blast,
> When the summertime is past,
> The cold, gray clouds will blind the skies,
> The wind will creep by with wailing sighs,
> Where I am sleeping at last.
> But what does it matter? I won't care
> How fast the world swings on
> When I am dead and gone.
> Cyclone and blizzard may howl 'round my bed,
> But I will sleep quietly on.

This tragedy made her seriously question her religious convictions and ability to continue life without her beloved Will. Over the following year, her grief gradually gave way to acceptance as Frank began filling the emotional chasm left by the sudden loss. Hattie would soon marry, raise a family, and welcome a daughter and grandchildren into her home. But she retained memories of Will for the remainder of her years.

After high school, she was undecided about her next steps and career options. The only future she ever envisioned—marrying Will and starting a family—was gone. Reluctantly, she decided to forego enrollment in the teacher's preparatory program at Adams Collegiate Institute, a program that included an eventual transfer to Syracuse University.[25] She continued giving piano lessons and began working as a clerk, cashier and bookkeeper at the general store of C.C. Moore & Son in Lorraine Center (the area known locally as "The Huddle"). She also worked part-time at her father's egg business in

---

25. Both these options were pursued in later years by daughter Laura.

The Story of Hattie and Frank

Hattie during her late teenage years, circa 1886 or 1887. Her elegant attire with jewelry and bustle skirt reflects the relative affluence of her family. Following the sudden death of her beloved boyfriend Will in 1885, she found herself reluctantly thrust into the local singles scene in Lorraine. A succession of brief, unsatisfactory encounters rapidly followed. Then, in 1888, a new guy arrived in town from Little Falls. (author's collection)

the basement, something she found disagreeable because it included removing chicken crap from massed cages. This was in no sense a happy or fulfilling time in her eighteen-year-old life.

As becomes evident in her writings, transient episodes of melancholy continually plagued Hattie throughout her lifetime, attributable no doubt to the traumatic events of September 1885. Family and church affairs are noted with an equivocation betraying a profound, underlying sadness. Her awareness of this handicap is evident, as she repeatedly chastises herself with remonstrances

PART II : JEFFERSON COUNTY & THE NORTH COUNTRY

A turn of the 20th century postcard featuring Hattie's alma mater in Adams. By all appearances, it was quite an imposing edifice for such a small town in rural upstate New York. Families able to afford tuition costs frequently sent their children to this school from neighboring communities, including Hattie's cousin Ethel in Lorraine. The school opened in August of 1870 as the Hungerford Collegiate Institute. It was renamed Adams Collegiate Institute in 1883 and then Adams High School in 1899. It included a chapel with seating for over 260 people. Prior to the opening of the Opera House in 1904, the chapel also served as the area's largest venue for public entertainment. The Chapel contained a pipe organ, something undoubtedly of interest to the musically inclined Hattie. Much of this structure was torn down in 1938 after suffering severe damage during a wind storm. (author's collection)

to forget about the past and start "living in the moment." On a Sunday in March following marriage, she records attending Church and finding she was "one of three brides there," as if to indicate even the spotlight of matrimony had been denied her. She concludes with the remark, "Frank and I had quite a pleasant afternoon. Of course, I had to have a fit of the blues to celebrate the day."

Following Will's death, her sudden availability on the singles market was not lost on the local boys, who began vying for her attention. Hattie was smart, attractive, and the daughter of one of the wealthiest men in town: attributes which undoubtedly sent up flares over the countryside. One of the young men (whose name was also Will) tested the waters in proper Victorian fashion by

Original location of C.C. Moore & Son's general store on Main St. in Lorraine center. Hattie worked here as a bookkeeper and clerk after graduating from high school in 1885. This picture was taken shortly before the building burnt down in December of 1893. The store soon reopened at a larger location across the street and is still run by the Moore family in the 21st century. A remarkable example of the continuity of life in rural America (courtesy of Bilkey Moore)

sending letters and imploring her for a response. Hattie records her reticence, but recognizes that etiquette demanded she at least acknowledge his approaches. What she eventually wrote back is unrecorded, but he soon gave up his quest because by mid-year no further correspondence is noted from Will.

Over the next several months, she describes a succession of encounters with potential suitors, including Ed, Charlie, Oren and others, recorded only by their initials. Most were presumably her age or a little older. One chronically inebriated sod several years her senior had a knack for getting on her nerves by "buzzing around me in the store" and other locations. His name was Eber, and he happened to be her cousin. It appears he was also employed at the family's egg-packing business, so Hattie had the pleasure of running into him

PART II : JEFFERSON COUNTY & THE NORTH COUNTRY

A photograph of Lorraine center in 1925. This congregation of buildings is known locally as The Huddle. The general store of E.H. Moore is visible to the right, replete with an antique gasoline pump visible to the left of the front porch. Increasing automobile ownership in later years resulted in the installation of a second pump on the opposite side. Hattie's father, Lafayette, ran his egg pickling and packing business on the basement level. The upper floor served as a hall for dances and town meetings of various local organizations. The Moore family still operates this local landmark in the 21st century. The town of Lorraine is smaller than neighboring Adams, and contains less population and commercial development. Logging and sawmills had been staple industries in the first half of the 19th century. By Hattie's day, the main occupations were crop farming, dairy, livestock production and sugar bush operations (courtesy Bilkey Moore).

nearly every day. To hear her describe it, the nuisance did everything possible to "provoke" her with unwanted attention. It is doubtful that, in this small, religious community, he entertained any serious thoughts of marrying his cousin. Something else must have been on his mind.

When Eber accompanied her father on a business trip, she prayed fervently for him to stay there and give her some peace. Elsewhere, she fantasized about moving to some faraway locale, like "Guinea," where hopefully Eber would not be found. The last mention of him was in October when she observed him "staggering for the first time" down the street. In a largely dry town, Eber was a notable exception. She notes he "suffered from mental derangement (and was) taken to Odgensburg in 1900." The State Asylum for the Insane in Ogdensburg was hardly as distant as Guinea but still a welcome relief.

By October, her shock and grief had ameliorated to the extent she was able to note with satisfaction, "I came to the conclusion that it is fun to flirt!" What prompted the change was a pleasant encounter with "Ora" at an evening church concert (it seems most social events somehow revolved around the church). Anyway, he hung by her side until after midnight, delighting her with conversation and unabashed attention. The public setting makes it unlikely he got much further than the talking phase.

Ora ultimately struck out, but another local proved more successful in attracting her lasting attention. Hattie and her mother were already acquainted with Frank and his family through their church affiliation, as well as frequent patronage at the store where he worked. An invoice dated October 19, 1888, itemizes $31.63 in purchases (a considerable sum) for a bustle (padded undergarment), silk, braids, thread and buttons. Frank's modus operandi was far too suave to simply "buzz" around Hattie or send her repeated letters. He took advantage of the store's recently installed telephone service to speak with her directly while both were at work. In this early period, very few places were wired for telephony. But fortunately for Frank, D.E. Taylor's fancy dry goods had a connection, as did her father's business in Lorraine. In December, she made plans to meet him to "discuss the things we spoke about on the telephone." What these "things" were specifically is a matter of conjecture, although it undoubtedly involved more than just another telephone call.

Her diaries for the next two years are largely lost, although a fragment for 1887 contains an entry on May 31st which reads, "Made a bet for five cents worth of candy that I am not married in one year. EG to pay if I am not and I to pay if I am." This "EG" was obviously a friend of the female persuasion. A second entry on August 10th includes the notation "Made a bet with Alice that I would not be married in a year. Amount of bet 25 cents" Hattie won both bets because it wasn't until the 3rd of January in 1889, at 3:30 in the afternoon, that she and Frank married at her parent's home in Lorraine. Her future father-in-law, the Reverend Gordon, took the express train from Utica to perform the ceremony. She notes how the clock in the parlor "struck the half hour while the ceremony was going on." Out of 96 invitees, a total of "about 50" were in attendance—not too shabby for a January afternoon with several feet of snow on the ground, leaving local roads all but impassable. An otherwise melancholy Hattie records "got some fine presents—Beautiful Day!"

Hattie's writings contain no end of idiosyncrasies and witticisms, which adds considerable charm to this otherwise mundane material. She makes frequent use of sarcasm to express displeasure: "Well then, that's just the way things have to be!" She also makes frequent use of the term "in good season" to imply promptness, e.g., "got up this morning in good season" or "tended to all the preparations in good season." Never once do we encounter the expression "in bad season" to infer lateness with anything. Underlining, multiple exclamation marks and capital letters also appear for added emphasis. The overall effect makes for more interesting reading than the stiff formality of Reverend Gordon or the more mechanical, matter-of-fact diction of husband Frank.

Another curious feature is her frequent mention of ridding her backyard garden of "*toads*" each spring. Hattie hated the little bastards and every year embarked upon a holy crusade to exterminate all within her midst. What impact they actually had on her plantings and property is questionable. Although northern New York is a natural habitat for several species of toads and frogs, these amphibians tend to thrive in swamps and other marshy environments, none of which were presumably present in her garden on Main Street. Yet every year, she complains of them descending like one of the Plagues of Egypt in the Book of Exodus. In bold, underlined, upper case letters, we encounter things like "**SPENT THE MORNING KILLING TOADS**" or "**KILLED TOADS IN THE FORENOON**." Hattie was born too soon to witness the impact ecological damages have taken on these little critters. Nowadays, she wouldn't have such a vexing problem.

Since childhood, Hattie and her mother had always been extremely active in church and community affairs. As an adult, her responsibilities on various committees took up a large portion of her day, including plans for the annual Corn Festival and Redpath Chautauqua. Her Sundays were almost entirely devoted to religious observances, including the Sunday school class she taught weekly for 35 years. These classes apparently attracted attendees from the Methodist Church in Lorraine, as well as other Protestant denominations. On Sunday afternoons, the average class size was over 100 people. In February of 1921, Hattie records teaching in front of an oversized crowd of 304 people.

After initially moving about for a few years, Hattie and Frank eventually settled into the house on Main Street for the remainder of their marriage. It was here in 1896 that she gave birth to her daughter Laura, who eventually married, moved upstairs and gave her two grandchildren. Hattie was at home in 1898 when notice came of her father's sudden death in Lorraine. Her mother, Julia, later moved in and eventually died there in 1903. By all accounts, Hattie remained an honest, dedicated and hardworking daughter, wife, mother, grandmother, teacher and friend her entire lifetime.

She had been married for 33 years when her husband, Frank, passed away at home in June of 1922. This tragedy was followed in 1924 by the death of her beloved niece, Ethel. Hattie spent time over the next several months reading old diaries and reminiscing about experiences the couple had shared during their time together. Her periodic bouts of melancholy resurfaced, and she was compelled to visit the town doctor for medication to *"steady my nerves."* In mid-1923, she travelled to Lorraine to attend the golden wedding anniversary of old family friends; and recalled bittersweet memories of having accompanied her parents to the couple's wedding back in 1873. But now her parents were gone, and so was Frank.

That same year, she sat down with mother-in-law Flora to compile an inventory of family possessions. The listing only partially survives but contains an impressive collection of Colonial-era furniture, and other heirlooms brought over from New England at the turn of the 19th century. In September of 1923, she also felt compelled to sell the farmland her great-grandfather Joel had purchased in 1805. Frank always maintained a keen interest in their farming and dairy operations, but as a widow, she felt the time had come to move on. She sold the farmland, livestock and buildings to their property manager for many years but retained half ownership of dairy operations in Lorraine and Worth. She had previously sold her half-ownership of sugar bush operations to her brother Everett. Hattie was now 55 years of age and felt compelled to limit her focus to what mattered most at this point in life.

Her diaries from the end of the 1920s up to her passing in 1934 survive only in fragments. But it is known she became so ill around 1932 that she was no longer able to maintain her duties for church and community. She passed away at age 66 while at home on Main Street in September of 1934. Her daughter Laura, son-in-law Herbert and grandchildren were at her bedside when she died. In the final days, one of her Sunday school students was taken on as a nurse and remained at the bedside up to the end. A local obituary attributes her passing to "hardening of the arteries and an embolism," with the latter diagnosis as the immediate cause of death. She had outlived Frank by a decade and lies interred by his side in Adams Rural Cemetery. On the 1st of November in 1925, she had attended the dedication of two stained glass windows behind the church pulpit which were gifted in memoriam of Reverend Gordon and Frank. In 1934, a third stained glass window was added by her Sunday school students in recognition of her 35 years of instruction. The dedication ceremony included this benediction:

PART II : JEFFERSON COUNTY & THE NORTH COUNTRY

"Dedicated to the memory of our beloved teacher, friend and guide, who has passed from her earthly home . . . She was a woman who devoted nearly all her time to helping others in their Christian lives and has labored with us in The Lord's Vineyard for over thirty-five years. Think of her the same, I say. She is not dead; she is just away."

Group portrait from around 1890 with Hattie and other ladies of the Methodist Episcopal Church. Like her mother, Julia, she was active in several benevolent committees run by the Church. She was also involved with a number of civic organizations, including the annual Corn Festival and the scheduling of the annual Redpath Chautauqua in Jefferson County. Another notable activity is her 35 continuous years of teaching Sunday school. In adult life, daughter Laura continued her participation in most of these same groups. Hattie is standing at the center in the second row. Despite of average height, she comes across as a real shrimp in this group portrait. (author's collection)

FRANK GORDON

Not much is known about Frank prior to his family's relocation to Adams at age 21. We know that Frank Gordon was born to Flora and the Reverend in July of 1861 at Bennett's Corners in Madison County. The name Frank was common in the family. There were two relatives by this name on his father's side and a Franklin on Flora's side. Only three years separated him from his younger brother Charley, who typically accompanied him on daily walks to and from school. Frank seems to have inherited his father's aptitude for mathematics, and the Reverend would tutor him in this subject whenever asthmatic attacks kept him out of class. After high school, Frank initially planned to follow his father into the ministry and enrolled at Whitestown Seminary in Oneida County. For reasons unknown, his plans soon changed, although he remained extremely active in church affairs his entire life. In 1882, the family moved to Adams, where the Reverend had been assigned as minister. Once settled in town, Frank was able to secure work as a postal clerk at the office on Main Street.

In 1885, he was given the opportunity to work in some capacity at the hardware firm of Taylor, Cook & Company in Little Falls. The placement was only temporary because, in 1888, he was back again in Adams, where he appears in the 1890 "Child's Business Directory of Jefferson County" in partnership with D.E. Taylor at a fancy dry goods store on Main Street.[26] The store's trade cards and other advertisements boast of "a full line of Staple and Fancy Dry Goods," including such items as silks, linens, dress goods, cloaks, shawls, gloves and mittens, hosiery, white goods, hats, caps, corsets, ladies' and gents' underwear, umbrellas, trunks, traveling bags, "a full assortment of Mme. Demorest's Reliable Patterns" and "Austen's Forest Flower Cologne." The business was hardly the size of a modern superstore, and Victorian propriety would have prohibited Frank from selling underwear to female customers. They apparently employed at least one female clerk for this purpose.

Sometime in 1888, he made the acquaintance of Harriet Irene (Hattie) through mutual association with the Methodist Church, where his father was a minister. The couple fell in love and married in January 1889. After marriage, Frank continued to work at the apparel shop up to 1908, at which time he ceased playing an active role, although he retained a financial investment. By the time of the 1910 census, his occupation was listed as "Life Insurance Sales," a business he maintained as an agent and broker for various insurers. By 1920, he entered into partnership with son-in-law Herbert, who continued the business after Frank's passing in 1922. The motivations for Frank deciding to exit the retail trade are as murky as his reasons for abandoning the ministry earlier

---

26. The Taylor family in Adams appears related to the Taylors in Little Falls.

in life. Several critical years are missing from his diaries; material which would certainly have shed light on these matters.

In 1910, he spent what was then the princely sum of $1.50 for a business advertisement in the local telephone directory. The strategy apparently worked because he subsequently kept lists of newspapers and periodicals with notations as to whether ads had been placed by himself or by trusty assistant Hattie. Frank was undoubtedly an honest and likable fellow, but like most salesmen he couldn't help interjecting "the insurance game" into every encounter with friends and neighbors.[27] After all, salesmanship was his livelihood. The effectiveness of his approach is evidenced by the rapidity with which commercial, residential and automobile lines were added to his business. The latter became especially lucrative in response to skyrocketing levels of ownership. Between 1910 and 1920, living the "American Dream" included the mandatory smart upgrade from horsepower to motor vehicle. He records writing his first automobile policy in the spring of 1910 for $500 of coverage on a new Buick. The following month, he issued a second policy, which rapidly expanded into one of his most profitable "insurance games."

Amongst the material mercifully spared by the flames in the attic were several of his Sanborn Fire Insurance Maps for Jefferson County and Thousand Island Park. In 1866, the D. A. Sanborn National Insurance Diagram Bureau in New York City began compiling maps and statistics for use by fire departments, and also the insurance industry for underwriting purposes. These maps were minutely detailed and contained such information as the layout of each street and building (home, business, factory, mill, church, school, etc.), the material used in construction (wood, brick, stone, etc.), the locations of fire apparatus, alarms and hydrants (if any), railroad stops and crossings, water and gas mains, population density and prevailing wind directions. Frank undoubtedly maintained whatever maps were available for the towns and properties he insured, although most of his copies are lost.[28]

In the early years of marriage, Frank also served as a correspondent for several newspapers in Utica, in nearby Oneida County. These assignments likely coincided with his father's appointment to a church in the city. He carried a number of Correspondent's Cards for the year 1891, including the Utica Morning Herald and Utica Daily Press. Diaries in the 1890s record his ongoing struggles to meet deadlines, a problem likely attributable to his ill health. Hattie would periodically intervene by getting dispatches off to the publishers.

---

27. This verbiage or wording, to the same effect, appears consistently throughout his writings.
28. Prior to discontinuation in the mid-20th century, the Sanborn Bureau compiled detailed maps of over 12,000 cities and towns in North America.

Unfortunately, examples of his reporting have not been located but were no doubt related to affairs of the Methodist Church.

In addition to his journalistic endeavors, Frank was an amateur photographer. A number of surviving 3 x 5 glass negatives were included in storage, all of which date to the turn of the last century. Several salvageable negatives have been developed and included in this story. Somewhere on the family property was a darkroom, because he makes frequent mention of spending the evening hours developing his snapshots. In all likelihood, the camera he used was the model chosen by most Americans at this time: the Eastman Kodak Brownie. After its introduction in early 1900, it became the first ready-to-use, out-of-the-box model marketed specifically to non-professionals. The Brownie was lightweight, portable and easy to use. At the consumer-friendly cost of only $2 for camera and film, it easily sold over 100,000 units in the first year of production. No more sitting for lengthy exposure times in stodgy Victorian studios. The era of candid snapshots capturing people in the midst of their everyday activities had suddenly arrived.

A turn-of-the-century photograph likely taken by Frank, as the glass negative was found in storage on Main Street. The scene typifies the simplicity and gentility which is often associated with life in the Victorian Era. The oversized wooden wheels were common on passenger carriages in these years. Several other negatives contain interior views of the house pictured in the background. The inscription on the envelope with the negative reads "August 28, 1899 - Q. Colfax with Vinnie & team." (author's collection)

PART II : JEFFERSON COUNTY & THE NORTH COUNTRY

Another photograph was salvaged from Frank's undamaged glass negatives. The scene is a Fourth of July picnic in 1900. The location is uncertain, although possibly the yard on the side of the family home on Main Street. Hattie's large extended family also held get-togethers at places such as East Rodman, Southwick Park, Campbells Point or various spots along the St. Lawrence River. The man at left is holding a Brownie camera, the latest and greatest in 1900 photographic technology. It is also the type of camera likely used to take this snapshot. For some reason, the elderly matron at the center is making stinky eyes at Frank. Maybe she heard rumors about him and the lady with the cake. The person standing in the background at the upper right appears to be Hattie. She is probably keeping a close eye on her husband. (author's collection)

THEIR LIFE TOGETHER

Hattie and Frank were born around the time of the Civil War into small, rural communities in upstate New York. Their families could trace their paternal and maternal lineages back to the early 17th century, with one of Hattie's ancestors arriving on the Mayflower in 1620. She was the daughter of a prominent resident with several successful business ventures in the area. He was a minister's son and distantly related to owners of general merchandise stores in southern Jefferson County. The time and place of their initial encounter is unknown, but in all likelihood through their affiliation with the Methodist Church in Adams, where his father had been assigned in 1882. Frank would have been about twenty years of age at that time. Hattie was only about fourteen and deeply infatuated with her beloved Willard (Will). The two certainly gained greater familiarity during Hattie and her mother's frequent shopping trips to the fancy goods store where Frank was employed.

In the months following Will's death, Hattie was on the rebound and anxious to start a new relationship to add structure and meaning to her life. Most young men and women in small towns ended up marrying someone from amongst the local community; but her encounters with several potential suitors proved to be dead ends. However, someone of real interest soon arrived upon the scene. Frank was new in town but possessed sufficient qualities to be of interest to Hattie. The attraction was apparently mutual and no doubt moved along through Frank's use of some persuasive salesmanship skills garnered from his time in the retail industry.

While premarital dalliances were commonplace in early America, one's choice of life partner was subject to a number of qualifications, most notably ethnicity, religion, personal habits and family background. In rural communities, marriages were rarely arranged in the European dynastic sense but subject to caveats to safeguard the family's name, wealth and status against social climbers and interlopers. Fortunately for Hattie and Frank, their relationship was met with widespread approval on both sides of the family. It was an ideal match based on physical attraction, similar interests and the mutual desire for marriage.

Details regarding their courtship are largely unknown, as Hattie's writings from 1887 and 1888 survive only in fragments, and flames completely consumed Franks. Of course, public displays of amorous or raucous behavior, even excessive public gaiety, were unlikely to have occurred due to social and religious restraints. The *je ne sais quoi* and reckless abandonment of the Roaring Twenties was still decades away, and the couple undoubtedly conformed to the dictates of Victorian society, at least within the public sphere. In small-town America, the eyes of the community were always upon you, and your safest course of action was ready compliance with public expectations and sensibilities.

By this point, Hattie's despondency had largely been relegated to the subconscious. Family and community had duly examined her proposed mate and found no disqualifying defects, deficiencies or other overriding concerns. To everyone in town, Frank was obviously a decent fellow. He was also a devout Methodist and the son of a local minister. Matrimony could proceed as planned, so there was never any need to consider eloping and escaping to a safe distance. The prescribed Victorian courtship being duly completed, the couple was formally joined in holy matrimony on the third of January in 1889.

PART II : JEFFERSON COUNTY & THE NORTH COUNTRY

Cabinet card of Hattie and Frank taken shortly after their wedding in January of 1889. Huested Studios in Adams arranged the images into an artsy format making it appear the photographs are affixed by pins to a black background. The Maltese Cross on Hattie's necklace was probably an heirloom. Those puffy shoulders on her dress were all the rage on women's clothing in the final decades of the 19th century. Frank finally broke down and shaved off that debonair mustache à la Victoriana in 1912. (author's collection)

It is remarkable how quickly the newlyweds became engrained into the civic, educational and religious fabric of the community. Throughout their lives, they maintained membership in an impressive array of religious and secular organizations, all of which came with responsibilities that occupied considerable portions of their time. Frank's involvement with the Church included the Board of Trustees, where, over the years, he served as financial secretary, treasurer, and superintendent of the Sunday school. He also received the distinction of election as a lay delegate to the Methodist General Conference in 1908. He belonged to the Temperance League and Chautauqua committee and was Vice President of the Epworth League (Chapter 1485).[29]

---

29. In their youths, both Hattie and daughter Laura belonged to this movement, in existence from 1889 to 1939. It took its name from the village of Epworth in England, the birthplace of John Wesley, the founder of Methodism.

His civic duties included the Adams Board of Education, Board of Trade, Election Board, town Republican Committee, trustee of the Adams Collegiate Institute, trustee of a local bank, and organizer of the annual Corn Festival. In addition, he served as Vice President of the Lorraine Milk Company and the Dairy Men's League and was Vice President of the Regional Conference of Insurance Adjusters in Watertown. In his spare time, he belonged to the Pomona Grange (No. 117, Order of Patrons of Husbandry), Independent Order of Odd Fellows (Lodge 806), Masonic Rising Sun Lodge (No. 234 F. & A. M), and the Chautauqua Literary and Scientific Circle (C.L.S.C.). How Frank found time to be, as he would say, "about sick" is a mystery.

Hattie was no slouch in her regard. She served on the Board of the Lorraine Milk Company, was an organizer of the annual Corn Festival and Redpath Chautauqua, the Church Temperance League, Sunday School Board, Woman's Foreign Missionary Society, Woman's Home Missionary Society, Ladies Aid Society, Ladies' Freedman Fund, Daughters of Rebekah Lodge (IOOF 23), the Epworth League (Chapter 1485), International Order of the King's Daughters and Sons, and the local Pomona Grange (No. 117).[30] In addition, she taught a dedicated Sunday school class in Adams for thirty-five consecutive years. In recognition of this steadfast devotion, in the month following her death, her students raised funds for a stained glass window in her honor in the Methodist Episcopal Church. Her entire class of over 100 students attended the dedicatory ceremony, at which time the following oration was read:

"Dedicated to the memory of our beloved teacher, guide and leader . . . We, the members of her class, feel deeply grieved at the loss of a sincere friend and spiritual adviser . . . who devoted nearly all her time to helping others and labored with us in the Lord's vineyard for over thirty-five years."

During their early marriage, Hattie and Frank alternated stays at the homes of their parents in Adams and Lorraine. But like most newlyweds, what they really wanted was a place of their own. They record months of house hunting in Adams and Lorraine, which failed to result in a suitable setting. In May of 1889, they rented a flat above a store in the commercial district for $2 a week until "the old Smith house" was ready for occupancy. The house was also leased and by October was determined to be equally unsuitable, forcing them back out house hunting on local streets.

In March of 1890, Hattie records their month-long stay in Utica at the residence of her in-laws during the Reverend's assignment at a local church. The

---

30. Founded in 1882, the Women's Home Missionary Society was a charitable organization devoted to social causes, including funding for orphanages and homes for the elderly. The King's Daughters and Sons was an interdenominational fraternal and philanthropic organization founded in New York City in 1886.

PART II : JEFFERSON COUNTY & THE NORTH COUNTRY

ADAMS, N.Y. NORTH MAIN STREET.   Published by Mrs Nellie E. Warriner.

A postcard of North Main Street in Adams at the turn of the 20th century. The imagery is similar to many small towns in New England during this period. Note the telephone and electrical poles which began appearing on American streets in the late 1800s. People loved their new utilities but loathed the necessary infrastructure, which they considered an ugly intrusion into the landscape. Hattie and family walked up and down this street nearly every day to church, stores and post office. Starting in 1914, they could show off by driving through town in their new Model T. (author's collection)

size, commercial development, and social activity in the city took her aback. All the bright lights and bustle made quite an impression on the newlywed, who had not yet attained her 22nd birthday. With 44,000 residents, Utica was considerably larger than anything she had seen. In Jefferson County, the largest population center was Watertown, with a population of 14,000 in 1890. Her trips to the city had been limited to brief stays while her father was on business.

Her time in Utica provided the opportunity to visit her friend Clara, who was either an acquaintance from Jefferson County or someone she met during Frank's trips to the city. The thought occurred to her what an ideal setting the city would make for life with Frank. She alludes to some dissatisfaction at having to return home: "(Frank and I) talked of our year together," she writes, "I wish we could go to Utica to stay." Up to that point, she had led a relatively isolated small-town life amongst the farms and dairies back home. Since childhood, her social interactions had also been limited to small groups of family and acquaintances at home, farm, church and school. The sentiment in the song "How Ya Gonna Keep 'em Down on the Farm After They've Seen Paree?"

THE STORY OF HATTIE AND FRANK

Church Street in Adams around 1910. The scenery is again reminiscent of many small communities in New England around the turn of the last century. Note the automobile in the driveway at the far right. A considerable degree of affluence is evident from this photograph. Those large Victorian homes started appearing in the mid-1800s, resulting in some mighty picturesque neighborhoods. Frank's insurance trade required him to traverse this section of town regularly, servicing clients, soliciting new business and distributing his yearly insurance calendars. (author's collection)

adequately summarized the changes to small-town boys after fighting in France during the Great War. It also describes Hattie's altered state of mind after visiting Clara in the big city.

The move to Utica never materialized, and in April of that year, the newlyweds returned to Adams, where they moved into the upper level of the house on Main Street. Soon after, with his church assignment completed, the Reverend and his wife, Flora, also took the train back to Adams. The succeeding months were busy, with both couples engaged in renovating the upstairs rooms into a livable space. Frank and Hattie slowly moved their belongings into their new home, where they continued to reside for the remainder of their lives. Judging by her journal entries, Hattie the Blues Queen was overall quite happy with her new living arrangements. After all, it was the culmination of her longtime desire for marriage, which had monopolized her thoughts since her teenage years in Lorraine. But with four adults in such proximity, life was not always a bowl of cherries.

She records the standard anxieties and disagreements newlyweds experience while adapting to their new situation. Hattie's diaries are peppered with all the

PART II : JEFFERSON COUNTY & THE NORTH COUNTRY

An elegant cabinet card was found amongst Hattie's possessions in storage. As per the inscription on the reverse side, the portrait was taken at Lewis studios in Carthage and likely depicts her friend Clara from Utica. In the early years of marriage, Hattie and hubby made frequent trips to the city while Frank was a correspondent for a number of local newspapers. The hustle, bustle and bright lights of Utica dazzled Hattie and made her question her loyalty to the old hometown. (author's collection)

sly sarcasm she reserved for whenever someone or something managed to get under her skin. In March of 1895, she records "quite a talk with (mother-in-law Flora) over money matters and other things. I do not know what to do or how to remain patient." The family was far from destitute, so precisely what these "money matters" were is difficult to determine. Maybe Flora considered her young daughter-in-law too much of a spendthrift and made suggestions to tighten up a bit on the family budget. The following month, Hattie alludes to another disagreement with this facetious and rather cryptic entry: "They (Gordon and Flora) have gone to Watertown. Have had all doors and windows open and done what I liked with nobody to look at me." Maybe Flora liked the shades drawn and doors locked to deter all the peeping Toms along Main Street.

With the Reverend's passing in April of 1905, Hattie, Frank, and eight-year-old daughter Laura moved downstairs with newly widowed Flora, an arrangement maintained until Frank died in 1922 and Flora's in 1926. Rather than leave the upstairs rooms vacant, they rented the flat to a succession of families on a twelve-month lease. This arrangement continued until September of 1919 when newlyweds Laura and Herbert moved into the second floor and eventually welcomed son Gordon and daughter Marion into the family. After Frank's passing, Hattie would journey upstairs to watch the "kiddies" while their parents went out and about, an activity she cherished for the remainder of her years.

Later in life, one tends to wax nostalgic and think back over the people and events of the past. In this respect, Hattie and Frank were no different. Aside from wintering down south and seasonal sojourns to Thousand Island Park,

Postcard containing a photograph of how Hattie and Frank's home appeared shortly after the Civil War. Constructed between 1810 and 1811, it was one of the oldest houses in Adams and celebrated as the birthplace of J. Sterling Morton, founder of Arbor Day in 1872. The structure was sold in 1889 to Hattie's father, Lafayette, and Frank's father, the Reverend Gordon. Lafayette never lived in the house, although the Reverend resided there periodically up to his passing in 1905. In 1890 Lafayette later conveyed his half interest to Hattie, who became the sole owner upon the deaths of husband Frank in 1922 and mother-in-law Flora in 1926. When Hattie passed in 1934, ownership was transferred to daughter Laura and spouse Herbert. With their passing, ownership was conveyed to their daughter, Marion. In subsequent years, the house has been renovated and expanded and is still visible on South Main Street in Adams. (author's collection)

PART II: JEFFERSON COUNTY & THE NORTH COUNTRY

Their home on Main Street around 1900. Reverend Gordon and Flora are standing at the center, with Hattie and Frank pictured at right. Shortly after marriage, the newlywed couple renovated the second floor and resided there until Reverend Gordon's passing in 1905. They then moved downstairs and lived with the widowed Flora. When daughter Laura married in 1919, she and her husband Herbert took possession of the upper level, where they eventually raised a family. Compare the additions and embellishments in this photograph to the rather austere appearance of the house shortly after the Civil War. (author's collection)

they resided on Main Street through the death of numerous family members and friends, as well as the welcoming of grandchildren into the home. In 1921, Frank recorded his despondency over Flora accidentally knocking over and breaking an old reading lamp in the sitting room. He laments it "was one of the first things we purchased when we moved in" (in 1889). The lamp was kerosene and apparently unlit, or he would have had more to worry about than a broken fixture. A few years later, Hattie lamented the tearing down of a decrepit old picket fence in the backyard. "It had been there since before we moved here," she writes. "It was like losing an old friend."

Frank passed in 1922, living just long enough to bask in the glory of National Prohibition and its ostensible curtailment of the scourge known as demon rum.

Frank's side of the family in an unidentified yard in the late 19th century. Judging by all the mallets, hoops, and balls, someone was planning on a little croquet. Pictured left to right are cousin Crane and wife Mary, Reverend Gordon, Flora, Crane's parents Almira and Spurgeon, and Hattie. To her left is a rather ominous-looking Frank, deciding whether to obey the voices and bonk Hattie on the head with his mallet of mass destruction. The inscription on the reverse side lists the people on the hammock as "Harrie, Laura, May, Flora, Arthur" Faces of a family well known to others in their time. Today, how many are still recognizable, even by their lineal descendants? (author's collection)

Had he lived to witness the gaiety of the new decade, it is questionable how much would have met with his approval. He would have hated all the bathtub gin and bootlegging wars. Elegantly appointed movie palaces might have been ok, but dance halls and speakeasies would elicit a big two thumbs down. It's doubtful he would have appreciated jazz music, as even the syncopated rhythm of ragtime had been too radical for his tastes. Hattie lived until 1934 and got to see much of the restructuring of post-war America, including the precipitous rise and fall of Wall Street, the free love movement, the Charleston, bobbed hair, raised hemlines and Al Capone. But the Gilded Age just passed was the time during which their generation had been born; and the society in which they came of age and moved about for the majority of their years.

PART II : JEFFERSON COUNTY & THE NORTH COUNTRY

Frank the Salesman

Frank's insurance trade added considerably to their income from the wife's side of the family. He cultivated strong salesmanship skills during his association with D.E. Taylor and put them to good use in networking with contacts at church and various civic and professional organizations. His technique was undoubtedly similar to the modern sales repertoire: prospective buyers would do themselves an enormous favor and end up in a much better place if they spent their loot on whatever they happened to be peddling at the time. In advertising, it's always the same old shtick but with a new set of words. The more things change, the more they remain the same.

Take, for example, the millions of trade cards circulating in the 19th century, one of the most popular forms of advertising in the Victorian Period. Frank and Hattie accumulated quite a collection over the years, including several from his dry goods store. They remain impressive examples of antique lithography, with colors still clear and vibrant on postcard-sized pieces of creased and chipped cardboard. The front side of one example displays an elegant young platinum blonde enveloped in a bouquet of roses, peonies and lilies. Quite an attention-grabbing lead-in to the standard sales pitch on the back. In the interest of historical veracity, this rather bizarre bit of antique hubris is rendered verbatim:

The Secret of Beauty! All women know that it is beauty, rather than genius, which all generations of men have worshipped. Women know that when men speak of the intellect of women, they speak critically, tamely and coolly. But when they come to the charms of a beautiful woman, their language and eyes kindle with an enthusiasm that shows them to be profoundly, if not ridiculously, in earnest . . . There stands the eternal fact that the world does not prefer the society of an ugly woman of genius to that of a beauty of less intellectual acquirements. The world has yet allowed no higher mission to woman than to be beautiful . . . and all women now to whom Nature has denied the talismanic power of beauty may correct the deficiency by the use of a most delightful toilet preparation known as the 'BLOOM OF YOUTH' . . . With the assistance of this American invention, female beauty is destined to play a larger part in the admiration of men and the ambition of women than all arts employed since creation. Ladies, beware of worthless imitations of Laird's 'BLOOM OF YOUTH.' Sold by all Druggists and Fancy Goods Dealers.

Let's face it, ladies, your intellectual achievements amount to naught! An utter, unequivocal turnoff to the men in your midst! Nature has decreed no higher mission than becoming eye candy to the superior sex! One can imagine how the commercial would appear if television had been around in 1889:

Announcer: Ladies, do you weep bitterly at your reflection in the looking glass? Do you fear your gentleman suitors will get a decent look and promptly lose their morning oatmeal? Fret not, ugly women of genius, to whom Nature has denied the magical talismanic power of beauty! By the use of a most delightful toilet preparation known as the Bloom of Youth, you may now correct this most egregious deficiency! Your beauty is destined to play a dramatic role in the admiration of mankind. Try this wonderful preparation, and be prepared for legions of suitors swamping your parlor, competing for your attention! Let us observe an actual conversation prompted by the daily use of this miraculous formulation:

> THE SCENE: two smartly dressed gentlemen sauntering down Main Street
> ORVILLE: "I say, might that be Lily Langtry by yonder hitching post?"
> WILBUR: "Why, no! It is none other than our good neighbor Prunella, magically transformed by Laird's Blossom of Youth!"
> ORVILLE: "And smelling sensationally besides!"
> ANNOUNCER: "Ladies! With Laird's Blossom of Youth, you, too, may smell like daisies! Accept no imitations! On sale by all druggists and fancy goods dealers."

The verbiage in Victorian times may have differed a bit, but the message was the same. Don't be left out! Buy this new product before it's too late! Your happiness and welfare are literally contingent upon splashing liberal amounts of our stink solution from head to toe. Laird's *Blossom of Youth* a truly a life-altering experience!

PART II : JEFFERSON COUNTY & THE NORTH COUNTRY

Interior of D.E. Taylor & Co. in the late 1890s. D.E. is standing at left in his stylish three-piece suit, replete with a pocket watch and fob. The dapper gentleman in the hat and overcoat is unidentified. Behind the counter at the left is Frank. Standing beside him is Neelie Dodge, the gal likely tasked with assisting female customers shopping for new foundations or other apparel. Holding the bundle of fabric is someone named on the back as "Beamer" or "Boomer" Unidentified is the lady seated at far left in front of a sewing machine or other apparatus. Also unidentified is the rather ominous-looking little gremlin lurking behind Frank (possibly talking him into bonking Hattie on the head with a croquet mallet). A sign for Butterick Patterns appears at the upper right, which Hattie utilized along with Mme. Demorest's Patterns for much of her clothing. Note the incandescent lamps hanging from the ceiling. (author's collection)

Front and back of a trading card from D.E. Taylor & Co., the fancy dry goods shop where Frank was in partnership between 1888 and 1908. These antique advertisements featured colorful lithographs with many of the same motifs seen in modern advertising: pretty ladies, adorable children, frisky kittens and lavish floral arrangements. Formulated by W.J. Austen & Company in Oswego, New York, Austen's Forest Flower Cologne was widely promoted as "The richest and most fashionable perfume of the day. Permanence and delicacy of odor have won for it the FRONT RANK. Produced by a combination of the finest perfumes known, obtained from French and Oriental laboratories, it presents a perfect bouquet of unsurpassed delicacy and strength where no one odor predominates but all unite to please. Forest Flower Cologne has had many rivals but NEVER AN EQUAL! Look out for counterfeits and accept no other. Price 25 cents per bottle. Large bottles 75 cents." In all likelihood, the fragrance was too overpowering for modern tastes. In an era prior to daily bathing, deodorants and regular laundering, these intrusive industrial-strength preparations were a convenient way to mask unpleasant odors. Still, one hopes Frank brought home a bottle for Hattie and not just these trade cards. (author's collection)

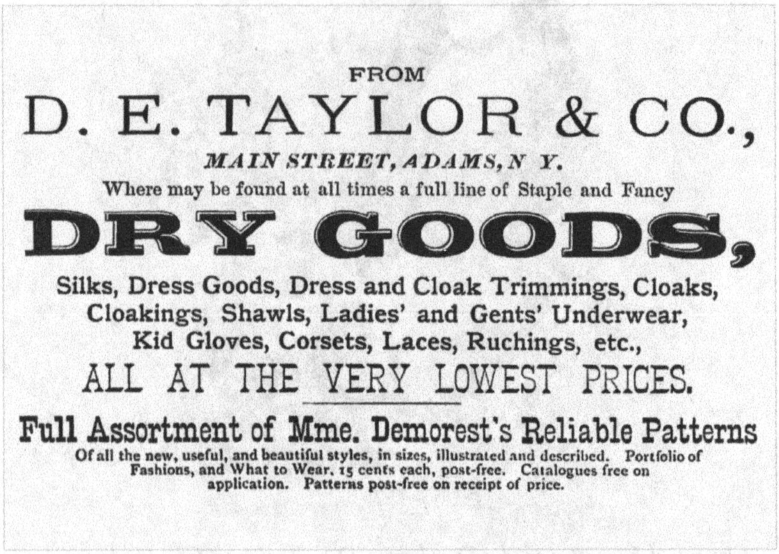

PART II : JEFFERSON COUNTY & THE NORTH COUNTRY

FROM
D. E. TAYLOR & CO.,
MAIN STREET, ADAMS, N Y.
Where may be found at all times a full line of Staple and Fancy
DRY GOODS,
Silks, Dress Goods, Dress and Cloak Trimmings, Cloaks,
Cloakings, Shawls, Ladies' and Gents' Underwear,
Kid Gloves, Corsets, Laces, Ruchings, etc.,
ALL AT THE VERY LOWEST PRICES.

Full Assortment of Mme. Demorest's Reliable Patterns
Of all the new, useful, and beautiful styles, in sizes, illustrated and described. Portfolio of Fashions, and What to Wear. 15 cents each, post-free. Catalogues free on application. Patterns post-free on receipt of price.

The reverse side of another trade card from D.E. Taylor & Co. It Seems unlikely Frank was the point person for assisting female customers shopping for new underwear. In the 19th century, much clothing was made at home from commercial patterns, such as Mme. Demorest's Reliable Patterns. As she grew older, Hattie purchased more and more of her clothing from retail outlets. What she didn't do was periodically weed out her prodigious assortment of trade cards. Literally, hundreds of these colorful, antique relics were found in storage in varying states of decomposition. Their survival provides a unique window into advertising practices in the second half of the 19th century. (author's collection)

Another trade card for Austen's Forest Flower Cologne from the attic on Main Street. The survival of such fragile antique advertising into modern times is really quite remarkable. Any attention-grabbing imagery that makes you part with a little cash is utilized over and over again. What Victorian lady could resist buying a bottle after getting a gander of this little charmer with that colorful bouquet? Trade cards were amongst the most common forms of advertising in the late Victorian Era. The colors on many of these antique lithographs remain vivid after almost a century and a half—a feature unfortunately lost in this black and white illustration. (author's collection)

PART II : JEFFERSON COUNTY & THE NORTH COUNTRY

Frank's Lousy Health

Unfortunately for Frank, his overall health was never very good. Since childhood, he suffered from a number of chronic maladies, including severe asthma, abdominal pain from "bilious complaints" (liver and gallbladder disorders), digestive issues and headaches. His pulmonary problems were particularly troubling because attacks of bronchitis and shortness of breath prevented his participation in most sports and often kept him out of classes for weeks at a time. As an adult, recurring bouts of asthma curtailed his ability to engage in strenuous activities or even take long walks with family, friends and business associates. Effective treatments such as nebulizers, bronchodilators and steroidal therapy were still a long way down the road. It's a wonder he managed to live as long as he did, having passed away in 1922, just one month shy of his 61st birthday.

Hattie also records her husband passing "colored water" (discolored urine), which was likely symptomatic of his biliousness or some undiagnosed renal disorder. Throughout the years, the expression "I am about sick" is frequently encountered in his writings, which is an antiquated way of stating "I am sick today." When symptoms subsided, he always stated "Am some better today," which in modern idiom means "I feel somewhat better." For his entire life, he was also railthin. Although over half a foot taller than Hattie, their weight was usually about the same, and Hattie was never an overweight woman. Considering his bewilderingly busy social and professional schedule, he probably also just ran himself into the ground as the years went on.

The treatments he sought were typical of those available in rural and small-town America. For most, medical care consisted of whatever was available from the family doctor, who acted as an internist, pediatrician, obstetrician, surgeon and psychiatrist to everyone in town. Much of the care was rendered in the patient's home, with diagnostic and therapeutic support limited to whatever he happened to be carrying in his little portable leather bag.[31] Medical specialization was in its infancy, and the little available in the city was still pie in the sky to most in the countryside. The only possible upside to these deficiencies was the now-endangered art of personable, doctor-to-patient rapport. In the olden days, the town doctor came to your home to treat your illness. You would not have first to visit your "primary care physician" to get a referral to see a specialist, who would lateral you over to some other specialist, who would order up a king's ransom in tests and pricey pills before advising you to go home, get some rest, and call him in the morning. Our convoluted, modern medical

---

31. The antiquated custom of your physician making what were referred to as "house calls" is regrettably as obsolete as holiday sing-alongs by the player piano in the parlor.

practices would make old-time farmers spit, cuss and head home for a stiff swig of whiskey to feel better.

Frank also suffered his entire adult life with inflamed, bleeding piles (severe hemorrhoids). In 1921, his family doctor was finally forced to enlist the help of two other area physicians for a badly needed hemorrhoidectomy—on Hattie's kitchen table. She graciously donated two-bed sheets for use as drop cloths. Whether she washed and reused them is not recorded. One physician administered the anesthetic while the other two performed the procedure. Their Main Street residence was hardly equipped with a sterile operating suite, recovery room or ancillary medical support. If Frank had hemorrhaged or developed any other inter-operative or post-operative complication, he would have been in one helluva pickle. Ambulance services were exceedingly primitive, and the nearest hospital was over 25 miles away on country roads.

Frank's lousy health was undoubtedly exacerbated by the severe northern climate and his rigorous family, church and business schedules. His periodic internment from asthma, bronchitis and headaches were related to fluctuations in temperature, with acute flare-ups leaving him out of commission for weeks at a time. In the late 19th century most travel about town was done by walking. Longer distances were by open carriage or steam locomotive, which could be frigid in winter or sultry in summer. One aspect of his insurance trade was the annual distribution of promotional calendars, a task accomplished in the early years by slogging up and down hills and streets in Adams, Lorraine and neighboring communities in wintertime. The purchase of their first automobile in 1914 greatly eased this annual burden.

Even in early adulthood, he prayed fervently for the strength to continue and make something of himself in this world. Typically, on New Year's Eve, he offered prayerful thanks for his domestic life and business success. In 1915, he wrote, "What the New Year will bring to us we cannot tell. The year that is passed with its joys and sorrows are fresh in our memories. I realize I have not long to stay here and am trusting God for the days to come . . ." His fervent Methodist faith and deep love of family were sustaining factors through increasing bouts of illness. Unfortunately, by 1920, Frank's infirmity rendered him unable to manage his bewildering responsibilities. He was compelled to resign as Sunday school superintendent and other posts and became increasingly dependent upon Herbert to maintain operations in their insurance business.

The most miserable year of his life came in 1922. In early February, his beloved church in Adams caught fire and burnt to the ground. The loss was as devastating a blow psychologically as it was financially and spiritually to this close-knit community. His father had served there for two terms as a minister, and it was there the family attended religious services and taught Sunday school for many years. Frank was also on the Board of Trustees, serving as financial secretary and treasurer. Of immediate concern was his role as a church insurance agent, which meant he must summon the wherewithal to address damage assessment and rebuilding issues. That he acted as quickly and effectually as he did is a testament to his strength and integrity in the closing months of life.

By April of 1922, he was extremely emaciated, and his weight dropped down to an unsustainable 115 pounds. He had always been rail thin, but at 5'10", always at least 20–30 pounds heavier than 5'4" Hattie. Now, his wife outweighed him by 25 pounds. His despondency increased after a candid appraisal from the family doctor, who had been summoned to the house due to Flora's illness. He was taken aback by Frank's pallid and emaciated appearance and blurted out, "You are in a very bad way." Attendance at Sunday services fell by the wayside, and solicitation for insurance became his son-in-law's responsibility. His health declined to the extent he was consigned to an invalid's existence, with days limited to lying on the sofa reading the paper or sitting by the front window to watch the activities on Main Street. He rebounded somewhat after undergoing surgery on the kitchen table but soon suffered a relapse of the "bilious complaints" that had long plagued him.

Hattie chronicled his final weeks, during which he became progressively weaker and thinner and ultimately unable even to sit up or take small amounts of nourishment. He was completely bedridden, with intermittent lapses into delirium and unconsciousness. On a Saturday morning, he suffered a stroke, attended by hemorrhaging from the nasal passages. Frank passed away on the 17th of June, just five weeks shy of his 61st birthday, and was buried alongside his parents in the family plot at Adams Rural Cemetery. Friends and neighbors eulogized him as a quiet, unassuming man of high intelligence, deep spirituality and an inherent sense of civic responsibility. One wonders how much more he could have achieved in the political spectrum had he been blessed with a more robust constitution. His strong desire to serve the community is evidenced by the number of town boards and local organizations in which he served. But the leap from participating in town committees to running for public office never occurred. Like his father, he was a lifelong Republican, and active on the local Republican Committee and town election board. But that's as far as it ever went.

After the graveside service, Hattie returned home and continued to reside with Flora on the ground level, with Laura and her family upstairs. After thirty-three years of marriage, the loss of her husband tore another gaping hole in her psyche, something made manifest in her diaries. She had always been subject

The Story of Hattie and Frank

Modern photograph of the three stunning stained glass windows behind the pulpit in the United Methodist Church of Adams. The first two were installed in 1925 in memoriam of Reverend Gordon and son Frank for their years of service and dedication to church and community. The larger middle window was gifted by Hattie's Sunday School Class in 1934 in recognition of her thirty-five continuous years of teaching. The dedicatory inscriptions below each window are unfortunately not visible in this image. (courtesy of Judy Franklin)

to periods of melancholy, but now a pervasive sense of gloom compelled her to seek counsel in order to regain equilibrium and return to some sense of normality. She gradually came to terms with her grief, but their neighborhood church was gone, and now so was Frank. Hattie reflected on her deteriorating circumstances in her diary entry for the 31st of December in 1922: "The close of the saddest year I have ever known. Yet I am sorry to have the year gone. It seems like another link with the past has been broken."

Daughter Laura and Cousin Ethel

Hattie and Frank had one child, a daughter named Laura Fidelia, who was born at the house on Main Street in June of 1896. Her first and middle names were bestowed in honor of her maternal and paternal great-grandmothers. Growing up in an observant Methodist family, her activities naturally centered on the same church and social events as her mother, including the Epcot League, Standard Bearers, Rebekah League, and various Ladies' Aid and other committees. As a child, she accompanied her parents on their inspections of the family's farming and dairy operations. Once a bit older, she sometimes tagged along on her father's business trips to Watertown and other destinations. Laura was always extremely close to her cousin Ethel, with whom she shared a bedroom whenever they stayed over at each other's residence.

Laura graduated from Teacher's Training at Adams High School in 1915 and was one of twenty-five students (!) at Commencement to give an address between Invocation and Benediction. Her offering was *The Land of the Sky*, presumably a description of the 1876 novel by Christian Reid. The following fall, she transferred to teacher's college at Syracuse University, where she graduated in 1919 with a Bachelor of Arts. During her high school and college years, she assisted her father in his insurance business by completing paperwork and running errands about town. For these efforts, Frank paid her an exorbitant salary of $1 per week. While at school, Laura maintained daily correspondence with the folks back home, and their contents offer a classic study of the redundancy of letter writing in times past. Between her schoolwork and these long daily letters, she probably nursed a case of writer's cramp.

While few of Laura's letters back home survive, she retained mountains of written correspondence from the folks in Adams. Ongoing discussions occupy multiple pages on matters now resolved by simple text or telephone calls. Sometimes, the *tête-à-tête* goes on for months, much the way Victorian chess players engaged in matches by mail: Here is my move. Kindly write back with your next move. Hattie continually clips fashion advertisements from newspapers and magazines, sending them off as suggestions for smartening up Laura's wardrobe. If Laura were on the hunt for a new dress, Hattie would query her as to choices in material and styles, and whether she preferred to have it made by pattern or purchased at a local shop. Laura would perpetuate this interminable exchange with a few new thoughts on the matter. On one occasion, Hattie warned that choices in shoes and other accessories were still dangerously undecided for some upcoming event. Laura's available fashions weren't her parent's only concern: they also had her ship all dirty laundry back home by rail for cleaning. As in grade school, her academic progress remained of critical concern, and she unfailingly included all test results and class grades with her daily letters.

While at college, she met and fell in love with her future husband Herbert, a student from a Methodist family from Wallkill in Orange County, New York. The September following graduation, they married at the family home on Maine Street, settling into the upstairs rooms along with Winkles the cat. It was here they raised two children: son Gordon, born in 1923, and daughter Marion, arriving in 1927. These kids represented the fourth generation of the family to reside in the house on Main Street. In 1920, Herbert joined his father-in-law's insurance business, a partnership lasting until Frank's death two years later. While raising her family, Laura taught French and mathematics at Adams High School and assisted Herbert with all the clerical aspects of his business. She also remained active in church and town affairs, including the annual Corn Festival and Redpath Chautauqua committees.

In 1925, the couple began putting up a seasonal tent on the campground at Renshaw Bay, a holiday destination in Oswego County, south of Adams. They also purchased a small boat to do a little fishing during their stays. In 1927, they ditched the tent and purchased Mallard Lodge, a waterfront cottage near the Bay. This was in addition to the family cottage they maintained at Thousand Island Park. Mallard Lodge was nestled amongst the dunes on the 17-mile-long peninsula separating Sandy Pond from Lake Ontario. It remained a seasonal destination before the land eventually eroded into Lake Ontario, taking with it generations of summertime fun and spectacular sunsets.

After Hattie had married and moved to Adams, she remained in close contact with her brother Everett and other family members in neighboring Lorraine. While growing up, one of Laura's closest friends was Cousin Ethel, who was born in Lorraine in May of 1892 and was thus four years her senior. Ethel was the daughter of Everett and his wife Martha; the latter a daughter of Lorraine store owner C.C. Moore. Laura and Ethel shared similar trajectories in social, religious and educational matters. They made frequent trips to Lake Ontario and Thousand Island Park, as well as accompanying one another to moving picture shows, musical presentations, picnics and ice cream socials in town. Ethel bordered with Laura while attending Adams High School, where she graduated from Teacher's Training Class in 1913.

Ethel eventually married a local named George, and together, they welcomed daughter Arlene into the family in November of 1922. Together with Laura and Herbert, they made the rounds at social events and vacationed at Mallard's Lodge and the family's cottage on Wellesley Island. Ethel's married life was unfortunately cut short after contracting tuberculosis, from which she succumbed at age 31. George was left to raise their young daughter with some significant help from his mother. Arlene would continue living at her grandmother's home in Lorraine for the next 92 years, where she eventually married and raised four children of her own.

PART II : JEFFERSON COUNTY & THE NORTH COUNTRY

Ethel's symptoms had developed gradually over several years, but her youthful vibrancy always permitted her to rally to the extent everyone became hopeful for remission or recovery. But by July of 1923, she was again pregnant, and her physical condition deteriorated to the point her weight fell to an alarming 90 pounds. Her physicians felt the only chance of recovery was swift relocation to the Adirondacks, with its cool, crisp, rejuvenating mountain air. In July, a pregnant Ethel bade goodbye to George and Arlene and moved into a friend's cottage in Old Forge, New York.

Hattie and family drove up for a stay of several weeks in August, and it was then that Laura (who was also pregnant) went unexpectedly into labor, giving birth to a son, Gordon. Unfortunately, the mountain *rest cure* did little to improve Ethel's condition, and Hattie grew increasingly despondent as her niece steadily deteriorated to the point she was unable to rise out of bed. Her family consented to her wish to be brought back home to Lorraine, where she died in early April of 1924. As was the custom, the funeral was held in the family parlor. Hattie recalls how mournful family and neighbors overran the house, porch and lawn. Ethel lies interred in the family plot at Lorraine Rural Cemetery.

The Story of Hattie and Frank

Absolutely charming snapshot of young Laura planting a big wet one on the cheek of Cousin Ethel. The location is possibly Ethel's home in Lorraine. Despite the slight age difference, these girls were inseparable during their formative years. Ethel lived in neighboring Lorraine but moved in with Laura and her family while attending classes at Adams High School. Their large extended family was utterly devastated when, as a young mother, Ethel succumbed to tuberculosis at age 31. (author's collection)

PART II : JEFFERSON COUNTY & THE NORTH COUNTRY

A. H. S. SENIOR CLASS, 1915.

Laura's high school graduation picture from 1915. The problem is that the album doesn't identify each student in the photograph. The consensus, after comparison with other photographs is the gal at the upper right in the third row is probably Laura. In days past, people didn't move around as much, and marriage partners were often chosen from amongst the local population. More people being related results in greater similarity in appearances, as evidenced by this class picture from Adams High School. A century or more on, how many in today's pictures will be readily identifiable, once almost everyone that person knew is gone? Even the elderly who dimly recall a meeting in their youth will be hard-pressed to identify that person from a photograph taken earlier in life. The immutable destiny of all is to fade away, along with our photographs.. (author's collection)

A resplendent Laura in her Edwardian finery. Wrinkle releaser sprays weren't around back then to help smooth out a lady's cotton attire. One of several photographs was taken in 1916 during her freshman year at Syracuse University. In the early years of the new century, respectable women were still expected to pin their hair up off the shoulders while out and about in public. By the 1920s, most began chopping off their long locks for the bobbed look so fashionable in the Jazz Age. (author's collection)

CHAPTER 14

Southern Pines and Hot Springs

DUE to chronic health conditions, in the early 1900s, Frank sought respite from severe North Country weather through seasonal relocations to the southern States. For several winters, the family joined other local Methodists in their annual migration to Southern Pines, North Carolina, a burgeoning destination for "snowbirds" in the late Victorian Era. For six seasons, they rented a small cottage, where Frank experienced nominal relief from recurring bouts of asthma and bronchitis. The change of scenery also afforded them an opportunity to engage in recreational activities unavailable near Lake Ontario.

Unfortunately, in the first decade of the century, there was no Methodist Episcopal Church in Southern Pines. They were forced to compensate by attending services at the local Baptist, Congregational, and Episcopal Churches rather than trekking over on Sunday mornings to the Methodist services at Doubs Chapel in neighboring Pfafftown or Bascom Chapel in Robbins. For the family to spend the season without some form of religious observance was, of course, inconceivable. Frank also records a service they attended at a nearby AME church, something impossible back home because the first chapter in Jefferson County—Thomas AME Zion Church in Watertown—didn't open until 1909. The following Sunday, the family returned to watch a children's presentation at the Sunday school.

The local Independent Order of Odd Fellows chapter provided Frank with a familiar diversion. There was also a Daughters of Rebekah lodge, but Hattie makes no reference to it in surviving diaries. Laura was enrolled in the local Kings Daughters and Sons chapter, something she was involved with back home. Laura was duly enrolled in the local school system, although they record her reluctance to attend on a daily basis. She was probably having too much fun in the sun to bother with reading, writing and arithmetic. Fortunately for everyone, Southern Pines was a scheduled stop on the local Chautauqua circuit, which appeared outside of town in early spring.

The warmer climate afforded them a number of activities, including golfing at a nearby country club.[32] Croquet and roque were other popular outdoor activities. Although Frank considered himself an ace at croquet, to his embarrassment, he really stunk up the joint at roque (poor baby). He probably found the more rapid ball movement too much for his asthma. On the whole, their indoor and outdoor activities picked up dramatically during their stays each winter. But Frank still found time to complain of bad health when asked to walk long distances with family and friends. At least, this was his excuse to head back to the cottage to read the paper. For more sedentary evening pleasures, there was the Southern Pines Opera House, which offered a more varied program than they were accustomed to in Adams.

Nightly sightings of Halley's Comet begin to be recorded in the spring of 1910. Frank notes everyone's wonder at watching this daily phenomenon in Southern Pines, as well as later when back home in Adams. The comet's tail remained visible for months, much to the delight of millions across the country. Some of the more religious-minded feared it a portent of the coming apocalypse, a curious social phenomenon that had also occurred during previous sightings in 1758 and 1835. The theological implications of this celestial visitation were keenly debated in homes and churches by a society still enraptured in the afterglow of the Second Great Awakening.

Rather than returning to Southern Pines in 1909, they headed down to Hot Springs, Arkansas. This up-and-coming town was another destination for snowbirds escaping the winter drudgery up north. It featured an extensive resort section adjacent to their celebrated therapeutic baths, a feature which undoubtedly influenced the family's change in destination. Another selling point was the Hot Springs Methodist Hospital and Sanitarium, which opened in 1908. During their stay, all mail was rerouted to a hotel across from the Central Methodist Episcopal Church on Park Avenue, another feature unavailable in Southern Pines. And like Southern Pines, Hot Springs was also a scheduled stop on the Chautauqua circuit.

For reasons unrecorded, they stopped wintering down south after 1910. Frank had left the retail trade and embarked upon a fledgling insurance career, in which his initial sales were less than spectacular. The monetary factor alone might have incentivized them to stay local and concentrate on building the business. They did maintain regular correspondence with friends they made in North Carolina, as well as local Methodists during their winter sojourns. These snowbirds also helped arrange shipments of pine trees up north each Christmas

---

32. Golfing appears unavailable in Adams this early in the century.

PART II : JEFFERSON COUNTY & THE NORTH COUNTRY

season. Hattie mentions that, upon arrival, one would be set up, one in the parlor, with the others adjacent to the church pulpit. The maple syrup they shipped down each season was likely quid pro quo for these Christmas trees.

The first year they stayed home, Old Man Winter treated everyone to an impressive display of brutal North Country weather. The thermometer consistently registered sub-zero temperatures in tandem with record snowfalls. Frank notes several weeks of intermittent blizzard-like conditions, with impassible snowdrifts across the roads and against the house. His temperature log records days between -10 and -22 degrees, with a record low at Lorraine Center in excess of -30 degrees. The drain pipe from the kitchen sink froze and cracked open, but they had to wait until the spring thaw to initiate repairs. Frank complains of his mother's repeated remonstrations this was exactly why she wanted them all to go south that winter.

The North Country family and friends at Christmas dinner while wintering in North Carolina in 1905. Yuletide dining al fresco was certainly a rarity back in Jefferson County. The writing on the tablecloth includes the notation "81 degrees in shade." The location is the town of Tryon, which is about 200 miles west of where they stayed in Southern Pines. Few people had a motor car this early in the century. Seems likely Hattie and company took the train to Tryon for their visit. The back of the photograph is inscribed "Christmas dinner Tryon N.C., Fannie and J. Hart Waite, Florilla, Frank, Harriet, Laura." (author's collection)

CHAPTER 15

Thousand Island Park

"The fire that warms us can also consume us. It is not the fault of the fire."

—SWAMI VIVEKANANDA

Hattie and Frank were from families fortunate enough to own property at Thousand Island Park, a Methodist retreat on Wellesley Island along the St. Lawrence River. Beginning in the late century, their two cottages, Bide-a-Wee and Restmoore, became a welcome family retreat in a setting that also strengthened their bonds to the Methodist community. One of the Reverend's first tasks upon arrival was to walk over to the Tabernacle and greet the Presiding Elder. The Tabernacle was a massive outdoor chapel that easily accommodated up to 1500 worshippers. Over the years, he was frequently invited to assist with religious services at the chapel.

The Thousand Islands region along the Canadian border had long been a popular destination for vacationers from the northern states. The Methodist Park on the southwest tip of Wellesley Island had its inception amidst the religious fervor of the Second Great Awakening, an evangelical movement that also gave rise to the Chautauqua movement in upstate New York. The Thousand Island Park Association was founded in 1875 by John Dayan, a Methodist minister from Jefferson County who endeavored to create a safe retreat where families could go and enjoy respite from all the noise, vices and temptations of town and city life. Reverend Gordon records a two-hour family tour of the Park in the summer of 1876. They traveled by steamship from Cape Vincent to Alexandria Bay and from there to Wellesley Island, where they marveled at all the new construction and activity.

During the next quarter century, the Park underwent a rapid transformation from a small religious camp to one of the most popular vacation spots in

PART II : JEFFERSON COUNTY & THE NORTH COUNTRY

New York. It was reported that, by 1900, more steamboats headed from the mainland to Wellesley Island than to the remaining 1864 (actual count!)islands combined. A rapid building boom commenced within the original allotment of 100 acres. By 1895, numerous hotels had opened, along with a seasonal community of over 600 cottages. A reliable water supply was established, along with electric lighting and a modern sewage system. By 1905, the Park reported a summertime population of between 10,000 and 12,000 vacationers, an enormous increase over previous years. In winter, the population dwindled to between 100 to 150 residual staff, including maintenance workers, watchmen and stowaway girlfriends.

There were a number of embarkation points along the St. Lawrence River and Lake Ontario shorelines for people traveling to the Thousand Islands. Among these were Alexandria Bay, Fishers Landing, Clayton, Sackets Harbor, and Cape Vincent further southwest. By the 1870s, railroad and trolley terminals opened on the mainland, which brought vacationers over to coastal terminals teeming with steamships and sailboats, all destined for the Islands. In the 1930s, rapid improvements in roadways and increased automobile ownership led to sharp declines in railway and trolley usage. However, a convenient ferry service was established to transport both vacationers *and* their cars to their destinations.

From its inception, the religious nature of the Park was evident. Methodists from Canada and the States brought families along for a vacation free from alcohol, gambling, cavorting and other sinful activities. Relative to other recreational sites such as Coney Island, the Park was considered a safe and wholesome alternative, a place where businessmen could send their families on Monday mornings and then join up with them on Friday evenings. Turn-of-the-century photographs show train stations crowded with men in derbies waving goodbye to women and children at the commencement of their journey.

However, the park hierarchy soon realized the impossibility of attracting sufficient crowds for financial viability while simultaneously maintaining such draconian restrictions on membership, activities and moral character. Several incremental steps were taken, and in its second decade of operation, the Park was opened to visitors of all Christian denominations. Most original prohibitions were eased or entirely rescinded, including restrictions on alcohol, tobacco, card games and late-night gatherings. All people of good character were now welcome to spend their leisure time in this idyllic setting amongst the archipelago of a thousand lakes. A new summertime family fun place had opened for business. Attendance at Sunday services was suggested but no longer required.

The newly renovated Park attracted national attention, with visits from such luminaries and public speakers as Teddy Roosevelt, Susan B. Anthony and Frederick Douglas. Anthony utilized the Methodist platform for progressive causes in her crusade for women's suffrage. Douglas drew attention to the growing disenfranchisement of African Americans under Jim Crow legislation in the southern States. The strongly Christian character of the Park didn't prohibit interactions with people of other religions. In 1895, the Hindu monk and spiritual leader Swami Vivekananda arrived for a rest after his exhausting tour of America, during which he addressed the Parliament of the World's Religions at the 1893 Columbian Exposition in Chicago.

For two weeks the Swami resided at the cottage of Miss Libby Dutcher, an acquaintance made during his lectures in New York City. Although a devout Methodist, Dutcher was also an artist of note, as well as liberally minded and receptive to new ideas. The Swami visited, taught and meditated with crowds of followers and curiosity seekers attracted to the cottage during his stay. Frank and Hattie somehow ended up being introduced to the Swami. To most Americans at the time, any dialogue with a turbaned Hindu mystic must have seemed tantamount to philosophical discussions with a moon man. The Vedanta and Upanishads *vis-à-vis* the ineffable word of God in the Holy Bible? They no doubt remained respectful but later recorded the encounter as more of a curiosity than a genuine opportunity to expand their religious *weltanschauung*. The Indian holy man was just another sight to see and nothing more. In 1947, his followers returned to the cottage and became appalled at the state of disrepair. Raising the necessary funds for its purchase, it was renovated and reopened as the Vivekananda Cottage. To this day, it remains a Hindu sacred site where members of the Vivekananda Society teach classes and meditation sessions.

Each new season, their visits to the Park involved more than simple fun and relaxation. Both cottages had been boarded up since last year, and needed much cleaning and maintenance to ensure their habitability. This upkeep was also necessary because instead of leaving them vacant in their absence, they were rented to friends and acquaintances for weeks at a time. Upon arrival, Frank, the Reverend and hired men would be busy at work with hammers, screwdrivers and other essentials. Hattie was out and about, soliciting help for all the time-consuming domestic and gardening chores.

The labor of closing and winterizing the cottages at the end of each season was no picnic either. One year, Frank realized that not only was the roof on Restmoore leaking and beyond repair, but the entire structure had begun sinking into the soft soil of Wellesley Island.[33] By the early 1900s, these structures were sorely in need of modernization as they lacked such basic utilities as running water, indoor plumbing and electricity. A water closet wasn't installed at Restmoore until the fall of 1921. Until then, everyone had to use the privy at Restmoore or walk over to the public conveniences elsewhere in the Park.

Mornings involved a lot of chores, including trips to the pump to fetch water for cooking, cleaning and daily grooming. In the 1890s, the Reverend makes mention of arising at daybreak and chopping wood to "build a fire and put over a tea kettle" to start his day. On cold spring and late summer mornings, extra wood was required for the stoves to stave off the chill. As late as June of 1917, they were still debating whether to install a gas line and fixtures because their indoor lighting was solely by sunlight and kerosene lamps. For some reason, they waited until 1920 for the upgrade, only to have everything replaced with electrical wiring and fixtures in 1925.

By modern standards, Park decorum was inhibited by all the formalities and restrictions inherent to Victorian and Edwardian social life. A communal dinner was served at noon, followed by a mandatory rest period to replenish one's physical and spiritual constitution. Afternoon and evening events were attended in full dress. Except while at the shoreline, everyone was expected to remain fully dressed: ladies in skirts, jackets and hats and men in collars and waistcoats. It didn't matter if the temperature was ninety degrees and you were trying to soak in some rays on the beach. Anything more form-fitting than those infamous Victorian woolen bathing suits would probably get you thrown off the beach. In the interest of developing strong moral character, bedtime for the kiddies was kept crazy early. While mothers tucked them away and read their bedtime stories, the gentlemen would gather on the veranda to enjoy some cigars and a few glasses of port. Although excessive alcohol consumption was consistently frowned upon by the church, the overall lack of enforcement is obviated by photographs of picnickers consuming mass quantities of wine at their grassy hideaways.

Activities included more than religious events and parading down the promenade in fashionable attire. Boating, hiking, swimming, sightseeing, picnicking, berry picking, lawn tennis, croquet, concerts, lectures, afternoon tea parties and evening social rounds were all common activities. At the turn of the century, the Ocean Grove Orchestra regularly performed before packed audiences. They had been a mainstay on the Chautauqua circuit and mixed gospel

---

33. Hattie sold Restmoore cottage shortly after Frank died in 1922 but retained Bide-a-Wee (the latter an old Scottish expression for 'stay awhile').

music, traditional songs and current hits from Tin Pan Alley. Originating in Ocean Grove, New Jersey, they were also a frequent attraction at Methodist Love Feasts across New Jersey, New York and the northeast. At Asbury Park in 1905, they performed the "Hallelujah Chorus" from Handel's "Messiah" before an enthusiastic crowd, including a delighted President Theodore Roosevelt. Earlier that year, they performed in front of 12,000 "singing, shouting and gesticulating" congregants at the 31st annual Methodist camp meeting at Ocean Grove. The August 28, 1905 edition of the New York Times described it as the largest religious gathering ever held in this country.

Fishing was a pastime that provided a steady supply of fresh food for the dinner table. Most catching was done by men and boys on small fishing boats, although Hattie, Laura and Ethel often tagged along for fun. Of course, catching them was the easy part. Then, the womenfolk stepped in for preparation time in the kitchen, including the scraping off of scales, cutting off of heads and removal of entrails prior to frying on the stovetop or baking in the coal-fired oven. In the early years, the Park lacked running water or organized garbage disposal, so when dinner was over, the ladies then had to clean up all the smelly and messy fish residue. Fortunately for Hattie, her long familiarity with animal butchering back home was a decided advantage when it came to all this disagreeable stuff.

PART II : JEFFERSON COUNTY & THE NORTH COUNTRY

A picturesque view of Restmoore Cottage around 1900. One of the family's two retreats at Thousand Island Park on Wellesley Island. On the back of the photograph is the inscription "Restmoore cottage TI Park corner Eden & Ontario St." Hattie and Laura are seated on the steps. Behind them are Reverend Gordon, Hattie's mom, Julia; and Flora. Frank is apparently between asthma attacks, and revved up to do a little bicycling around the Park. In spring and summer, these cottages became magnets for vacationing members on both sides of the family. After Frank passed in 1922, Hattie sold this cottage but held on to Bide-A-Wee.. (author's collection)

THOUSAND ISLAND PARK

A picnic at Thousand Island Park in 1912. These unidentified people were likely acquaintances of Hattie and Frank from their mutual affiliation with the Methodist Church. Here, we find the picnicking party enjoying their afternoon with bottles of sparkling Saratoga spring water (?). Most beverages were presumably non-alcoholic, in observance of Park recommendations. Actually, by the turn of the century Park management was resigned to their utter inability to restrict alcohol consumption by residents and guests. Potables of all kinds began to be enjoyed ad libitum up to the enactment of national Prohibition.. (author's collection)

CHAPTER 16

Evangelicalism and the Methodist Faith

THE Methodist Episcopal faith into which Hattie and Frank were born was a factor in virtually every aspect of their lives. Religious services were attended without fail, even when it involved trudging across town during a snowstorm. If illness or other extenuating circumstances obligated them to miss a church function, an explanation is unfailingly noted in their diary. As was their parents' custom, their weekly schedule revolved around nearly endless church-related activities. On Monday evenings, Hattie attended a lady's Bible study at a neighbor's home. On Tuesday evenings, both Hattie and Frank attended (or taught) Bible classes. Thursday evenings involved a prayer service at the Parsonage. Saturday afternoons included various church committees, as well as fundraising activities such as rummage and bake sales and canvassing for subscriptions to religious periodicals. On Sunday mornings, the entire family attended weekly service, including Holy Communion at designated times. Sunday services were followed by Sabbath school, in which they were both active. Sunday evenings included yet another prayer service at Church. It seems the only day they had off was Wednesday.

Similar to the demographics in neighboring Adams, the town of Lorraine was comprised almost entirely of Anglo-Saxon Protestants, with this same demographic remaining fairly consistent well into the 20th century. Construction of the town's Methodist Church commenced in 1853 and opened in 1857. In June of 1939, the original building was struck by lightning and burnt to the ground, an unimaginable tragedy that shook this small and tightly-knit community to the core. A new church soon opened at the same site and remains in service as the United Methodist Church of Lorraine.

In Adams, the First Society of the Methodist Episcopal Church was formed in October of 1828, with services originally held at the old Presbyterian Church. This arrangement continued up to the dedication of their church and parsonage between 1853 and 1854. In 1922, a fire erupted in the church basement. The building was wooden and, as occurred to the church in Lorraine a few years later, a total loss—although the next-door parsonage was thankfully spared. This tragedy overwhelmed the congregation and dominated entries for weeks in their diaries. As an insurance agent for the churches in Adams and Lorraine, Frank was responsible not only for damage assessment but—as a member of the finance and rebuilding committees—planning a replacement structure as soon as funds permitted. Expenses fell mostly to the local congregation, with fundraising activities such as bake sales, rummage sales and door-to-door canvassing occupying much of the family's time in ensuing months. In the interim, the congregation in Adams attended Union Services at the Baptist or Episcopal Church. It was a shocking and stressful time for Hattie, Frank, Laura and the rest of the Methodist community.

Expressions of religious piety take many forms but are perhaps most admirable in tangible acts of benevolence and charity. Hattie and Frank always found time to visit with sick neighbors and go door to door soliciting bereavement funds after a local death. Through bake sales, charity drives and similar events, the Methodists of Jefferson Country were able to address the needs of destitute people in various sections of the country, as well as financial support for missionary activities in numerous countries. During and after the First World War, the Church sponsored a number of Belgian and French children who became orphaned following the loss of parents during these years. The amounts given by most were no doubt modest but extended a critical lifeline to people in need. The family also kept up regular written correspondence with several of these children well into the 1920s.

The *summa totalis* of their religious beliefs was contained within the Holy Scriptures as interpreted by John Wesley and other early Methodists. Their Protestant faith was among the most idealistic organizations in England and America during the 19th century and involved with such progressive social causes as abolition, temperance, women's suffrage and prohibitions against child labor. The camp meetings so prominent since the earliest years were a blueprint for the creation of Thousand Island Park on Wellesley Island, a place where families could vacation in an idyllic setting also conducive to the maintenance of strong moral values. The Chautauqua circuits so prominently in the American entertainment scene between 1880 and 1930 also developed from Methodist activities along Lake Chautauqua, southeast of Lake Erie in upstate New York.

The Methodist Society originated as a Christian revivalist movement in 18th-century England, primarily through the efforts of the Anglican cleric John

Wesley. It flourished amidst the evangelicalism of the First Great Awakening, a populist movement that had a lasting impact on religious thought in England, continental Europe and North America. The revivalist and evangelical aspects have often been interpreted as a backlash to all the scientific skepticism and secular humanism inherent in the Age of Enlightenment. From its inception, Methodism placed heavy emphasis on the born-again conversion experience during their large outdoor gatherings. Early recruitment was greatly facilitated by circuit riders, a veritable army of lay preachers who traveled the countryside with a Bible in one hand and sermons of John Wesley in the other. Their grassroots efforts were so successful that by 1850, Methodist societies had been established in virtually every town and city in America. Early converts were drawn primarily from the lower classes, including the rural poor, day laborers, former slaves and other groups who felt marginalized by mainstream religion.

The religious fervor of the First Great Awakening received further impetus during the Second Great Awakening movement between 1800 and 1870, during which time American membership in the Methodist Church grew by leaps and bounds. Religious services occurred in various settings, including private homes and outdoor camp meetings adorned with temporary wooden tabernacles. Soon, large tent tabernacles (Tents of the Faithful) became a prominent feature. These larger services typically included the Love Feast or Agape Meal, an interactive liturgy including the ceremonial sharing of bread and Loving Cup among the congregation. This tradition had been modeled upon biblical feasts between Jesus and his Disciples, including the Last Supper. John Wesley incorporated these practices into the early faith after witnessing a Moravian religious ceremony during the early 18th century, as he later recalled in his memoirs:

> After evening prayers, we joined with the Germans in one of their love-feasts. It was begun and ended with thanksgiving and prayer and celebrated in so decent and solemn a manner as a Christian of the apostolic age would have allowed to be worthy of Christ.

The Love Feast became an integral component of camp meetings and was believed to promote faith and brotherhood within the congregation, as well as a desire to spread the good word to others. Most ceremonies proceeded in a well-defined order. They began with an opening hymn or chorus, followed by spoken or sung prayers, an address or personal witness to the Scripture, the passing of the communal bread, a collection for the poor, circulation of the loving cup, and testimonies, prayers and singing of hymns. A closing exhortation, benediction and formal dismissal concluded the ceremony.

In this era, people became mesmerized by the fiery rhetoric of clergymen and the raucous, ecstatic responses they elicited from the congregation. The drama and intensity of camp meetings and Love Feasts became dynamic tools in the conversion of more and more people to the faith. In time, increasing church wealth led to the construction of permanent wooden churches for indoor services. In later years, these wooden structures were largely replaced with the impressive stone churches so prominent in the modern faith. In 1870, the U.S. federal census listed church membership at nearly one million. In New York State alone, 1100 preachers were servicing 165,000 congregants in over 1600 churches. When Hattie passed in 1934, the national organization had grown to nearly five million members.

Around the time of the Civil War, Amanda and her family in Northfield, New Hampshire, began attending services at the Methodist Episcopal Church in Sanbornton Bridge. Whether they formerly realigned their religious identity to the tenets of this new denomination is not recorded. It was mentioned that, as teenagers, Belle, John and Joseph attended either a Methodist camp meeting or a Great Awakening revivalist event somewhere in the area. Aside from these entries, this New England family does not appear to have been particularly observant, and certainly, no mention is made of their participation in Methodist functions or organizations. Their religious faith appears limited to riding in the wagon to church a few Sundays each month and observance of major Christian holidays. The fire and brimstone theology so influential in these years never resulted in any personal epiphanies nor altered their focus from their usual preoccupations.

The sponsorship of domestic and foreign missions was another hallmark of early Methodism. By 1870, a total of 388 missions had opened across five continents, which included a clerical and lay staff of nearly 35,000. There occurred a concomitant rise in Sunday School Union enrollment, with the number of weekly participants just shy of 14,000. Significantly, Church records for this period list a total of 152 institutes of higher learning, including biblical colleges and male and female seminaries. In Hattie and Frank's lifetime, 21 of these centers were operating in New York. From its humble beginnings as a splinter group of the Church of England, Methodism had grown into a worldwide phenomenon, the likes of which John Wesley could scarcely have imagined.

Significantly, Methodism was also the first Protestant denomination to organize on a national level. By the late 1800s, it was the largest and most efficiently run national organization in America, aside from the federal government. The Methodist Episcopal Church was the most prominent among several branches prior to its consolidation in 1939 as the Methodist Church, at which time the term Episcopal was dropped. The remaining branches merged in 1968 to form the United Methodist Church, with the exception of the African Methodist Episcopal and African Methodist Episcopal Zion Churches. Methodism remained the largest Christian denomination in America prior to the massive influx of Roman Catholics in the closing decades of the 19th century.

Protestant Christianity has always been the most prominent faith in the northeastern States, with adequate representation within the Methodist, Presbyterian, Baptist, Congregational and Episcopal denominations. A smaller number of Seventh-Day Baptist and Seventh-Day Advents Churches have also been active. Historically, a small number of Catholics settled in these areas from French-speaking Canada or arrived subsequent to the large-scale Irish immigrations of the mid-1800s. The first Catholic parish in Adams was incorporated in 1890, with the dedication of their first church in 1903. There were few, if any, Orthodox Christians in the North Country. A number of Jewish families lived in upper New York State, resulting in the formation of Degel Israel Synagogue in Watertown in the 1890s. There were no Muslims, Hindus, or Buddhists to speak of in these parts. For Hattie and Frank, adding some variety to their religious experience meant attending services at other Protestant churches. The people in their families were never religious zealots nor overtly exclusionary or fanatical in their beliefs. It was just that, considering the homogenous demographics of the area, few had ever encountered anyone from a radically different ethnic or religious background.

A person's faith was influential in determining the type of people you met, socialized with, and eventually married. However, belonging to a certain denomination never excluded you from participation in other church services and events. As was the custom with Reverend Gordon and Flora, Frank and Hattie always opened their homes to visiting ministers of other faiths. The religious divide was only a factor when it came time to welcome someone into the family through marriage. The expectation was that everyone would know enough to retain their Protestant identity when shopping for a life partner. Frankly, the *sine qua non* for full acceptance in Hattie's eyes was whether the person was another Methodist. After meeting a friend's new beau, she mentions the fellow was "quite a good looking, but <u>Catholic</u>" (with "Catholic" underlined twice). Her girlfriend might as well bring over a gentleman with an eye in the center of his forehead. Can you imagine if the poor guy had been Jewish?! Hattie would have telegraphed New York City for an alienist to determine what, if anything, was inside the misguided woman's head. When another girlfriend introduced Hattie to her new squeeze, it elicited the comment "nice fellow, but <u>not Methodist</u>" (the latter two words underlined twice). In Hattie's mind, any impetus towards religious, cultural or ethnic diversity was still a long way off.

Turn of the 20th-century photograph of the Methodist Episcopal Church in Adams. This structure opened in 1853 and was in regular use until it burnt down in 1922. The sudden loss devastated the congregation in this small and tightly-knit community. The conflagration reportedly started on the basement level in the newly renovated kitchen and dining area. Frank was their insurance agent and was forced to respond during a time of rapidly declining health. The building to the right is the parsonage, which was fortunately spared from the conflagration. Until the new church was consecrated in May of 1925, the Methodist congregation attended Union Services at the nearby Baptist and Episcopal Churches.. (author's collection)

PART II : JEFFERSON COUNTY & THE NORTH COUNTRY

Photograph of the original Methodist Episcopal Church in Lorraine. This picturesque structure opened in 1857 and was in use until 1939, when it was struck by lightning and, like its counterpart in neighboring Adams, burnt to the ground. The sylvan setting is typical of the Lorraine landscape, which is more rural and less developed than Adams. In the Colonial Period, steeples and spires were quintessential architectural elements on churches in New England and the North Country.. (author's collection)

CHAPTER 17

Temperance Movements

ANOTHER prominent component of early Methodism was the temperance movement, a nationwide activity that lent considerable impetus to the passage of the Volstead Act in 1919 and the enactment of National Prohibition. In the latter half of the 19th century, anti-alcohol activism became common amongst religious leaders and social reformers, as it appeared society was slowly degenerating into a state of collective inebriety. Long before baseball became the national pastime, getting bombed had been a popular sport amongst both genders and at all levels of society—in both public houses and private settings. It is estimated that in Colonial America, the average adult consumed on the order of twice the modern national average of intoxicating beverages, including whiskey, brandy, rum, wine, beer, ale and hard cider.

This penchant for strong drinks has often been attributed to a scarcity of clean, safe drinking water in these years. People felt they had no choice but to consume mass quantities of alcohol whenever they wanted to quench their thirst—or so the story goes. Whether there is so much as a kernel of truth to this cock and bull baloney is debatable. But what is known is our original national pastime did nothing but pick up steam as the decades rolled on. By one estimate, the annual per capita consumption of alcohol rose from 8 gallons in 1878 to almost 17 gallons by 1898, an increase of 112.5 percent. Everyone was forced to acknowledge that alcoholism and its associated ills were rampant medical and social problems in virtually all cities and towns. In New York City alone, one Victorian reformer claims to have counted one saloon for every hundred male inhabitants—and most of those inhabitants liked to drink.

The Methodist and Baptist churches had a long history of influencing public sentiment against the sale and consumption of intoxicating beverages. Church leaders of both denominations realized it would be an uphill battle to reform people's behavior, let alone convince legislators to attempt to curtail such practices. Although strong opinions existed on both sides of the issue, a century and a half of religious activism—coupled with the widespread enactment of local restrictions—eventually led many to incline towards the side of prohibition. The Northfield family frequently attended temperance lectures given by traveling ministers at various churches in the Tilton area. Indeed, abstinence appears to be a common characteristic of this family, at least through the years chronicled in their diaries.

While growing up in Jefferson County, Henry Lyman refers to alcohol consumption at various local events. But it doesn't appear his parents were inveterate drinkers like so many others in this era. Even the *switchel* his mother mixed up to satiate the summertime thirst of family and farmhands was almost certainly alcohol-free. As members of the Epworth League, Hattie and Laura had taken oaths early in life to remain abstinent and to assist others in doing the same. The enactment of the Volstead Act was viewed by many within New England and the North Country religious communities as a vindication of these longstanding efforts.

By all accounts, everyone in the house on Main Street in Adams remained teetotalers their entire lives. They all professed strong religious convictions against both alcohol and tobacco and never once in their letters or diaries was the problem of selecting just the right potables for social occasions very high up on the agenda. All were longtime members of the Methodist Church Temperance League, whose efforts included sponsorship of regular "No License" referendums to ensure that "rum sellers" abstained from operations within the town's jurisdiction "for the purpose of manufacturing or selling anything beverage that may intoxicate, including malt liquors, wine and cider."

It is debatable the degree to which people complied with the periodic enactment of draconian anti-alcohol legislation. An anecdote is related to a gentleman in Lorraine who kept a bottle of special "cough medicine" handy under the stairway at work. Apparently the poor guy suffered regularly from a mighty powerful cough. There can be little doubt that, during National Prohibition, liquor continued to flow freely across the border from Canada into New York and other states. And folks in the North Country, of course maintained their hallowed tradition of fermenting hard cider and other intoxicants. All in all, countryside production of homemade hooch likely continued unabated, as it had for generations.

At Adams Center, the Union Temperance Society was organized in 1875, followed by the Women's Christian Temperance Union in 1886. Amongst her papers was a signed pledge Hattie made to the latter group on November 8,

1886, which reads: "I pledge my WORD and HONOR, GOD HELP ME, to abstain from the use, as a beverage of spirituous and malt liquors, ale, beer, wine or cider, and that I will, by all honorable means, encourage others to abstain." Even during Prohibition, Frank continued tithing support to the Anti-Saloon League in their ongoing efforts to keep the town dry. The Daughters of Rebekah and Independent Order of Odd Fellows Lodges had long advocated anti-alcohol legislation since the days when the Reverend and Flora became members in the years following the Civil War.

As previously indicated, not everyone in town agreed with these religious-driven restrictions. As early as 1803, a succession of taverns and other drinking establishments appeared in Adams and Lorraine. In the stagecoach era, it was common for taverns and inns to operate along the stage and postal routes as places of respite for weary, hungry and thirsty travelers. And, of course, there was always your neighborhood store, which kept bottles behind the counter for needy customers. A cider mill was operating somewhere in Lorraine between 1891 and 1906. These mills typically produced both hard and soft cider, as there was always a consistent demand for both. People working long, hot days in mills or fields worked up hearty appetites and strong thirsts.

In Adams, a distillery was operating as early as 1808. The first town brewery appeared in 1838. An innkeeper opened for business on Main Street in 1852, and a nearby saloon was in continuous operation between 1852 and 1867. The first tavern opened its doors on Main Street in 1860, joined by the notorious Park House Hotel in the late 1800s. Half of this latter establishment was situated in Adams, with the other half over the town line in Ellisburg. Each year, officials in both communities voted on whether to continue the sale of alcohol within their jurisdictions. In years when Adams went "dry," liquor was still offered on the Ellisburg side. In years when Ellisburg went dry, the cheer flowed freely in the Adams section. This ridiculous conundrum made little sense to anyone, and in 1892, the entire Park House Hotel was fully and completely prohibited from selling alcohol.

During prohibition years, even small towns were hardly immune to scrutiny by overzealous federal agents. Several raids were conducted at the Lorraine Hotel between 1923 and 1925, during which small quantities of "intoxicating agents" were confiscated, including several bottles of Canadian Ale. Acting on a tip, one raid uncovered ten "suspicious looking tin cans," which appeared to have been hastily drained of their contents. Over the decade, the hotelkeeper received several fines but was spared any jail time. In retrospect, these raids appear a monumental waste of time for a few lousy bottles of Canadian cheer.

PART II : JEFFERSON COUNTY & THE NORTH COUNTRY

In addition to their teetotaling, no one in the house on Main Street ever developed a smoking habit. Their strong anti-tobacco stance is periodically referenced in their writings and the church journals of Reverend Gordon. Hattie relates an incident in the mid-1920s when son-in-law Herbert returned home green and nauseous from all the cigar smoke at a Board of Trade meeting. Whether Herbert and wife Laura refrained from liquor while at Syracuse University is unknown. They both attended classes in the years prior to prohibition, and booze was never a scarce commodity on college campuses. Whether they remained abstinent in later life is also unknown. Both were devout Methodists, for whom abstinence—or at least moderation—was always the order of the day.

Temperance Movements

Period illustration of anti-saloon activist Carrie Nation engaged in one of her patented hatchet jobs at a tavern in the Midwest. Caroline Amelia Nation (née Moore) was born in Kentucky on the 25th of November in 1846 and became the personification of faith-based temperance activism in America. As a child, she underwent a religious conversion while attending a Methodist revival meeting in Missouri and became subject to periodic mystical visions for the remainder of her years. In June of 1900, she received a "call from God" to rid Victorian society of the many evils of demon rum.

Armed with a Bible and a bagful of rocks, she led a merry band of female crusaders on a righteous rampage through saloons in Kansas and neighboring states. Their modus operandi was to storm in and methodically smash all the liquor bottles with a volley of rocks. She later substituted a battle axe after being apprised she could do more damage that way. Her notoriety escalated in tandem with her arrest record. Between 1900 and 1910, she was jailed and fined a total of 30 times, but she continued storming about, quoting scripture, singing gospel songs and exclaiming, "Men, I have come to save you from a drunkard's fate!" Saloons began hanging signs reading "All Nations Welcome But Carrie." A prominent member of the Women's Christian Temperance Union, she later retired her hatchet and embarked on a career as a fiery temperance lecturer and advocate for women's suffrage. Supporting herself through touring fees and sales of souvenir hatchets, she was even promoted on the vaudeville stage in Coney Island as the Kansas Cyclone. Yet despite all her ardent efforts, she passed away in 1911, nearly a decade before the enactment of National Prohibition. (Public Domain)

PART III

Everyday Life in the Victorian Era

WHAT follows are a series of vignettes illustrating the lives of the vast majority of Americans throughout the 19th century. Most people in this period lacked the wherewithal to maintain seasonal "cottages" at Newport or spend their summers yachting off the Hamptons while their domestic staff tended to all the dirty work, like emptying chamber pots and slop pails and cleaning up the mess from last night's revelry. For the majority, all necessary tasks at home and work were their responsibility. As a result, daily activities were tedious, labor intensive and maddeningly monotonous. Only a little downtime afforded by regularly scheduled holidays and other festivities kept everyone from becoming completely psychotic and flinging themselves underneath the tractor. Life in Victorian times was far from the bowl of cherries it's often made out to be.

If the average person could be teleported back to the Victorian Era, their initial reaction after rematerializing on Main Street would be something like, "Look how cool everything is! Just like on TV and at the movies." But after the novelty wore off, they'd be dumbstruck at how shorter, sharper, smellier and more brutish life was back in the good old days. Fully 99.9 percent of the population didn't indulge in lives of leisure, like the rich and famous at the Vanderbilt Mansion in Hyde Park. One aspect that would certainly offend 21st-century sensibilities is that cleanliness in the modern sense simply didn't exist. Everywhere you go, you're surrounded by filth, bugs, heat, cold, horse poop, unwashed bodies, and a pervasive absence of modernity, with all its creature comforts and conveniences.[34] Luxury, lace and elegance are decidedly in short supply, also. And that whole Victorian thing you expected to encounter—assuming it ever existed at all—must be located somewhere else.

---

34. In Victorian times, the term convenience was often used to denote public and private restrooms. Here, it refers to things like appliances, devices and other mechanical/man-made constructs that facilitate everyday operations and make things easier in general.

Not only that, but God help you if during your surreal excursion through the 19th century, you came down with a sniffle. Kleenex hadn't been invented, and most people didn't own linen handkerchiefs. You'll probably end up blowing your nose on your clothing and hope nobody notices. But even if they did, it's no big deal because they do it too. Should the sniffle develop into a full-blown respiratory infection, your next step would be to query the hotel clerk for directions to the town doctor. Doc Holliday would do the few things he could do—check for fever, look down your throat—then advise you to go home, rest, and start guzzling some of the evil-tasting liquid he just sold you. If his bottle of desiccated mule's testicles in an alcohol base doesn't' cure you outright, and you develop pneumonia, your trip to the Victorian Era might be headed towards a disastrous and premature finale. The furniture maker who built the vile horsehair bed in your hotel room also happens to be the local undertaker, so best to have the clerk keep him on standby.

Assuming the rampant contagions of the era don't kill you, the realization eventually sets in you really wouldn't relish being mired in such antiquated and uncomfortable surroundings. The people around you don't seem to mind because it's the only existence they've ever known. Prevailing circumstances have always defined societies and their inhabitants, and the modern, interconnected and digitalized world into which you were born helped define you as an individual. Aside from the occasional esthete, anyone in the modern world endeavoring to revert to such a starkly simpler way of life might eventually find themselves mired in primitive surroundings analogous to life in some third-world country. Bygone times and places are fine to visit in a transient, fly-on-the-wall type of experience. But they're unlikely to satisfy over the long haul if you're already accustomed to anything better.

The rapid pace of modernization towards the end of the Victorian Era brought improvements to even mundane aspects of everyday life. Especially in the major cities, by the 1920s society had been so transformed as to be virtually unrecognizable from what it was merely half a century earlier. Changes came more slowly in rural areas, where life continued as it had for generations—with only a few newfangled bells and whistles to help shake off the stupor and make it apparent that, for better or worse, times were changing. Still, the complacency of the older generation was profoundly shaken, and many waxed nostalgic for the simpler, more orderly and religious way of life they remembered during their younger days in the Gay 90s.

This rapid transformation of American society is attributable in large measure to two hitherto unimaginable factors: electricity and the internal combustion engine. It's hard to fathom how all this profound restructuring between, say, 1890 and 1920 could have occurred without the integration of these radical new technologies. A paradigm shift is observable in people's outlook and routines through the gradual realization of new possibilities and an enhanced sense of personal mobility. People would still go on inhabiting their own mental spaces filled with self-doubt, contradictions and neuroses. But now, a rejuvenating sense of enthusiasm had been injected into the mix, and it became clear to most life could never return to the way it was in years past.

In addition to all these technological changes to society and conventions, American demographics were also undergoing a profound transformation. A nationwide backlash began in the early 1900s in response to all the dark, sinister-looking foreigners arriving in their millions from ports in eastern and southern Europe. To make matters worse, the majority of these immigrants were either Catholic or Jewish (name your poison). In addition, the ongoing migration of emancipated slaves and their families to the northern states only added to the overall anxiety. Racial, ethnic and religious persecution became widespread as the white Protestant majority railed against this influx of deplorables and their seeming debasement of American society and traditional values. Fortunately, programs like the nationwide Chautauqua Movement assisted in restoring a sense of equilibrium within the general population, especially amongst rural populations less familiar with the diversity in major cities. The Chautauqua would simultaneously entertain and provide reassurances the sky was not falling, and the country was still alive and well in this new age of uncertainty.

CHAPTER 18

The Chautauqua Movement

FORMER president Teddy Roosevelt once declared the Chautauqua "the most American thing in America." For over half a century, the various Chautauqua circuits were so popular they vied with attractions like fairs and circuses for the money and attention of millions across America. Mention is made by the Northfield family of their attendance one summer at some unspecified location in New Hampshire. The annual Redpath Chautauqua was eagerly anticipated in the North Country, where, for several days each summer, the entire family could gather under an enormous tent and enjoy varied entertainment as a welcome diversion from the drudgeries of life back home. It was one of the few things people of limited means could afford to do to get out, see other people and be entertained.

Although originally conceived as a form of religious instruction by the Methodist Church, the Chautauqua format was soon expanded to broaden its appeal to people of all denominations and interests. As lay officials of the church, Hattie and Frank were actively involved with planning and promoting this annual event in the flatlands just outside of town. This included regular meetings with church, town and business leaders, as well as door-to-door canvassing for subscriptions to the weeklong event. Daughter Laura and husband Herbert continued the family's active involvement with the annual Chautauqua after Frank had passed and Hattie's increasing illness prevented her ongoing participation.

The origins of this uniquely American social and cultural institution are traceable to 1874 when the Methodists organized the Chautauqua Lake Sunday School Assembly on a campsite along Lake Chautauqua in upstate New York. Envisioned as a way to provide religious and moral instruction to Sunday school teachers, the format soon expanded to include musical groups, dramatic presentations and educational lectures on artistic, literary, scientific, political and self-improvement topics. The eventual rise in popularity of the nationwide

Chautauqua movement is attributable to several factors, including an increasingly prosperous middle class, improvements in roadways, inexpensive and widely available railway service, and the gradual abatement of Victorian-age restrictions against many forms of popular entertainment.

In the late 1870s a number of daughter Chautauqua's were begun at fixed locations in the United States. These soon evolved into touring events, with promoters scheduling performances outside of towns with ready access to railway service. It soon accelerated into a national phenomenon, and by 1920, there were 21 Chautauqua circuits active across the country and Canada. Promoters assumed exclusive rights within their respective areas, much the way circuses had operated for almost a century. The Chautauqua became the first successful form of mass culture in America, reaching its greatest popularity in years just prior to and after the First World War. As lay officials of the church, Hattie and Frank were involved with annual planning sessions, as well as promotional meetings with town and business leaders.

The annual Chautauqua in Jefferson County was part of the Redpath Lyceum Bureau circuit, the largest of several active between 1904 and 1932. With regional headquarters in White Plains, NY, they booked thousands of performers and educators in engagements across rural New York and New England. Attractions included dramatic and comedic plays, musical presentations, and lectures by adventurers and world travelers, which captivated audiences with tales of exotic lands and strange customs. Other features included comedians, magicians, moving pictures, and animal shows for children at their "Junior Chautauqua." The *Redpath Chautauqua News* advertised a diverse, six-day program for their 1930 season, including a feature presentation of "Journey's End," a drama about the Great War written in 1928 by British playwright R.C. Sheriff. By the early 1930s, the national austerity of the Great Depression—coupled with the increased availability of radio and local movie theaters—led to the demise of Chautauqua circuits. Attendance underwent a steep decline, with the swan song for the Redpath Chautauqua in 1932.

One of Hattie and Frank's tickets for the 1921 Redpath Chautauqua season in southern Jefferson County. The Chautauqua movement had its origins in Methodist camp meetings along Lake Chautauqua in upstate New York. The entire family was involved in the promotion of this annual event. These shows were immensely popular and offered people in rural sections much cultural, musical, and informative content typically lacking in seasonal venues such as agricultural fairs and traveling circuses. The Redpath Lyceum Bureau was the nation's largest booking agency for Chautauqua tours between 1904 and 1932. (author's collection)

One of Hattie and Frank's (stamped) tickets to the Riverside Camp Meeting in 1892. From the earliest days, these outdoor congregations had been an integral component of the Methodist faith. This camp meeting occurred somewhere in New York, but precisely where it is uncertain. It was possibly held along the Niagara River in the Riverside section of Buffalo. Or the name may not refer to the location but to the refrain in the popular religious song "Down by the Riverside," in which the minister begins with "I'm gonna lay down my heavy load," to which the congregation responds, "Down by the riverside, down by the riverside, down by the riverside!" (author's collection)

CHAPTER 19

Racial and Religious Intolerance

"What's happening now is what happened before, and often what's going to happen again sometime or other."

—ORSON WELLES

A MARKED homogeneity in the gene pool defined American demographics up to the end of the Victorian Era. Most everyone in New England and the North Country was of Anglo-Saxon descent, with a minority of French Canadian, German, Scottish and Native American ancestry. Interactions with indigenous people are wholly absent in the surviving writings of these families. Most of Frank and Hattie's encounters with African Americans occurred while wintering in North Carolina. This is somewhat surprising when you consider the large number of stops on the Underground Railroad in Jefferson County prior to and during the Civil War. Some former slaves opted to settle in these communities, where their descendants are found to this day. In the 1860s, a young boy in upstate New York recalls having the pants scared off him when encountering a large black woman hiding up in the garret. His parents neglected to inform him their house was a stop for runaways on their way to Canada. Frank does mention peer to peer discussions with African delegates at the Church General Conference in 1908. Still, the appearance of *any* minority groups in rural areas of the northeast was a rarity in this period.

For most of the 19th century, the overall consensus on racial issues in these parts was never delineated by any intentional or well-defined ideology. Whatever opinions people harbored were habitual rather than doctrinal and consistent with the belief that the Creator preordained the prevailing social order and later enshrined in the nation's founding documents. Major racial, ethnic or religious differences were wholly minimal, as almost everyone in their midst was basically cut from the same cloth. The occasional outliers weren't much different, either. Some were French or Irish Catholic, or maybe Scottish. Mainstream Protestantism promulgated the prevailing moral and social beliefs and any religious intolerance attributable to aftereffects from the accelerating pace of mass emigration, as well as the exclusionary, fire and brimstone theology of the Great Awakening movements.

Those born again into the Lord crusades of the 18th and 19th centuries were often raucous affairs in which impassioned preachers brought audiences to a fevered crescendo of religious exuberance. Evangelical ministers were adept at convincing people of their sinful ways and guiding them into salvation through rebirth. The downside was all the exclusivity inherent to their core beliefs and the invectives hurled freely at all who believed otherwise. Acts of religious tolerance were never very high on their list of priorities. In their view, anyone harboring conflicting beliefs was simply earning themselves a one-way ticket to damnation. And the Almighty would forward one of his "Go to hell. Go directly to hell. Do not pass Go. Do not collect $200" cards. And there were no "Get out of hell free" cards available, either.

The mission of the faithful was to bring everyone into the fold for their own good, meaning before it was too late and their immortal souls had been consigned to the eternal flames of hell. Catholics were condemned as a heretical sect of Papists, beholden not to Jesus Christ in heaven but to their chief idolater on his throne at the Vatican. Jews were reviled because the ancient religious hierarchy in Jerusalem had infamously denied and betrayed the Anointed One. Islam was vilified as a conglomeration of demons damned for eternity for usurping the Holy Land from Christendom. In these years, the heathenous ideology of the Muslim had become personified in the State of Ottoman Turkey, the Sick Man of Europe.

Although slavery had been legally abolished after the Emancipation Proclamation and the enactment of the 13th Amendment, African Americans still carried the stigma of servitude and inferiority around their necks like yokes flashing in bright neon colors. Nothing approaching true freedom or equality would ever be attained by most, as they found themselves increasingly disenfranchised in ways analogous to the status of manumitted slaves in ancient Rome: they would never be fully accepted as members of the club. In New England and the North Country, people of color never experienced the levels of violence and systemic racism endemic to the states of the old Confederacy. But most harbored serious doubts of ever seeing genuine improvements to their status in mainstream society.

RACIAL AND RELIGIOUS INTOLERANCE

In the decades leading up to the Civil War, the status of Black America was grouped with foreign immigration as topics of discussion within social gatherings, newspapers and Sunday sermons. Issues regarding slavery and abolition became particularly contentious as new States endeavoring to join the Union were forced to decide whether to allow the practice. The feelings of most in Jefferson County mirrored the prevailing attitudes in the northern and eastern States. People in rural areas had largely been insulated from social problems endemic to the larger cities and newly founded States. But as the nation continued to expand geographically and demographically, the problems of slavery and the "Huddled Masses" were no longer subjects they could conveniently ignore.

In the late 1800s, the federal government was also aggressively consolidating control over vast swaths of Native American lands. The indigenous populations that had resided in these areas for millennia were systematically herded up and consigned to reservations in clearly designated locations. In this way, officials could keep a wary eye on the nations that wreaked such havoc during the years of Manifest Destiny. Simply put, most Americans neither liked nor trusted the red race. In 1886, future President Theodore Roosevelt was queried by the press on his thoughts regarding this remark by Civil War General Philip Sheridan: "The only good Indians I ever saw were dead." To this, Roosevelt responded, "I don't go so far as to think that the only good Indians are dead Indians, but I believe nine out of ten are, and I shouldn't like to inquire too closely into the case of the tenth." Similar to the status of emancipated slaves, the indigenous races found themselves ostracized in their lands, with little or no roles to play in mainstream society.

In 1899, British author Rudyard Kipling summed up the consensus on racial issues with the expression "The White Man's Burden." The Anglo-Saxons were inherently superior to all others, and *noblesse oblige* required a display of benevolence and charity to uplift inferior peoples so they might partake in or at least recognize all the blessings of enlightened civilization. Of course, there was never the slightest chance that once uplifted, they would ever become fully accepted in polite society. On American soil, racism and xenophobia had become as much a part of national identity and tradition as pumpkin pie on Thanksgiving and fireworks on the Fourth of July. But it was the resurgence of the Ku Klux Klan in the early 1920s that really brought the issues of racial, ethnic and religious intolerance into the national press and mainstream dialogue.

The KKK was originally founded in Tennessee in late 1865 by decommissioned Confederate officers who seized upon growing resentment of Union victory and their heavy-handed policies of Washington during Reconstruction.

PART III : EVERYDAY LIFE IN THE VICTORIAN ERA

By the 1870s, Klan chapters were active in all States of the former Confederacy. Their racist-fueled agenda of violence and vigilantism reached such a crescendo the Federal government was compelled to step in and curtail their most murderous and clandestine activities. But by then, the group's main objectives had been achieved: the wholesale disenfranchisement of Black Americans in post-war society and the establishment of Jim Crow legislation to prohibit them from ever voting for anything different.

Although their most brazen activities had largely ceased, group activities continued underground, and by 1915, there reemerged a new and somewhat sanitized version onto the national stage. Unlike the small, secretive and clannish nature of the original incarnation, this new KKK took pains to portray itself as a legitimate sociopolitical movement, anointed to enlighten the white race on growing national menaces and the need for a swift and righteous response. However the group soon realized their original post-war business model was insufficient for expansion beyond the old Confederacy. What was needed was a public relations apparatus to convince the largely sedentary northern populations to join in and preserve their traditional way of life. These efforts were given impetus by the unforeseen success of *The Birth of a Nation*, a silent movie in 1915 that portrayed Klan ideology and activities in a most favorable light. Through the modern miracle of moving pictures, their message was successfully broadcast across the nation: this righteous band of holy warriors had been anointed to save white America from virtually everyone else.

Their rapid resurgence is attributable to a number of factors, including the growing synergy between white nationalism and certain Anglo-Saxon Protestant ideologies and objectives. The religious incentive became a powerful tool for recruitment: by the mid-1920s, national membership included untold thousands of Protestant ministers. This figure excludes all the sycophants who, for one reason or another, never officially announced their allegiance. But mere religious aversion to the evils of alcohol, tobacco and all the immorality in modern society was insufficient to attract church members whose perception of the Klan vacillated between ambivalence and outright revulsion. Further, Klan enrollment became contingent upon the identification of new enemies and threats to their proscription lists. To people of color, virtually all immigrant groups, and especially Catholics and Jews arriving *en masse* from Southern and Eastern Europe. The urban elite in major cities were also vilified, as were the blasphemous white tower intelligentsia embedded at universities, which, the righteous were reminded, had recently repudiated the biblical account of creation during the Scopes Monkey Trial.

These effective marketing tactics convinced many of their legitimacy as just another mainstream movement within American society. People were assured this was not your grandfather's murderous old band of hooded thugs prowling about looking for someone to lynch. Although members retained their signature masks and robes, they weren't the ragtag bed sheets worn by the post-war bunch. These new duds were immaculately tailored to exacting specifications and so stylish that discerning Klansmen and Klanswomen could feel proud to wear them in public. This "new Klan" also modeled its organizational structure and initiatory procedures after such groups as the Freemasons and Odd Fellows. Nighttime meetings were carefully choreographed and filled with awe-inspiring flourishes like secret rituals, esoteric symbols and gestures. Being a racist and xenophobe was suddenly fun.

Their public relations *shtick* included a cadre of locally born recruiters who organized such mainstream activities as neighborhood flea markets, bake sales, marching bands, and carnivals with free food and fun rides for the kiddies. Most importantly, they reassured their neighbors they were merely a band of brothers and others who finally gave voice to all the legitimate fears of true blue Americans. Face it: the country was going down the collective crapper, and this was your opportunity to do something about it. Membership in the Klan identified you as an insider and entitled you to affix one of the colorful Klan crosses to your wagon or Model T.

All this grandstanding succeeded far beyond expectations. By 1926, several million male and female members had been recruited from virtually every State in the Union. In September of that year, the national organization felt so empowered they brazenly paraded 30,000 members in full Klan regalia down Pennsylvania Avenue in Washington, DC. These promotional tactics and dramatic displays resonated all too well with many in New England and the North Country, as it legitimized the growing concern that hoards of unseemly, unwanted foreigners were inundating the nation. In August of 1921 a Klan unit for Jefferson County was formed in Adams, with membership drawn from all neighboring communities. In an effort to disassociate them from the original Southern Klan, they called themselves the Northern Ku Klux Klan and the Knights and Ladies of the Blue Cross.

Their first public meeting in Adams occurred on Labor Day of that year and attracted large crowds of observers from around the area. Between 1922 and 1926, membership in the local chapters had swelled into the tens of thousands. Group activities were fortunately short on lynching but long on public displays, including fiery cross-burnings in neighboring fields and hilltops. In more sedentary settings, members worked on recruitment strategies and distribution of Klan literature, including their newspaper, *The Fellowship Forum*. Their initial appearance in Hattie's diaries occurs in 1923, with a brief notice regarding a gathering at a neighbor's home. Her entry was written with such nonchalance and matter-of-factness it might have escaped notice except for the telltale *KKK* initials as an identifier. She apparently considered the meeting of no more importance than any other social or political noisemaking in town.

In August of 1925, an estimated 15,000 onlookers were drawn to Adams to witness a sizeable number of hooded Klansmen parading down Main Street on their way to the obligatory cross burning outside of town. Newspapers recorded the event as the largest display of Klan influence ever witnessed in the North Country. Residents from nearby communities dressed up in their Sunday finery and lined the streets as they would for any parade or holiday celebration. With a combination of nonchalance and *naïveté*, Hattie penned the following entry for the 30th of August: "Anna came down (from Lorraine) and was here to supper with Arlene. Herbert, Laura and Gordon came down, and we all went to see the KKK parade, then up to the field (to see the) cross burned and fireworks." The event made quite an impression, as nothing remotely similar had ever occurred in the area. Fortunately, it was the Klan's first and only public spectacle in Adams.

Of course, however innocuously they portrayed themselves, Klan activities were never limited to incendiary diatribes and showy public displays. Wherever they went, mayhem was never far off. Hattie's next mention appears in an entry for the 15th of November, where she relates a neighbor had been "shot in the woods" somewhere near Watertown during Klan activities. The man soon died from his wounds, requiring the family to travel to the city to retrieve the body. At the funeral three days later, she describes a "big crowd and quantities of flowers, among them a Klan cross of red flowers."

But despite all their public largesse, gala parades and dramatic rituals, their reemergence on the national stage faded as quickly as it appeared. By 1927, membership had dwindled from several million to less than half a million, and the Northern Ku Klux Klan and Knights and Ladies of the Blue Cross were no longer viable social or political entities in Jefferson County. In the minds of most, they were never more than a flash in the pan and had run their course the same as so many other movements in years past. Whatever additional goings-on Hattie witnessed between 1926 and 1929 are unknown, as her diaries for these years are largely lost.

It is doubtful the KKK could have maintained more than a transient foothold in Jefferson County. Throughout her life, Hattie clung fast to her

Methodist convictions; including the belief all people were equal in the eyes of God. Progressive social issues like anti-slavery and social plurality had been core tenets of Methodism since its inception in the early 19th century. In the church's formative years, most converts had, in fact, been drawn from the most marginalized segments of society, including paupers, day laborers, immigrants, free blacks and runaway slaves.

It is difficult to know what Frank would have made of all this had he lived to see it. In all likelihood, his religious beliefs would have preempted any strong sense of pleasure or identification. As did Hattie, he would have noted everything with the same matter-of-factness, evincing neither resonance nor strong disapprobation. They were just another social movement making their way across the landscape. In Jefferson County, strong sentiments regarding racial superiority never acquired the immediacy so prevalent in the southern and border states. In every society, whenever the political pendulum swings too far in one direction, a course correction inevitably occurs to restore a sense of normality and equilibrium to everyday life.

CHAPTER 20

Telephones, Radios and Phonographs

IN the late 19th century, the most significant innovation in interpersonal communications was the installation of telephone services in people's homes and businesses. In these early years, people were amazed at the sudden ability to transmit their voice unimaginable distances through this newfangled and rather peculiar looking device hanging on the wall. The farmstead in Northfield was without a telephone connection for the entire period covered in their diaries. As with most remote sections of the country, the task of fully wiring isolated neighborhoods remained a work in progress well into the 1920s. For most in the 19th century, the fastest form of communication was still the telegram, and the local telegraph office was to remain a staple of small-town life throughout the 1940s. For many well into the 20th century, using the telephone meant traveling into town and accessing one of the public connections.

In northern New York, Frank began his courtship of Hattie by calling her on the newly installed telephone in the dry goods store. Telephony grew in leaps and bounds through the implementation of increasingly sophisticated and interconnected networks. The ability to speak to others across town soon expanded to the ability to call anywhere in the State, then across the region, and eventually most of the nation. But all this wizardry was still accomplished through a system of wires and other metal parts, which constituted a traceable, physical connection between sender and receiver. This mechanical nexus, however, was missing with the development of *wireless* communications in the first decades of the new century. The ability to send messages through the *aether* with absolutely *no* physical connections whatsoever would have seemed inconceivable to people of Reverend Gordon's generation.

Wireless technology had its inception during 19th century research by Guglielmo Marconi, Nikola Tesla and other inventors who wanted to improve upon the system of wired telegraphy as pioneered in the 1830s by Samuel Morse. In public demonstrations, people became dumbstruck at the ability to transmit data with absolutely no discernable link between sender and receiver. The earliest practical application of this new technology was station-to-station transmissions by the Navy and maritime industries to ships at sea. In 1909, the *First Annual Official Wireless Blue Book of the Wireless Association of America* was published, listing all registered public service, governmental and amateur radio transmitters in America and southern Canada. By 1913, there were 322 licensed wireless radio operators in America. By 1917, this number increased to several thousand, a figure that didn't include the legions of *unlicensed* operators across the country.

The early years were strictly the domain of hobbyists, as amateur enthusiasts sought to gather the parts needed to assemble these first primitive sets in their homes and workshops. Always eager for more tax revenue, licensure laws were soon enacted in many States. Within a few years, the technology had advanced to the extent that senders and receivers were no longer limited to the transmission of simple dots and dashes. Improvements in frequency modulation now allow the transfer of vocal and musical data to any unit capable of tuning in to the appropriate frequency. The exciting new radio fad spread like wildfire across the country, with assistance from the newly created electronics industry, which eagerly supplied the necessary parts for these homemade sets. More sophisticated, ready-assembled radios entered the market during the 1920s. The first units required users to plug in a headset to hear broadcasts, which greatly limited the number able to listen in at one time. The marketing of sets with built-in or external speakers soon rectified this deficiency. Now, the entire family could gather in the evening and tune in to the thrilling new world of radio broadcasts while drinking near beer and snacking on Cracker Jack.

By this time, most Americans had lost interest in the ability to transmit data and became obsessed with receiving the increasing array of commercial programming. Prior to this time, if you wanted to hear live music or other programs, you had to leave home and travel to wherever the show happened to be. Now, the technological wizards had devised a way to beam the shows directly to you, wherever *you* happened to be. In November of 1920, KDKA in Pittsburgh was the first radio station to offer regular commercial programming. Additional stations quickly appeared, and by 1924, the number nationwide had increased to 600, with another 50 across the border in Canada. While early broadcasts were limited to the evening hours, stations and sponsors soon saw the potential to expand their programming throughout the day. This led to a remarkable paradigm shift in people's utilization of their leisure time. And in the wink of an eye, the age of the couch potato had arrived.

PART III : EVERYDAY LIFE IN THE VICTORIAN ERA

In these years, the country underwent phenomenal growth in the entertainment and advertising industries. Early stations were hampered by the short range of their signals, which could only be received by sets in relative proximity to the transmission antenna. By the 1930s, more powerful signals were being generated to reach increasingly wider audiences. Broadcasters began devoting enormous resources to satiating the public's demand for new shows, like comedies, mysteries, serials, musical presentations, news broadcasts, sporting events and religious programs. Advertisers invested millions of dollars in creating more and more ridiculous advertisements for products like cigarettes, shaving creams and laundry detergents.

The first commercial station in upstate New York was WFBL in Syracuse. Hattie records her trip upstairs to listen in to Laura and Herbert's new radio, which was capable of pulling in broadcasts from as far away as Troy (NY), Newark (NJ) and Pittsburgh (PA). Some stations came in so clearly you could actually sit back and enjoy them. In all likelihood, what they heard was either classical music or the latest popular tunes from Tin Pan Alley. A full panorama of musical and dramatic entertainment was suddenly available to anyone with a radio in rural America. In most homes, this ubiquitous device remained the premier form of domestic entertainment throughout the first half of the 20th century.

A further enhancement to home entertainment occurred in 1877 with Thomas Edison's invention of the talking machine or phonograph, which had the capability of both recording and replaying sounds on small, portable wax cylinders. Further refinements came a decade later when Alexander Graham Bell devised the Graphophone, which reproduced sound on flat discs called gramophone or phonograph records. Commercial versions of these products appeared in 1895, followed two years later by the opening of the Edison Phonograph Company, which offered a wider variety of recordings. These machines were run by a small internal motor powered up by a hand crank on the side of the cabinet.

Like early automobiles, the first phonographs were expensive and perceived as yet another plaything for the wealthy. But for the first time, prerecorded music by popular composers and musicians could be enjoyed without the obligatory trip to the opera house or other venue. The national impetus to incorporate all residential sections into the electrical grid resulted in the marketing of electrically powered phonographs by the late 1920s. The first mention of these wondrous auditory devices appears in Hattie's diary for 1904, where she recalls the scratchy sound of "Daisy Bell" wafting from an open window during a trip to Watertown:

> Daisy, Daisy,
> Give me your answer, do!
> I'm half crazy,
> All for the love of you!
> It won't be a stylish marriage,
> I can't afford a carriage,
> But you'll look sweet on the seat
> Of a bicycle built for two!

By 1910, literally, everyone in the country wanted to own one of these prestigious devices. Hattie records their visit to a neighbor's home one evening in 1912 with the specific intent of listening to their new *Victor Talking Machine*, or *Victrola*. It is hard to envision the trajectory of 20th-century commercialism without the mass introduction of electrical service into American homes and businesses. Virtually all future developments were, in one way or another, contingent upon this revolutionary power source. Except in isolated areas, the age of animal and steam power was by now all but relegated to obscurity. The sky was truly the limit with this innovative new array of consumer gadgets.

PART III : EVERYDAY LIFE IN THE VICTORIAN ERA

A gaggle of Victorian party animals wired into an early Edison jukebox circa 1888. Hard to imagine how the DJ in the back managed all these giddy patrons while tending to the musical selections. Most early recordings were made on wax cylinders, which limited musical offerings to whichever selections happened to be brought out for the presentation. The wires to the earbuds were intentionally kept short to inhibit disruptive outbreaks of karaoke or ecstatic dancing. The guy with the derby at right looks like the bouncer, who would spring into action whenever anyone hesitated to make way once their nickel's worth of entertainment was up. (Public Domain)

CHAPTER 21

Weather Readings

MAKING careful notation of daily weather conditions is a consistent feature of antique journals in 19th-century America. The family in Northfield didn't own a thermometer or barometer but recorded overall conditions each day at the beginning of their entries. In years past, most people spent considerably more time outside, either working, playing or traveling by foot, horse, or in an open wagon or carriage. And they needed to know when conditions might make them wish they had stayed at home. Everyday trips for shopping, mailing letters, attending social gatherings or church services were done mostly on foot. People in the countryside relied upon their trusty almanac for such essential data as weather predictions, rising and setting times for the sun and moon, lunar phases, tide tables and more. In southern New England, *Beckwith's Almanac* was particularly noted for the accuracy of its long-range forecasts.

As had been Reverend Gordon's custom in upstate New York, Hattie and Frank began each day by recording overall weather conditions, as well as temperature and barometer readings from their front porch. Periodic updates were made if conditions changed significantly during the day. Some of their entries were quite lengthy and occupied almost half the available space for each day: "Pleasantly warmer this am. Temperature 27 degrees with 29-6-7 barometer at 7 am. The morning remained fair, with a slight west wind in the forenoon. Growing colder in the afternoon with some flakes in the air. Full blown storm by early evening." The unstable weather patterns in Jefferson County were due to the proximity to Lake Ontario, as well as arctic cold fronts sweeping down from Canada.

Since Colonial times, attention to the weather had been a critical tool for tending crops, raising livestock, repairing buildings and fences, and a host of other outdoor activities. People were wholly dependent upon local newspapers, almanacs and personal observations for insights into changing conditions. Still, the assiduous daily reporting on Main Street appears to be more habit than necessity. How many times did Frank dust off an old diary to verify the weather on any given day? Seems unlikely anyone would query him with "Hey Frank! What was the temperature and barometric pressure ten years ago this May the eleventh?"

Winters in the North Country and upper New England could be bone-chillingly cold for weeks on end. Sleigh travel over frozen lakes and landscapes was a regular feature of winter in most sections of New England. In upstate New York, these diaries recorded numerous January and February days with temperatures around -20 degrees. In 1890, Frank wrote with much satisfaction his ability to heat the downstairs rooms to a balmy 30 degrees after purchasing a portable wood-burning stove. But not all townspeople were so fortunate. He notes how one neighbor went over a month with an inability to cook, take a drink, clean up, or even shave due to solid ice buildup in every water spout and receptacle. Prior to central heating, indoor water closets were prone to freezing almost as readily as other water sources in the dead of winter. In times like these, people were thankful for access to their old-fashioned outdoor privy.

The weather in summer months could also be a problem, with severe winds, thunder storms and protracted spells of high heat and humidity. Amanda and her family often record skipping the daily chores because it was too bloody hot to do anything other than go swimming or fishing. The Dog Days in Jefferson County could be just as brutal. The family records an average temperature hovering around 80 degrees. Frank recorded a heat wave in July of 1911 that lasted an entire week. Their thermometer on the front porch registered 102 degrees, which he records as "the hottest day we ever knew." The entire family "lay out on the lawn" until sunset because it was just too hot to go inside. Electric cooling fans for domestic use were available by 1910, but there is no mention of anyone making a purchase this early in the century. People did the only things they could to mitigate their summer discomfort: they put on lighter clothes, stayed in the shade, drank lemonade and prayed for cooling rain.

The Great Blizzard of 1888 as experienced on a street corner in New York City. Victorians spent more of their time out of doors, and keeping careful tabs on the weather helped keep them from getting caught in some meteorological nightmare, like the hapless bunch illustrated here. The guy atop the mailbox (?) seems to be directing traffic, which at the time consisted of flying people, hats and umbrellas. This mother of all nor'easters began rather innocuously on March 11th, but before it ended, it dumped up to 50 inches of snow on coastal sections from Maine to New Jersey. Destructive wind gusts of 80 miles per hour were reported in some areas. Years later, one eyewitness recalls that when it started snowing, her parents reassured her it was "just a few flakes and nothing to worry about." She awoke the next morning to find snowdrifts blocking the view from their third-floor windows. Literally, everything in the northeast shut down for days. People remained stranded wherever they happened to get caught, without access to food, water, fuel or medical attention. Anyone needing to journey out back to the privy was in a world of hurt (public domain—courtesy Library of Congress).

CHAPTER 22

Clothing and Laundry

ONE of the things Hattie brought with her into married life was her mother's old, pedal-driven sewing machine. As with most girls in Colonial and Victorian times, as soon as she could thread a needle, she was initiated into the domestic arts of spinning, weaving, sewing, needlework and embroidery. Sewing and mending were primary female responsibilities both before and after marriage. Amanda and Belle in New Hampshire spent a portion of most days sewing, darning, dying and otherwise fixing up the family's wardrobe. Traveling into Tilton to shop for fabric and accessories always went down as a notable event in their diaries. Most girls honed their techniques on the ubiquitous sampler, surviving examples of which are amongst the most endearing legacies from these periods. In addition, working on her sampler was often a girl's initial exposure to numbers and letters, things she invariably incorporated into the piece. While still at home, Hattie makes mention of cutting and sewing her clothing based upon commercially bought patterns, in addition to near continuous mending for other members of the family.

Prior to around 1900, most clothing was made at home from locally obtained textiles, including flax, linen, wool, hemp and cotton, with the occasional silk, satin and lace trim. The ability to walk downtown and purchase ready-made attire would have seemed miraculous to most Americans in the 18th and 19th centuries. Although well-to-do families relied upon staff or hired help for their clothing needs, most women and girls still passed the time by working on their embroidery and needlework. One Victorian farmer recalls how, in his grandfather's day, the usual way people measured for new clothing was to have the person lie on the ground while another traced their outline on the ground. The finished products were undoubtedly coarse, ill-fitting, and the antithesis of high fashion. But it was all the country people had in these years.

What all this homemade clothing lacked in stylishness was partially offset by its increased durability. Around 1900, author Emma Bell Miles describes how, back home in Appalachia, their homespun articles tended to last forever, while store-bought clothing rarely lasted the season.[35] Most people had an extremely limited wardrobe, so any torn or tattered items were repeatedly mended for as long as they would hold together. If something no longer fit, it was handed down to someone else. Anything beyond repair was cut up and used as towels, rags and toilet paper. Almost nothing went to waste in the good old days.

People in the New England countryside almost always made their clothing. Throughout her marriage, Hattie in New York was in a financial position to have seamstresses stop in periodically and assist with mending and fashioning new articles from commercially made patterns. In the latter half of the 19th century, a number of manufacturers issued a regular succession of new patterns to satiate demand for up-to-date wardrobes. Among these were Mme. Demorest's Reliable Patterns, which Frank sold at D.E. Taylors on Main Street. Another popular series was Butterick Sewing Patterns, which Hattie purchased through a subscription to *The Delineator*, an early fashion magazine. As she grew older, she purchased more and more of her clothing from retail shops in Watertown and elsewhere.

Of course, regardless of whether one's wardrobe was made from homespun flax or tailored from silk, satin and lace, most people spent so much time out of doors that everything ended up really dirty, really fast. Laundering was a lengthy and backbreaking manual process that occupied most of the day—or sometimes two. Any homemaker with two pennies to rub together sought outside help to ease some of this burden. Professional scrubwomen were readily available in towns and cities, which offered higher concentrations of indigent and immigrant populations. In the countryside, homemakers were forced to canvass about soliciting help from friends and neighbors. One of Hattie's first duties upon arrival at Thousand Island Park was to find someone to assist with laundering and general cleaning duties at the cottages.

Detergent options were limited to whatever coarse, evil-smelling, all-purpose soaps could be made at home or purchased locally. *Twenty Mule Team Borax* was one of the first commercial products to hit the shelves when it made its debut in 1891.[36] But country homemakers and people of limited means often scoffed at the idea of paying for something they could make themselves

---

35. As described in her memoir *The Spirit of the Mountains*. Emma Bell Miles wrote about life amongst the hills of Appalachia rather than the North Country or New England. However, many of her observations remain valid for rural residents of the eastern and central States during the late Victorian Era.

36. In the late 19th century, the Borax brand of laundry detergent was formulated from naturally occurring sodium compounds isolated from within salt deposits at Death Valley, California. The chemicals were mined and then transported out of the desert by teams consisting of two lead horses and 18 mules. In the 20th century, some components of Borax were determined to have toxic effects on human developmental and reproductive health. Around this same time, manufacturers switched gears and began marketing the product as an insecticide.

for a pittance. Regardless of their choice of detergent, white articles still had to be boiled to start the process or at least soaked overnight in a vat of bleach. Manual scrubbing then commenced on a wooden washboard, followed by the feeding of individual articles through the wringer to remove excess soap and water. The ability of clothing to survive these repeated regimens is a testament to old-fashioned materials and workmanship.

Assuming the weather cooperated, everything was hung outside to dry and then hauled inside for a little ironing and folding. In these days the domestic iron was an unwieldy block of metal with a wooden handle so homemakers could heat them on stovetops. Between the constant risk of fire from wood and coal stoves and reliance on nearly red-hot irons, instances of fire and severe burns were commonplace. Newspapers described a litany of horrific injuries and deaths from simple, everyday activities such as laundering, cooking and lighting kerosene lamps.

Considering such washday horrors, it is no wonder people wore the same smelly, soiled articles as long as they could get away with it. No one relished the thought of adding to mother's misery by laundering anything before it's time. And, although it's truly miraculous how well these antique fabrics held up under repeated ordeals, what about the wear and tear on the homemaker's skin? Can you imagine regular immersion of hands and arms into scalding hot water, bleach and caustic detergents? Washer's gloves were nonexistent, and commercial moisturizers were a rarity. The December 1879 edition of the *American Agriculturist For The Farm, Garden & Household* offered this simple solution: "The hands should be washed in Borax water, and afterward rubbed with melted suet and glycerin, half and half. Apply plenty of this mixture at night by the fire, then put on a pair of old kid gloves before retiring." Vegetarians and people with limited access to raw animal fat might mitigate the damage to whatever was left of their hands by slopping on the oil, lanolin or other palliatives most families kept around the house. Either way, forget about nails or manicures.

CLOTHING AND LAUNDRY

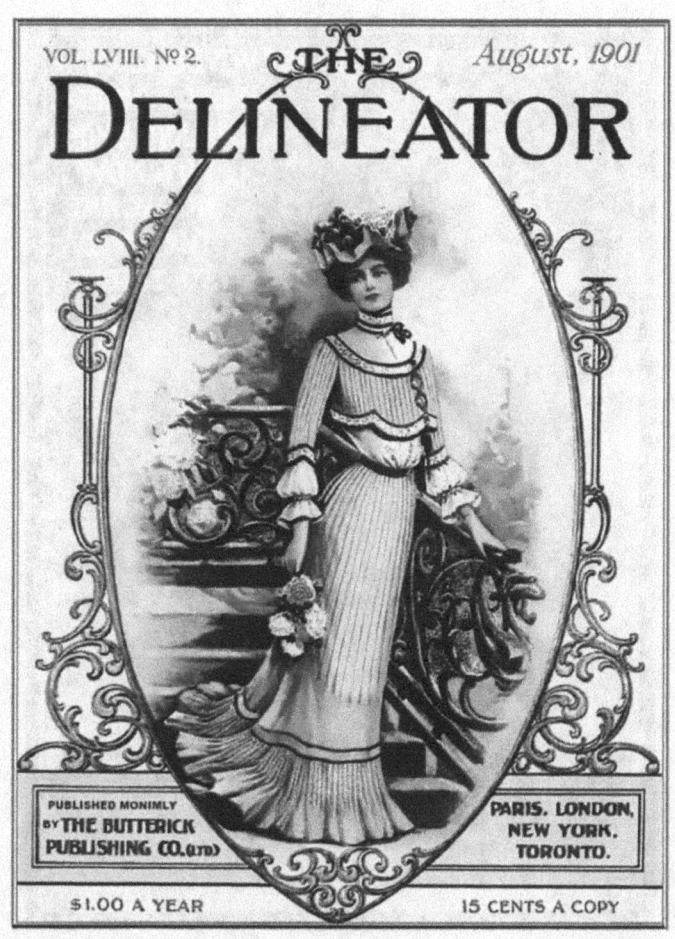

Cover of the August 1901 edition of The Delineator. Hattie subscribed to this early illustrated fashion magazine, which made its debut in 1875. It was published in New York City by the makers of Butterick Sewing Patterns, which she used for much of her clothing. In later years, many women began purchasing their apparel from retail shops. Clothing from sewing patterns and ready-made articles were both vast improvements over the rustic Colonial method of lying down on the ground while an outfitter crudely traced your outline to arrive at just the right fit. (Public Domain)

PART III : EVERYDAY LIFE IN THE VICTORIAN ERA

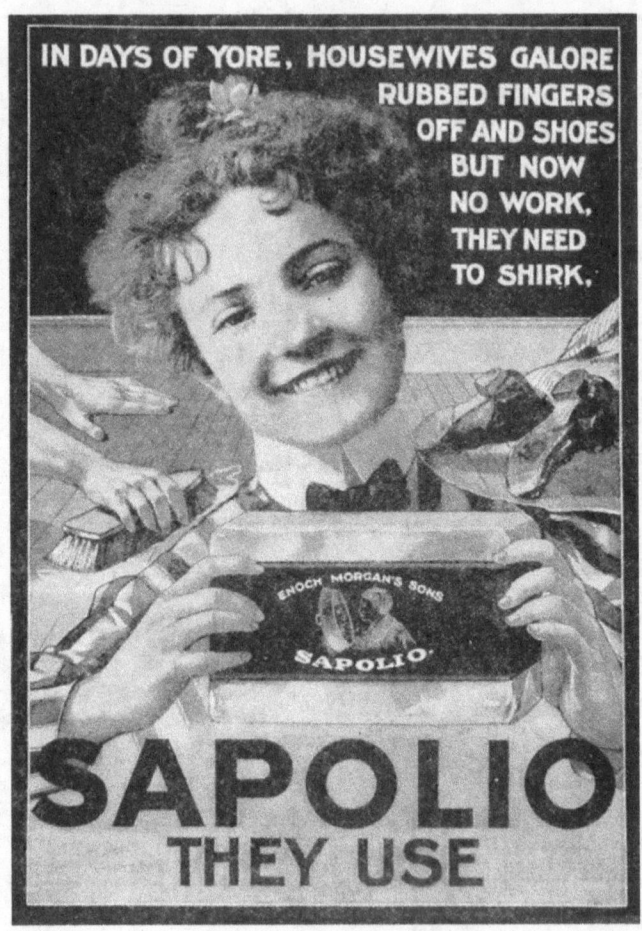

Illustrations from two-period advertisements for Sapolino, which was marketed as "a solid cake of scouring soap. All grocers keep it." It was among the first commercially made cleaning products when it hit the shelves in 1869. The name derives from a combination of the Italian word for soap (sapone) and the verb to polish. This brand of ready-made soap revolutionized household cleaning by transforming even the most backbreaking chores into pleasurable experiences no sane homemaker could resist. Their marketing blitz between 1870 and 1940 made it one of the most widely advertised products in America. The advertising team included King Camp Gillette, who soon left the company to market his creation, the Gillette safety razor.

Clothing and Laundry

Above, we see the typical Victorian homemaker, beaming from bouffant to bowtie after scrubbing the floor on hands and knees with Sapolino. Above are a series of characterizations from another of their many advertisements. Then, as now, whatever attention grabbing imagery the mind can conjure was used to sell the product. It makes no never-mind these depictions of common Victorian types have absolutely nothing to do with household cleaners. The original advertisement contained the caption "Is Marriage a Failure?" followed by "A man with his money may have ease through life. But without Sapolio, there's no ease for his wife." If this drivel doesn't make you want to scour the kitchen floor, nothing will. (Public Domain)

PART III : EVERYDAY LIFE IN THE VICTORIAN ERA

Laundry day has never been considered a fun day, regardless of when or where it occurred. But in Victorian times, it was positively abhorred as the most insufferable activity on the homemaker's to-do list. Something Hattie undoubtedly ran across in the newspapers was this advertisement for the 1900 Gravity Washer. Far from being the standard inert tub, this technological wonder featured an inner drum creating an oscillating motion as the hand crank was rotated on the side. Just pour a cupful of Twenty Mule Team Borax into this baby, turn the crank and watch the excitement. Another advertisement boasted this labor-saving miracle transformed the domestic sphere by "making washing almost fun . . . it is the machine every woman will have when she knows it." Homemaker Hattie might have "known it," but whether she convinced her thrifty husband to pony up and let her have tons of fun is another matter. (Public Domain)

CHAPTER 23

The Old Time General Store

IN terms of archetypal, old-time businesses, a number of readily identifiable types have been enshrined in the collective lore of Americana. Among these are the blacksmith shop, stable and livery, feed store, telegraph office, sheriff's office and lockup, the corner saloon, and the all-purpose country or general store. These institutions were once as ubiquitous to Main Street as gas stations, convenience stores, nail salons and Chinese take-outs are today. While virtually every settlement in America had at least one steady blacksmith, in some areas, drinking establishments maintained a precarious existence due to periodic activities of temperance movements and fluctuating local prohibitions. Town ordinances forced the intermittent closure of many saloons, taverns and distilleries in the decades leading up to the Volsted Act in 1919. But despite periodic changes in ownership, the general store has consistently remained a venerated feature of the American landscape.

This quintessential retail establishment was often situated near the center of town and served surrounding residents as the Walmart of their day. They were combination hardware, stationary, grocery, clothing and dry goods stores, and often the town post office and local meeting spot, all under one roof. Here, anything and everything you could imagine was crammed into every conceivable nook and cranny with a deftness, making the hoarders of television notoriety green with envy. If these places didn't carry it, you probably didn't need it. And in most cases, you would certainly go without it.

Nearly every settlement in the country had one or more mom-and-pop variety stores somewhere in the vicinity. A case in point was the retail store of C.C. Moore & Son in Lorraine center, where Hattie worked as a cashier and clerk after high school. The business opened in 1870 but tragically burnt down in December 1893. The family reopened at a nearby site, where it remains in operation by descendants of the original owner. From the street, the view is rather deceptive, as the store's narrow frontage belies its sizeable length and

PART III : EVERYDAY LIFE IN THE VICTORIAN ERA

square footage. Most retail activities transpired on the main floor, but the building includes a full basement, as well as an upper level where lodge meetings, dances and other activities took place in Hattie's day. After a century and a half, this store is as much engrained in local culture as any other topographical feature in the vicinity.[37]

Including the town's post office was a common feature of these stores, where services and inventory have always reflected the needs of the local farming and dairy community. In Hattie's day, interior lighting was by oil lamps and heating by two sizeable pot-bellied stoves, one in the front by the register and the other in the rear. The store was stocked to the rafters with all the necessities for country living, including stamps and stationary, money orders, school supplies, footwear, clothing, sewing supplies, jewelry and pocket watches, tobacco (cigars, chewing plugs and snuff), soap, medicines (Epsom salts, castor oil and tincture of opium), painting supplies, lanterns, (including kerosene and matches), kitchen and housewares, tools, building and farm implements, animal supplies, and plate glass cut to order. By the 1920s, a hand cranked gasoline pump was installed by the front porch. Motoring needs were also facilitated by the addition of two 55-gallon barrels of motor oil.[38]

Amongst the available grocery items were sacks of potatoes, flour and corn meal, 40-pound wheels of cheese cut to order, bread, fruit, sugar, coffee, tea, milk, potatoes, popcorn, crackers, candy, canned goods, dried fish, salt pork and bacon, cracker barrels full of cookies, industrial-sized containers of cereals including corn flakes, shredded wheat, farina and oatmeal, cooking and baking essentials like lard, flour, sugar, baking powder, baking soda, salt, vinegar and molasses. Modern notions of store cleanliness were virtually unknown in this era. Whatever statutes there were would probably have been overlooked as unnecessary intrusions.

These old-time general stores were as much gathering spots as shopping destinations. In the front section were usually the post office station, cash register and heating stove, where local women gathered to trade complaints about their husbands. Further in the back was another pot belly stove, surrounded by chairs and several strategically placed spittoons. Here, the men would congregate while discussing farming and other vital social issues, all while taking turns missing the spittoon with their tobacco chaws. Close by in the Lorraine shop

---

37. The author is indebted to Bilkey Moore for the use of the material from his late father, Donald, who ran the store for many years. Donald had taken over the business from his father, Edward, who had taken over from his father, the store founder C.C. Moore. The family still operates the facility as a store, diner, maple syrup bottling center, and town post office.

38. An overview of this store's impressive inventory during the early 20th century is contained on pp. 11–22 of *The Huddle-The Way It Was*.

was the men's urinal, situated against the rear wall in full view of unfortunate passersby. As antiquated as they appear today, these homey establishments were once as familiar in American towns as village greens, gazebos and hitching posts. Their allure never completely disappeared for reasons including convenience, tradition and nostalgic value. Most rural sections maintain their fair share of these quaint reminders of everyday life in Colonial and Victorian times.

The general store of E.H. Moore (Edward Moore) was on the corner of Main and Egg Street in Lorraine. Edward was the son of C.C. Moore, who opened the shop in 1870. In modern America's overly commercialized society, overrun from coast to coast with strip malls and megastores, it's hard to fathom how essential these old-time businesses were to the well-being of the community. In addition to her stint as cashier and clerk at the store, Hattie in Jefferson County also worked in the basement level at her father's egg pickling business. The entrance to this subterranean pickling paradise is visible on the right side of the building, below the sign and behind the concrete loading platform. The uppermost level was a multi-purpose hall used for various functions, including town meetings, dances, dinners and early moving pictures. Popcorn and Coca-Cola were both popular at the turn of the 20th century, but this facility probably lacked a concessions stand. The upstairs was also used for meetings of the various lodges to which Hattie and Frank belonged, including the Odd Fellows and Sisters of Rebekah. The ground floor establishment was renamed Moore's Friendly Store in 1946 by Edward's son, Donald O. Moore. In more recent years, the space has been remodeled and is still run by the family as a diner, maple syrup bottling facility and town post office. (courtesy of Bilkey Moore)

PART III : EVERYDAY LIFE IN THE VICTORIAN ERA

Another picture developed from glass negatives amongst Frank's possessions. It features a late 19th-century view of S. A. Moore's general store in East Rodman. Frank bought cigars here shortly before his wedding. He was also the owner's insurance agent in later years. There were a number of merchants in southern Jefferson County with the name Moore, including C.C. Moore and E.H. Moore in Lorraine. Enshrined in the annals of Americana as the old-time general store, these ubiquitous establishments were the supermarkets of their day and offered an astonishing array of otherwise unobtainable goods. They often included the local post office and served as a congenial meeting spot around heating stoves during long, bitter winters. The sign at the top is an advertisement for "Foley's Kidney Cure," which claimed to be "The most successful remedy for incipient Bright's disease, chronic inflammation of the bladder, gravel, irritation of the kidneys, diabetes and nervous exhaustion." God only knows what went into this silly glop. (author's collection)

CHAPTER 24

Health, Hygiene, and Medicine

RELATIVE to modern times, there were a number of notable differences in the diseases common to 18th and 19th populations. People's anatomy and physiology were, of course, the same, but they tended to get sick more often, and the available treatments did little to abate illness or, with serious conditions, increase their likelihood of survival. In 1885, Hattie was anticipating her engagement to a local youth who unfortunately succumbed to one of the many contagions making the rounds in these Victorian communities. The precise killer is unrecorded, but likely smallpox, typhoid or scarlet fever. Life was far shorter and more precarious in centuries past. The common bedside prayer of Victorian children contained immediacy not readily apparent to the modern reader:

> Now I lay me down to sleep,
> I pray the Lord my Soul to keep.
> If I should die before I 'wake,
> I pray the Lord my Soul to take.

In 1800, the life expectancy for the average American was less than 40 years. Due to advances in sanitation, microbiology, medical treatment and pharmacology, the average life expectancy by 1900 had risen to between 45 and 48 years. But infant mortality rates remained appallingly high. Even children who survived infancy ran the risk of succumbing to disease before they reached adulthood. In the 21st century, it is common for children to know their grandparents and, in many cases, their great-grandparents. Children of two centuries ago rarely knew any more about their grandparents than things related by adults at the fireplace or table.

Prior to effective methods of birth control, it wasn't unusual for women to give birth to six or more children, of which only a few would survive until adulthood and possibly give their grandchildren. Mothers also experienced high mortality rates both during childbirth and afterward from hemorrhage, postpartum infections and other complications. The advent of antibiotic therapy was still a long way off. Even the ability to lower fevers to alleviate suffering was nearly non-existent prior to the marketing of aspirin around 1900. The only conceivable upside to shorter life spans was the lessened risk of contracting disorders normally associated with aging, such as cardiovascular disease, dementia and certain forms of cancer. The longer you linger in the middle of the road, the greater your chances of getting run over. Of course, in times past, you were always at heightened risk, regardless of where or how long you lingered.

The concept of microorganisms as disease vectors was still in its infancy in the late 1800s, and many medical practitioners remained skeptical of their role in the etiology and transmission of disease. Children were particularly susceptible to the ravages of measles, smallpox, chicken pox, dysentery, whopping cough (pertussis), scarlet fever, typhoid fever, typhus, influenza, meningitis and diphtheria. Periodic outbreaks of communicable diseases cut broad swaths of mortality across all age groups in these tightly-knit communities. Influenza was especially problematic due to the complication of developing pneumonia, for which there were no effective treatments. Anyone coming down with a fever became a magic carpet for transmission to others within the household.

As a child in the 1860s, Belle in New Hampshire was afflicted with a debilitating middle ear infection, which kept her out of school and essentially bedridden for over a month. Whatever treatment was forthcoming from the local medicine man had little effect, but the condition eventually ran its course and resolved on its own. And apparently, no permanent hearing loss eventuated from the infection. As a teenager in early 1912, Laura in Adams was diagnosed with what Frank described as "a light case" of Scarlet Fever. Over the years, their writings mention a number of deaths of local children from this disease, but due to the relatively minor nature of her case, everyone remained hopeful for a full recovery. In 1912, the mortality rate from Scarlet Fever was around 25 percent, with much higher rates during the periodic pandemics that ravaged the nation. Her doctor posted the standard quarantine sign on their front door, restricting anyone from entering or leaving the premises until the infection had passed. After approximately three weeks, Laura's fever subsided to the point her doctor felt confident she was on the mend. The dreaded quarantine sign was promptly removed from the front door.

The roles of sanitation and hygiene in the prevention of disease went unrecognized for most of the 19th century. In many respects, domestic and environmental cleanliness had not advanced much, if at all, over the last several centuries. There was but a rudimentary understanding of the need to separate food preparation and water sources from areas of waste disposal and privy locations. Contagions from contaminated water and food supplies were endemic. Young and old suffered from dysentery and other gastrointestinal disorders from waterborne pathogens and other sources of contamination.

Contemporary health and mortality statistics illustrated the universality of these conditions in the 19th century. Although now more common in overcrowded urban areas and underdeveloped countries, in the past, the spread of airborne and waterborne pathogens was still endemic in most wealthy and ostensibly less dirty neighborhoods. Instances of parasitic infections like hookworms, flatworms and roundworms from contaminated water sources were common. This danger persisted up to the identification of causality and statutory mandates for healthy food storage, construction of secure water supplies and segregated waste disposal areas.

A medical treatise from the 1880s stressed three key factors towards the maintenance of health: no intoxicating beverages, no cigar smoking, and bathing once a week, followed by a change of underwear. People putting on the same filthy, sweaty underwear day after day was cited as a major cause of marital dissension. Everyone simply stank, and their appallingly unhygienic habits were largely to blame. Although commercial toilet paper was available in the 1880s, in most places, the age-old dependence upon newspaper strips, torn rags and leaves continued unabated well into the following century.

The concept of bathing once a week seemed radical in an age when most people bathed no more than once a month if that. Some medical practitioners even cautioned against taking a weekly tub, stating that over-exposure to soaps and bath water might prove injurious to those with delicate constitutions. Some religious authorities advised against tub baths, believing the sensual titillation of envelopment in warm water might lead the righteous into temptation. A sponge bath behind some makeshift curtain in the kitchen would more than suffice. With all these conflicting opinions and bogus recommendations, it is no wonder that widespread acceptance of good personal hygiene didn't become standard practice until well into the 20th century. And even then, such elitist lifestyles remained largely ignored in impoverished and underdeveloped areas.

Filthy clothes and unwashed bodies are also ideal breeding grounds for the spread of body and hair lice. The custom of females pulling their hair up off their shoulders into buns or coiffures before entering public was also problematic, as parasites tend to proliferate in these warm, tightly constrained environments.

PART III : EVERYDAY LIFE IN THE VICTORIAN ERA

Once infected, they were difficult to eradicate because eggs became cemented to the hair shafts. Early methods for removal—assuming one knew they were there in the first place, which was hardly a given—were exceedingly caustic and disagreeable. The simplest method was to let your hair down each night and brush the dickens out of it to remove the daily accumulation of filth and vermin. In Colonial and earlier periods, the removal of body and head lice was traditionally family fun time each evening. People would gather by the fireside and take turns ridding each other of these hideous intruders. The excitement came when you flicked them into the flames and listened to the crackling sound as they vaporized into eternity. Face it, there wasn't a whole lot going on at night in most antique homesteads.

The *Woman's Book* from 1894 recommended you wash your hair once a month, even if you considered such a regimen a bit excessive. The rationale, of course, was that most people washed it even less often. Suggested cleansers included diluted ammonia and onion juice, which not only cleaned the hair but also helped rid the scalp of lice and whatever else had festered up there since last month. Elegant images of Victorian ladies with their hair pulled up into elegant coiffures belied the fact that most times, it was indescribably caked and matted with perspiration, dirt, dust and every other impurity the antique environment had to offer. The Gibson Girl look of the Gay 90s was mere window dressing, which obscured the reality of scalps and bodies that, in modern society, are mostly associated with homeless people in the inner city.

Another disincentive towards regular bathing and laundering was the gritty and unpleasant nature of most early soaps. Prior to the late 1800s, rural home-makers didn't have an arsenal of cleaning products to select from for bathing, laundering, washing dishes and general housecleaning. Most relied on the same multi-purpose brown cakes they made at home from animal fat, water, and a lye solution extracted from stove and fireplace ashes. Soap making was such a smelly and messy process it was usually done out of doors and no more than once or twice a year. For some obscure reason, certain almanacs recommended putting off the chore until the moon was full. But regardless of when in the lunar cycle it occurred, homemakers still had to combine the same basic ingredients into a large iron kettle, followed by tedious boiling and stirring until the mixture had sufficiently thickened. At that point, the disagreeable slop was ladled out into smaller containers and allowed to harden in the sun before being cut up into manageably sized squares. *Voilà!* The family now had an ample supply of gritty, nasty-smelling brown soap to keep everyone and everything tip-top and scrupulously clean until the next backyard soap-fest.

Health, Hygiene, and Medicine

In years past, the universal disregard for hygiene and sanitation were major factors in the spread of disease and high rates of mortality in communities, both large and small. Americans were no more progressive in this regard than their European counterparts. During the First World War, a popular saying amongst the doughboys was, "You can tell a Frenchman by his smell." Men in wartime have always had fewer opportunities to freshen up and change their clothing. The assumption that Frenchmen were even filthier and smellier than most is a misnomer: they were no worse off than anyone else on the battlefield. But the Frenchman's habit of liberally splashing on scented toiletries to mask bodily odors seemed extraordinary to their Yankee compatriots. So, without a doubt, the French *poilu* did constitute a full frontal assault on American olfactory sensibilities.

This wartime lack of cleanliness, hygiene and separate spaces for food preparation and sanitation added significantly to already unprecedented casualty statistics. The universal prevalence of vermin, body lice and intestinal parasites made life intolerable within the filthy, shell-ridden trenches of the First World War. The colloquialism cooties originated on the battlefield as soldiers became enveloped by swarms of sickening lice and other vermin. One witticism at the time was if you took your shirt off and laid it down, it might get up and walk away. If the bullets and shrapnel didn't get you first, the rats and cooties certainly would.

The towns of New England and the North Country sacrificed considerable blood and manpower during the armed conflicts of these periods, including the American War of Independence, the War of 1812, the Civil War, the Spanish-American War and the Great War. Army camps and battlefields were always notoriously filthy and disease-ridden places, which added considerably to casualty rates both during and long after the cessation of hostilities. The total number of Civil War veterans buried in Adams, New York, is 123, of which 19 are recorded as dying on active duty. Of these, the number succumbing from disease is 15, which represents 37 percent of combat-related fatalities. This figure does not include the number succumbing later in life from diseases and disabilities resulting from their military service. The number of disease-related deaths from other 18th and 19th-century conflicts is unrecorded but undoubtedly similar to those from 1861 to 1865.

This inability to provide for basic cleanliness and hygiene was never limited to wartime: they were routine aspects of everyday life in Colonial and Victorian times. Routine factors like regular bathing were absent from most daily regimens because homes lacked such basic amenities as running water and bathtubs. Prior to central heating, winter temperatures inside many homes dropped below freezing, meaning their scant water sources often froze, leaving precious little liquid for grooming and cleaning. The family's primary source of drinking water in Northfield was their backyard well. In New York, Reverend Gordon records melting ice on the kitchen stove for his morning toilet. Wells were often dug too close to outdoor privies, resulting in fecal contamination and the spread of waterborne diseases like typhoid, cholera and dysentery. As late as 1905, the Reverend still relates going into the kitchen each morning to "wash myself," implying their bathing was done in the same domestic space as food preparation. Wash tubs were often small, portable jobs wheeled out of storage and into the kitchen, which was often their only source of running water. Several pots of hot water off the stove would be mixed in with cold well water, and needed to suffice for however many were bathing that day.

Even relatively minor afflictions that are now readily treatable could be life-threatening back then. In the antique countryside, there were no such things as ambulances, diagnostic apparatuses, blood transfusions, antibiotics or intravenous therapy. Available treatment options were limited, and people often succumbed to conditions like appendicitis, kidney stones, gallstones, blood clots, systemic infections and complications from diabetes. Even if they survived a surgical procedure, the patient was still not out of the woods due to the near-universal prevalence of lethal post-operative infections. Outside the city, summoning treatment for any emergent condition meant traipsing by foot or galloping off on horseback to fetch a doctor who was often miles away on unpaved roads. If the route became impassable due to deep snow or mud buildup, the patient's best hope was to open the family Bible and pray for divine intercession.

Although treatment options were exceedingly limited and primitive, most were at least within the patient's economic reach. For some reason, Hattie waited until 1923 to have her tonsils removed. Possibly some infectious condition forced the issue at the relatively advanced age of 57. On the day of admission, she paid the $200 hospital fee, which included her two-night stay in the post-surgical ward. Early the following year, she paid the surgeon's bill of $62 "for removing tonsils and making vaccine." No medical insurance or second mortgage was needed to finance the procedure. If Hattie had her tonsillectomy done today, her $267 total expenditure might cover 25 percent of the monthly bill for medical insurance. The total bill for this three day extravaganza would likely approach $90,000, against which her insurance may not pay out much due to her high annual deductible. At least in the 21st century, Hattie would be entitled to in-network pricing on most medical bills for her astronomical monthly premium.

In the 19th century, people's choice of therapeutic drugs and other medical treatments was often determined by whatever "cures" were being actively promoted by physicians, apothecaries, medical almanacs and itinerant salesmen. These offerings were, of course, wholly unregulated and often of dubious value, if not downright injurious. The proverbial snake oil of Victorian times was an actual product hawked at fairs and medicine shows from coast to coast. Not only did you not know what was in this stuff, there was no reliable way of finding out. You never knew whether it would cure you or kill you. Any number of poisonous substances and contaminants could and did make their way into these formulations, which were often concocted in giant, filthy vats in someone's basement or warehouse. The situation became of national concern due to skyrocketing sales from increasingly sophisticated railway distribution networks.

Congressional passage of the Pure Food and Drug Act of 1906 was the first federal legislation to impose a degree of quality control over the pharmaceutical industry. This landmark Act mandated drug makers to list all active ingredients on the label clearly and to provide sample bottles upon demand for chemical and qualitative analyses. These new laws not only ushered in regular product testing but also implemented litigation to quash the most egregious practices, including unsanitary manufacturing conditions, lack of quality control and exaggerated claims of health benefits. Studies determined most of these products actually contained little, if any, therapeutic value whatsoever. Ingredients like alcohol and opium derivatives tended to predominate, providing enough sedation and analgesia to dupe users into believing they were being "cured" of tuberculosis and other serious disorders. Over the next two decades, the majority of these hucksters and their quack remedies quietly disappeared from the marketplace. But until then, the safety and efficacy of most patent medicine was anyone's guess.

Then as now, aggressive marketing campaigns are what created the demand for these wonderful new treatments and cures. Manufacturers based their advertising strategy upon a number of factors, including the public's gullibility, fear of death and disease, and near-total ignorance of human anatomy and physiology. Take, for example, the Victorian infatuation with catarrhal disorders. The antiquated term catarrh refers to the inflammation of mucous membranes and discharges of mucous, particularly in the nose and throat. When Frank passed away in June of 1922, the obituary listed his cause of death as "cerebral

PART III : EVERYDAY LIFE IN THE VICTORIAN ERA

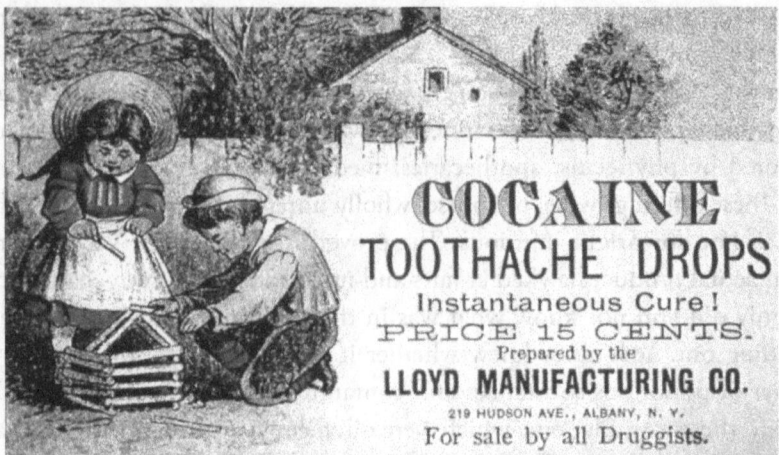

Something difficult to comprehend in this day and age was how readily available cocaine, morphine and opium were prior to the enactment of the federal Harrison Narcotics Tax Act in 1914. Literally, anything you wanted was available over-the-counter at pharmacies, grocery stores and other retailers. The so-called efficacy of many patent medicines was, in fact, due to their liberal narcotic and alcohol content. In the 1880s, cocaine was widely promoted as a miracle drug due to its efficacy as a topical anesthetic and myriads of other applications. Teething children would certainly benefit from the application of cocaine tooth drops. Mothers up all night with sick children after having scrubbed the floors all day with Sapolino would also get a lift by gulping down a wee bit themselves. One enterprising Victorian pharmacist created a soft drink sensation by mixing cocaine and cola nut extract into soda water. Until the psychoactive ingredient was finally removed from Coca-Cola, the drink certainly did live up to its advertising as "The pause that refreshes." The heyday for ready availability of these substances was over once everyone got serious about their addictive and other deleterious properties. (Public Domain)

hemorrhages, following an attack of catarrhal grip." A stroke (cerebrovascular blockage or rupture) was the likely cause of death. The "catarrhal grip" probably referred to nasal hemorrhaging from a ruptured blood vessel.

Throughout his ministry, the Reverend Gordon suffered from a number of chronic conditions, including depression, hearing loss, gastrointestinal disorders, asthma and, of course, that dreaded arch nemesis of Victorian society—catarrh! In 1903, he recorded receipt of "the Catalpa Remedy for Catarrh and Deafness," which was widely advertised in medical almanacs as a "cure" for multiple disorders. Since Colonial times, portions of the Northern Catalpa tree had been ground up, brewed and drank as a medicinal tea. Like many Victorians, the

Reverend was an avid tea drinker, so this seemed a logical thing to try. It is unknown what flavoring agents, if any, were added to make the brew a little more palatable. It may not have been a flavor sensation, but at least it wasn't loaded with all the bizarre stuff that went into most patent medicines. The final verdict on whether his tea time treatments proved efficacious was not recorded.

An innovative cashing in on not only the dread of catarrh but also the Victorian infatuation with spiritualism and psychic phenomenon was Dr. Hector McLain's Astral Ozone Inhalant. This innovative product, the unfortunate sufferer, was assured, "will positively destroy the devastating germ and promptly heal the sore and tender tissues . . . a cure is positive in a few weeks. Write for testimonials." OMG! An aerosolized inter-dimensional wonder that cures your catarrh, balances your chakras & possibly puts you in touch with your late auntie Tootsie about where she hid the money. A turn of the 20th century must-have for an amazingly low price of $3.50, nifty inhaler included.

Another classic case of 19th century hubris was advertisements for Pe-Ru-Na, that "remarkable new treatment" for dreaded catarrh.[39] Advertisements included an endorsement from that eminent—and otherwise completely unidentifiable—"medical authority," Dr. S.B. Hartman. This renowned specialist in all things catarrhal assures the public this new treatment is "worth more than untold wealth to all who suffer from the many ills which are the outcome of catarrh." He proclaims, "More than half our ills are catarrhal in nature! Were I asked which condition sets up the system oftenest to diseases that destroy life, I would name catarrh. While catarrh rarely destroys life, it makes life miserable and leads to a host of conditions which are fatal to life." His spiel goes on to list a number of maladies directly attributable to catarrhal disorders, including eye infections, hearing loss, consumption (tuberculosis), appendicitis, hepatitis, digestive disorders, nephritis, colitis, bladder infections, endometriosis and vaginitis. Erectile dysfunctions hadn't been invented yet, or it would have appeared on the list. Regardless, the renowned doctor concludes by assuring everyone, "If there is a remedy for catarrh which can be relied upon to relieve it in all stages and locations, such a remedy would be Pe-Ru-Na." Case closed!

What sealed the deal and made people eager to shell out cash were not only effective sales pitches but also the relatively low cost of most medicines and treatments. Promoters were keenly aware of the cost-consciousness of most consumers and became adept at getting them to part with a sorely needed buck or two. The industry was well aware that no farmer was going to mortgage

---

39. The insertion of a horizontal separation between syllables was a common affectation in the late Victorian period. Probably made the product sound more scientific.

his property to try out some newfangled "cure." The pharmaceutical industry had a somewhat different business model back then, which did not include fixing prices at whatever the market was willing to bear. But their sophisticated schemes nevertheless pulled in millions each year, as well as providing a blueprint for future medical advertising.

Up to the mid-19th century, many small communities lacked a local apothecary (drug store). All available medical products were dispensed by the town doctor or purchased off the shelf at neighborhood stores. Amanda in Northfield was mostly dependent on the local doctor for the family's medicine. In upstate New York, Frank's cousin Crain was a physician who, as was common, operated his medical practice in the rear of the family drug store in Stockbridge, Madison County. He had taken over the business from his father, a retired surgeon who had inherited the practice from *his* father. Although there were drug stores in Adams as early as 1870, area newspapers still ran advertisements from general merchants with sales pitches like "Retail Dealers in Drugs, Medicines, Choice Liquors, Cigars and Fine Teas." To their credit, the majority of these North Country communities were diligent in extending some level of care to their sick and lame Civil War veterans.

Another factor worth considering is that the palatability of these products was never high on the manufacturer's list of priorities. After all, strong, efficacious treatments were supposed to taste bad. Possibly the most hideous of these antique horrors were the various bitters. Marketed primarily for digestive disorders and related complaints, they were comprised of plant matter and other botanicals dissolved into a base of alcohol and water. Supposedly, the bitter taste—from whence these products derived their name—was evidence of how good they were for you. Literally, hundreds of proprietary bitters appeared in the Victorian Era, with annual production in the hundreds of thousands of bottles. One of the most successful and long-lasting was Burdock Blood Bitters. Although consisting of 25 percent alcohol, it contained no other injurious substances or narcotics, so it survived Pure Food & Drug Act scrutiny and remained on the shelves until reclassified as an intoxicant during national Prohibition. A trade card from 1880 touts the life-altering benefits of this evil-tasting miracle:

> THE KEY TO HEALTH! LADIES, THIS IS FOR YOU! There are thousands of females in America who suffer untold miseries from chronic diseases common to their sex. This is largely due to their peculiar habits of life and fashion, and the improper training of girlhood. To all those women with hollow cheeks, pale faces,

sunken eyes, female weakness, nervousness and general debility bordering on consumption, we earnestly recommend that grand system-renovating tonic, BURDOCK BLOOD BITTERS. Sold by all druggists.

Finally! A way to rectify all that notoriously inadequate training of Victorian girls by their inept mothers! And far from being merely a specific for the weaker sex, this godsend was also a lifesaving tonic for men! Another trade card from the 1880s featured this testimonial from a burley blacksmith in Canada:

Who is A. Burns? He is a blacksmith living about three miles east of Cobourg, Ontario. What does he have to offer? Ten cents is what he says he wouldn't have given for his chances of living before he used BURDOCK BLOOD BITTERS. He suffered in his miserable condition for fifteen years and was cured by three bottles of this very excellent preparation. That's the exact truth, nothing else.

Federal analysis in the early 20th century demonstrated the product contained an alcohol base mixed with burdock root, dandelion, golden seal, senna and cascara. No doubt the latter two ingredients promoted good gastrointestinal health because they kept users running out to the backyard privy. Which means it was also a pretty decent cardiovascular tonic. What additional health benefits one should expect, if any, were not mentioned.

Most patent medicines were manufactured in liquid form, with the product name boldly embossed on the sides of the glass bottle. Some came in a peculiar and unsavory quasi-tablet form. These crudely compressed balls of unwholesomeness appear more akin to grade-school science projects than the uniform tablets of today. A number of topical liniments and other preparations were marketed with equally dubious health claims. In the 1850s, Dr. Thomas' Eclectic Oil derived its name from a clever combination of electric and eclectic, which capitalized on the public's fascination with the purported healing properties of electricity. The advertisements emphasized it could be used both externally and internally. Unfortunately, analysis by the Pure Food and Drug Act exposed the product as a potentially toxic mixture of turpentine, camphor, fish oil and eucalyptus. But that didn't prevent good Doctor Thomas from claiming it would "positively cure deafness, lameness, earache, toothache, colds, diphtheria, asthma, neuralgia and catarrh." Everyone knows nothing cures a bad case of catarrh faster than gargling with a little turpentine.

PART III : EVERYDAY LIFE IN THE VICTORIAN ERA

The Alcohol in "Patent Medicines"

THE following percentages of alcohol in the "patent medicines" named are given by the Massachusetts State Board Analyst, in the published document No. 34:

	Per cent. of alcohol (by volume)
Lydia Pinkham's Vegetable Compound	20.6
Paine's Celery Compound	21.
Dr. Williams's Vegetable Jaundice Bitters	18.5
Whiskol, "a non-intoxicating stimulant"	28.2
Colden's Liquid Beef Tonic, "recommended for treatment of alcohol habit"	26.5
Ayer's Sarsaparilla	26.2
Thayer's Compound Extract of Sarsaparilla	21.5
Hood's Sarsaparilla	18.8
Allen's Sarsaparilla	13.5
Dana's Sarsaparilla	13.5
Brown's Sarsaparilla	13.5
Peruna	28.5
Vinol, Wine of Cod-Liver Oil	18.8
Dr. Peters's Kuriko	14.
Carter's Physical Extract	22.
Hooker's Wigwam Tonic	20.7
Hoofland's German Tonic	29.3
Howe's Arabian Tonic, "not a rum drink"	13.2
Jackson's Golden Seal Tonic	19.6
Mensman's Peptonized Beef Tonic	16.5
Parker's Tonic, "purely vegetable"	41.6
Schenck's Seaweed Tonic, "entirely harmless"	19.5
Baxter's Mandrake Bitters	16.5
Boker's Stomach Bitters	42.6
Burdock Blood Bitters	25.2
Greene's Nervura	17.2
Hartshorn's Bitters	22.2
Hoofland's German Bitters, "entirely vegetable"	25.6
Hop Bitters	12.
Hostetter's Stomach Bitters	44.3
Kaufman's Sulphur Bitters, "contains no alcohol" (as a matter of fact it contains 20.5 per cent. of alcohol and no sulphur)	20.5
Puritana	22.
Richardson's Concentrated Sherry Wine Bitters	47.5
Warner's Safe Tonic Bitters	35.7
Warren's Bilious Bitters	21.5
Faith Whitcomb's Nerve Bitters	20.3

By the early 20th century, patent medicines came under increasing scrutiny by medical professionals, governmental agencies and the general public. The May 1904 edition of the Ladies' Home Journal featured an article entitled "The Patent Medicine Curse," which included the table shown above. Beneath the listing reads, "In connection with this list, think of beer, which contains only from two to five percent alcohol, while some of these 'bitters' contain ten times as much, making them stronger than whisky, far stronger than sherry or port, with claret and champagne way behind." (author's collection)

What is also remarkable is the frequent appearance of the term celebrated in patent medicine advertisements; in much the same context, "famous" is seen today. To emphasize their products' superlative qualities, the word is incorporated into the description, the brand name, or sometimes both. No doubt, it helped convey the genuine euphoria users experienced when finally cured of their lifelong afflictions. It made no never-mind the ingredients were actually rotting, ineffectual plant matter dissolved in an alcohol base. Patients suffering for years from a loss of vitality, female complaints, constipation or buildup of belly button lint were magically transformed after a single gulp of these Victorian wonders. In reality, the only celebrating occurred at corporate headquarters when the daily profits were tallied. Some manufacturers assuaged their guilty consciences through public largesse, including sponsorship of road paving or new libraries in their communities.

Based upon the astounding number of surviving bottles, patent medicines were cranked out in prodigious quantities, including such standards as stomach bitters, castor oil, laudanum (tincture of opium), Lydia Pinkham's Vegetable Compound (for "female complaints"), and, of course, the immortal Kickapoo Indian Sagwa. The latter claimed to be a sure cure for "Dyspepsia, Sick Headache, Sour Stomach, Loss of Appetite, Heartburn, Depression, Neuralgia, Female Disorders, Liver Complaint, Constipation, Indigestions, Rheumatism, Impure Blood, Jaundice, Bilious Attacks, Fever and Ague, and all Diseases of the Stomach, Liver, Kidneys and the Blood." The label assured you it was the *'secret elixir'* that accounts for the marvelous health and longevity of Native Americans. The fact that "Indians" were even more unhealthy and shorter-lived than other Americans was generally unknown prior to modern demographical and public health studies.

Undoubtedly, the oldest surviving material in the attic on Main Street was a tattered collection of home remedies inscribed in an elegant, late 18th-century cursive script. The yellowed and folded paper measures 8 x 6.5 inches and memorializes three time-tested remedies from the period when every man was his own doctor because he had little else to depend upon in the event of illness or injury. The first concoction is called "cough powder" and is a combination of skunk cabbage, wake-robin, hoarhound, bayberry bark, bitter root nerve powder and molasses. This last ingredient probably kept users from heaving it back up after swallowing such noxious ingredients. The write-up includes instructions to "take a half teaspoonful of the powder on going to bed to keep warm." God help the farmer who threw caution to the wind by taking a full teaspoonful.

The second remedy is a relatively innocuous tincture of myrrh, which combines this sap-like substance from tree bark along with high wines and water. All of these were mixed and "kept aside for seven days" before being "strained through brown paper." Yum! The resulting fermentation was thought useful in treating such maladies as diarrhea, intestinal worms, hemorrhoids, consumption, syphilis, toothache, bad breath and whatever else ails you. The third and final assault upon gustatory sensibilities is labeled cephalic snuff. This was a combination of bayberry bark, bitter root, nerve powder and "a few drops of the oil of goldenweed." Snuff was customarily inhaled and appears to be a precursor to modern nose candy, like cocaine. Please don't try any of these remedies at home.

In later years, Hattie experienced the onset of several chronic afflictions related to aging. She was diagnosed with an iron deficiency, and the family doctor began administering "iron by hypodermic" every week for several months. She became blind as a bat and required frequent trips to Watertown for stronger eyeglasses. It seems that, even by the late 1920s, Adams either lacked ophthalmologists and opticians, or she just preferred the choices in the city. So she began taking regular trips to the city with either Laura or Herbert behind the wheel (thank God). By the 1920s, the practice of medicine had advanced well beyond the era of small-town doctors in the Victorian Era. But cutting edge and high-tech treatments were still unavailable to most in rural areas. Although modern medicine doesn't guarantee everyone a long and healthy life, it vastly improves outcomes for the majority of the population.

CHAPTER 25

The Scourge of Consumption

PRIOR to the mid-1900s, the leading cause of adult mortality was tuberculosis, a contagious and often fatal condition popularly referred to as consumption or wasting disease. The causative agent for this prolific and indiscriminate killer was unknown prior to the identification of the *tubercle bacillus* in 1882 (renamed *Mycobacterium tuberculosis* in 1886). The contagion is spread through contaminated bodily fluids, usually by coughs, sneezes, kisses and similar modes of transmission. Once inside the lungs, it often enters the blood stream and spreads to other parts of the body. Classic symptoms include chronic cough, expectoration of bloody mucous, fever, night sweats, extreme pallor, progressive emaciation and weight loss. For the majority of those afflicted, tuberculosis was tantamount to a slow-motion death sentence. Sufferers would waste away over months or years, with absolutely no remediation aside from palliative efforts to alleviate pain and suffering and make them as comfortable as possible.

In the 19th century, one out of every seven deaths in this country was attributed to consumption, making it the leading cause of mortality in most communities. An estimated 400 to 500 Americans died each day from this affliction, irrespective of age, gender or economic status. Chronic overcrowding, urban squalor and the lack of sanitation endemic to larger population centers resulted in city residents being especially hard hit. The filthy, poorly ventilated tenements of New York City ensured all new immigrants their fair slice of this American Pie. The City may have been short on other amenities and entitlements in this era, but death and disease were always found right down the street from the Statue of Liberty. Once this unseen menace entered the household, other family members became subject to an infection rate approaching twenty-five percent in these decades. The common saying "your kiss of affection is the germ of infection" may sound morbid and fatalistic, but it underscored the risks city dwellers faced from simple, everyday activities like going to work or market, then coming home and kissing their children.

PART III : EVERYDAY LIFE IN THE VICTORIAN ERA

During the 19th century, widespread fear of this mysterious, deadly affliction gave rise to a genuine vampire scare throughout the northeastern States, a phenomenon later memorialized as the Great New England Vampire Scare. Particularly in coastal communities, certain people became convinced that anyone dead and buried from consumption was at risk of morphing into a revenant. These New Englanders believed such nocturnal encounters were responsible for spreading TB and other diseases across town. The corpses of formerly innocuous grandmothers, schoolteachers and ministers would rise as ghouls and stalk the streets at night in search of new victims. Whether a nibble on the neck also resulted in more ravenous vampires is not recorded. But the insidious nature of tuberculosis inspired no end of legends, artwork and literature, as people sought to contextualize the menace and make it somewhat manageable. In Colonial times, TB was caustically labeled the great white plague due to the stark, sickly pallor of those afflicted. By the Victorian Era, some women whitened their complexions in bizarre simulations of that fashionable, not-long-for-this-world look.

Another coping mechanism was the appellation of the romantic disease, possibly the most macabre manifestation of 19th-century Gothic humor. The sobriquet was indicative of widespread resignation as more and more young lovers were torn apart in the prime of life by illness and death. It fostered a new genre of Gothic romance, inspired by real-world tragedies as people all around dropped like flies from mysterious, unseen causes. But some were reconciled by the hope these star-crossed lovers would reunite in the afterlife. Consumption as a romantic, wasting disease was summarized by Edgar Allen Poe in the short story "Metzengerstein: A Tale in Imitation of the German":

> The beautiful Lady Mary!—how could she die?—and of consumption! But it is a path I have prayed to follow. I would wish all I love to perish of that gentle disease. How glorious! to depart in the hey-day of the young blood—the heart all passion—the imagination all fire—amid the remembrances of happier days—in the fall of the year, and so be buried up forever in the gorgeous, autumnal leaves. Thus died the Lady Mary.

Even after the identification of the *tubercle bacillus* in the late 1800s, the discovery of a truly efficacious treatment remained elusive prior to the manufacture of the antibiotic streptomycin in the 1950s. But until then, the sufferer's best hope for recovery remained the body's innate ability to heal itself before the disease had progressed beyond the point of no return. Over in Europe, the evocation of nature, the healing mistress, was affected through the rest cure, a rather simplistic regimen involving lengthy convalescence in quiet, mountain-top sanatoriums or other cool and isolated settings. Enterprising medical men soon imported this promising new treatment approach to the States. For most Americans, the luxury of a lengthy sojourn in a TB sanatorium was certainly far outside their economic reach. Even those fortunate enough to obtain treatment and enter remission were never really out of the woods due to the interminable specter of recurrence and, with it, the very real risk of death.

Beginning in the 1880s, the first private and government-run sanatoriums for the treatment of TB opened in the Adirondack Mountain region of upper New York. Modeled after similar clinics in Europe, their standard treatment was deceptively simple: rest, sunshine, cold mountain air, simple but nutritious food and plenty of peace and quiet. It was also believed the scent of massed pine and spruce trees in the Adirondacks were additional healing agents. In the years prior to antibiotics, these rehabilitative programs offered a glimmer of hope to sufferers from the polluted, overcrowded towns and cities of the Industrial Revolution. The terror and uncertainly this disease evoked in Victorian society are difficult to appreciate after the passage of over a century. But no matter where you lived or how well you lived, the threat was always in the back of your mind. Everyone knew someone who contracted and died of the disease. To 19th-century Americans, it was just one more health hazard confronting them in this gilded age of elegance.

PART III : EVERYDAY LIFE IN THE VICTORIAN ERA

A new genre of Gothic romance and tragedy appeared in response to staggering mortality rates brought on by any number of mysterious, infectious and incurable diseases. This type of Victorian coping mechanism included such literary and artistic works as The Vampire, an 1897 painting by Philip William Burne-Jones, son of Pre-Raphaelite artist Sir Edward Burne-Jones. The imagery of a seductress insidiously sucking the life essence out of her doomed lover is an allegorical reference to the kiss of death from consumption. (Public Domain)

CHAPTER 26

Green's Diary, Almanac and Inimical Quackery

THE pretentious and insanely ugly cover of *Green's Diary and Almanac* for 1882 and 1883. This publication was marketed as a combination diary and almanac by the inclusion of a blank, lined page with each month's entries so readers could "make memorandums of any event, business transaction, notes given, births, extreme weather, time of planting crops, hiring help, purchase of horse or cow, and any incident (they) may wish to refer to hereafter." Each issue included the assurance: "The superior advantage of this almanac over any other medical almanac is its simplicity and usefulness. It is a book which should be always kept in your counting room, offices, library, nursery, etc., and other places near at hand." The backyard privy being a logical albeit unspecified location amongst the "other places."

George Gill Green capitalized on the late 19th-century mania by patent medicine manufacturers to publish almanacs as promotional platforms for their products. Almost seventy-five percent of *Green's Diary and Almanac* is taken up with hyperbole extolling the many virtues of his three products: Boschee's German Syrup, Green's August Flower and Green's Ague Conqueror. Green had formulated these remedies around 1870 at his father's shop in Woodbury, N.J. His claim to medical fame was attending medical school for two years at the

University of Pennsylvania before resigning so he could get out and make some money. For years, he offered readers complimentary sample bottles of these products by simply mailing in a request. The business ended up distributing untold thousands of sample bottles, with regular sizes available at drug stores for 75 cents each.

He promoted his Boschee's German Syrup not as a palliative but as a "cure for consumption (tuberculosis), pneumonia, asthma, bronchitis, and coughs due to colds." Unfortunately for the almost-doctor Green, later analyses determined the product was a combination of alcohol (7 percent), opium and a small amount of hydrocyanic acid—also known as cyanide. Why he included cyanide is unknown, although probably not as a flavoring agent. The combination of alcohol and opium probably made tuberculosis sufferers lose tract of the fact they were about to drop dead from this incurable disease.

Green's August Flower claimed it gave "certain and permanent relief from biliousness, jaundice, amenorrhea, constipation, dizziness, headache, numbness, nervousness, palpitation, and dyspeptic symptoms, acid fluids and food coming up, especially at night." He neglected to mention it also keeps your rear end from falling off during attacks of catarrh. The gibberish continues with, "A large majority of the American people are to-day wearing out a miserable and unsatisfactory life from the effects of dyspepsia, liver complaint or indigestion. Paralysis, mental derangement, suicide, consumption, heart disease, apoplexy, and in fact almost every disease surrounding us to-day are brought on by deranged stomach and liver." Not to worry, dear sufferer! All these conditions were readily remedied through the use of Green's August Flower. Compared to the ingredients of Boschee's German Syrup, the composition of this flowery nostrum was later determined to be relatively innocuous, consisting of alcohol (7 percent), sodium bicarbonate, Aloe Socotrina (a homeopathic remedy), peppermint oil and capsicum.

Ague is an antiquated term for fever, chills and sweating from any of several infectious diseases, including malaria. Advertisements for Green's Ague Conqueror assured readers his product contained "'No Quinine - No Arsenic - No Poison." What he neglected to point out was, as per analysis in 1911, it did contain a whopping 45.47 percent alcohol and was certainly no more efficacious than his other quack concoctions. By 1906, the passage of the Pure Food and Drug Act gradually put Green and his fellow hucksters out of business. (author's collection-public domain)[40]

---

40. Two editions of *Green's Diary and Almanac* were utilized for this description. Both were originally owned in the 1800s by a farming family near the city of Ithaca, around 120 miles southwest of Adams in New York. As per their handwritten entries, the names of these people were also Hattie and Frank, and their family name differed from the last name of our heroine and protagonist by only two letters! Talk about eerie coincidences.

A Gentle Hint.

In our style of climate, with its sudden changes of temperature—rain, wind and sunshine often intermingled in a single day,—it is no wonder that our children, friends and relatives are so frequently taken from us by neglected colds, half the deaths resulting directly from this cause. A bottle of BOSCHEE'S GERMAN SYRUP kept about your home for immediate use will prevent serious sickness, a large doctor's bill, and perhaps death, by the use of three or four doses. For curing Consumption, Hemorrhages, Pneumonia, Severe Coughs, Croup, or any disease of the Throat or Lungs, its success is simply wonderful, as your druggist will tell you. German Syrup is now sold in every town and village on this continent. Sample bottles for trial, 10 cts.; regular size, 75 cents.

False Impression.

It is generally supposed by physicians and the people generally that Dyspepsia can not invariably be cured, but we are pleased to say that GREEN'S AUGUST FLOWER has never, to our knowledge, failed to cure Dyspepsia and Liver Complaint in all its forms, such as Sour Stomach, Costiveness, Sick Headache, Palpitation of the Heart, Indigestion, bad taste in the mouth, &c. Out of the 50,000 dozen bottles sold last year, not a single failure was reported, but thousands of complimentary letters received from Druggists of wonderful cures. Three doses will relieve any case. Try it. Sample Bottles 10 cents. Regular size 75 cents.

FOR SALE BY

W. H. WITHINGTON,
Adams, N. Y.

The reverse side of a trading card for Boschee's German Syrup and Green's August Flower. G.G. Green manufactured both patent medicines in the same unsanitary and unregulated warehouse in New Jersey. This Garden State huckster made a fortune by promoting his brand of worthless nonsense as the "infallible wonder cures of the age." Note the admonition for mothers to keep a bottle of Boschee's German Syrup handy for whenever the kiddies come down with sniffles or coughs. Failure to do so puts them at risk of needing one less egg to fry for the breakfast table. In modern times, medical advertising is a bit more suave and understated and only includes the word "death" among potential side effects. (author's collection)

CHAPTER 27

Early Automobiles

TRAVEL by foot, animal power or steam locomotive were the ways most went about in the Victorian Era. Beginning in the 1840s, an explosion of railway lines occurred across the continent, which vastly accelerated the movement of people and material across hitherto unimaginable distances. Railroad service had arrived in Tilton, New Hampshire and southern Jefferson County by mid-century, with the railroad depot opening in Adams in 1851. This original structure burnt down in 1896, to be replaced later that year with a larger, more modern facility. In the larger cities, foot power or horsepower in the literal sense was the only way to get around prior to the introduction of electric streetcars (trolleys) towards the end of the century.

But in smaller communities, walking or equine conveyance was still the way the vast majority of people got about town. Travel in rural areas had long been hampered by unpaved, packed dirt roadways that became nearly impassable in snow storms or from mud accumulation after heavy rains. In winter months, local navigation was facilitated by a changeover from wheeled vehicles to sleds to improve traction across icy or snow-laden roads. Some people replaced the wheels on their wagons and carriages with bobs (runners), which served the same purpose. But it was the invention of the internal combustion engine and the rapid ascension of the auto mobile which truly revolutionized personal transportation.

The switch from equine power to gasoline power in the 1900s resulted in changes to virtually every aspect of American society (a phenomenon similar in many respects to more recent transformations in the communications industry through wireless technology, including cell phones and similar devices). The advantages of motorized transport were initially slow in seeping into a public consciousness long inured to reliance on animal power. But the lure of this prestigious new technology became undeniable, even in rural areas, which often lagged behind the technological curve.

The specific year when the Northfield family began utilizing motorized transportation and gasoline-powered farm equipment, is unknown, as the years included in their surviving diaries end in the 1880s. In Jefferson County, Hattie and Frank first make reference to the technology shortly after the turn of the 20th century. They also began using the term auto in place of automobile in about 1920. Significantly, the former term usually appeared in quotation marks, denoting a slang expression.[41]

The automobile was also the impetus for improvements in town streets and roadways between neighboring communities. Without a sustained investment in the nation's transportation infrastructure, this transition from horse travel to motor vehicles would have been impossible. In most communities, these upgrades were a slow, costly and incremental process. In 1912, Frank watched a team of workmen applying a coat of oil to his street prior to laying down the tar pavement. The modernization effort was so significant his neighbors all came out to witness the event. Noteworthy also was the relatively late year in which this occurred. Their home was hardly in some inaccessible backwater, as their street was just downhill from a thriving commercial district.

Automotive sales and technology grew by leaps and bounds between 1905 and 1929, with literally hundreds of small, start-up manufacturing companies and repair facilities appearing in these years. The early models were exceedingly primitive and unreliable and prone to repeated backfires, breakdowns and flat tires. As was the experience of radio hobbyists in the early years of wireless, it was almost essential for the auto mobile enthusiast to possess sufficient mechanical skills to get the rickety contraption up and running and onto its destination. Despite a myriad of problems and setbacks, the lure of this new, ultra-modern technology was sufficient to ensure the rapid dominance of the automotive industry. By 1905, there were approximately 78,000 registered cars in the United States. A scant five years later, that number increased to almost half a million. By 1920, almost eight million cars were on American roadways, a figure ballooning to 23 million by 1929. Of course, such exponential increases came with corresponding decreases in demand for horse-drawn transportation and train travel.[42]

By the First World War, motorized vehicles were no longer perceived as a plaything of the rich but had evolved into a commodity essential to the viability

---

41. A few years earlier, the term aero plane had been commonly contracted to aeroplane.

42. After purchasing their first car in 1914, trips to Thousand Island Park became a whole lot faster and more convenient. Rather than taking the train from Adams to Fishers Landing, they now drove to the coast and parked the car near the ferry for 30 cents a day. In later years, the Park allowed visitors to ferry their cars over to Wellesley Island.

of modern commerce. Prior to their first car purchase, Frank ran his insurance business by either walking about town or riding Laura's bicycle—asthma permitting. For longer trips to Lorraine, Rodman and Worth, he hired a horse or team from the local livery. At the turn of the century, the customary charge for these round-trip rentals was $1 for a single horse and $2 to $3 for a team and wagon, depending upon the distance traveled. But traveling by horse power was far from our quaint and romantic conception of elegantly dressed people breezing by in finely appointed carriages. It was rather a dirty, arduous, uncomfortable and time-consuming experience on, for the most part, sub-standard equipment. Frank describes hitching a ride on a mule-drawn manure cart during a business trip in 1913: "I went down to (the customer's) new farm house to inspect it for builder's insurance. Rode down with his man on a load of manure." Whether he rode in front by the mule or in back with the manure is not specified.

Seems that by the second decade of the century, most of Frank's business associates had already made the transition to motor vehicles. He notes the steady increase of auto mobiles parading down Main Street each Sunday afternoon. The advantages of this new technology were undeniable, and with Hattie's prodding, he finally broke down and purchased their first motor car in 1914. Although their diaries for this year are lost, we know the purchase occurred then because, in the spring of 1915, he writes about getting "the machine" out of storage and "fixed up and ready" for the driving season. There had been no mention of car ownership in previous years, and in 1913, Frank was still hitching rides on manure wagons.

Exasperatingly, there is no record of the type of car purchased. However, a reasonable supposition can be made. For one thing, there was only one automobile dealership in Adams in these years: Greenley & Sons Auto on North Main Street, which opened in 1912. Until 1915, the only cars they sold were Fords (in August of 1915, they switched to Chevrolets).[43] It wasn't until 1916 that two additional dealerships opened in town, which vastly expanded the available choices. Frank was also Greenley's insurance agent for both business and personal needs. It seems extremely unlikely they would forego the local purchase by traveling to Watertown in search of an automobile. Another reasonable assumption is they opted for the Ford Model T, which at the time was

---

43. As late as 1920, this dealer advertised they were not only the exclusive Chevrolet Motor Car dealer for southern Jefferson County, but were also fully equipped to satisfy the needs of the motoring public. Their business included a service station for repairs, gasoline, motor oil, flour, corn meal, hominy, bran, malt sprouts, salt, feed, seeds, fertilizers, hides, pelts and raw furs. Sort of an early convenience store but with a different inventory.

away and by far the most popular car in America. After debuting in October of 1908, Tin Lizzy was a runaway success, with over sixteen million units sold during its twenty years of production. Henry Ford greatly increased sales by dropping the cost from $825 in 1908 down to about $550 in 1913, depending upon the type chosen.

Compared to later models, these first cars were clunky, archaic contraptions lacking in basic features that buyers now take for granted. For instance, starting the old relic involved a series of complicated steps if you entertained any notion of getting it going and onto the roadway. It included a number of turns of a hand crank the operator inserted into the designated opening below the front grille. The rotations turned the crankshaft and hopefully initialized the process of internal combustion. Problems arose when the engine started roaring before the crank was removed. Then, the operator was subjected to the same indignities as the hapless coyote in the roadrunner cartoons. Electric starters and even electrical headlights were unavailable prior to the 1919 model year, at which time they became optional upgrades. Fully electrical equipment did not become standard at Ford until 1926.

The Model T came with a three-geared manual transmission: two forward and one reverse. The drive train was connected to a minuscule, four-cylinder engine producing a staggering twenty horsepower at full tilt. These puny power plants were major liabilities when transporting a load of passengers or heavy freight up steep hills or across other inertial barriers. The engine would frequently stall, requiring passengers to disembark and help push the mechanical monster uphill. An added liability was when these episodes occurred while passengers were dressed in their Sunday best or the weather was stormy, snowy, icy, hot, or cold. Frank writes of impressing two friends by bringing them along in his Model T during an insurance inspection. The car couldn't make it up the hill, so they had to disembark and walk the rest of the way. At least before it stalled, they were treated to the transitory thrill of speeding at a breathtaking fifteen miles an hour down Main Street.

Surprisingly, in addition to slow acceleration rates and ridiculously low top speeds, during the first decades of production these tiny power plants were still exceedingly poor on gas mileage. Frank records around twelve to fifteen miles per gallon, which, in fact, matched the manufacturer's stated fuel efficiency. In 1917, the average cost of gasoline in New York was around 30 cents per gallon, equivalent to almost $6.50 today. Automobile ownership may have been more prestigious than piloting the old grey mare into town, but it was a lot more expensive, too.

PART III : EVERYDAY LIFE IN THE VICTORIAN ERA

Consider also the condition of most roadways vis-à-vis the early wooden wheels with their skinny 3-inch wide pneumatic tires—which appeared more suitable to mopeds or mountain bikes than motor cars. Jefferson County was hardly the untamed West, but road conditions were still far from ideally suited to this new technology. Most roads remained unpaved and mired with challenges and obstacles that often brought forward motion to a crawl or screeching halt, including mud, ruts, rocks, fallen trees, dead animals, ice and impassable drifts of North Country snowfall. At this early stage, there were few town or state resources to keep roadways clear and passable and scant tow trucks for stranded motorists. So riding in your car these first decades was as much adventure as convenience. Walking or horse travel was still the preferred way to go in and about town. But for trips too far for walking but too short for train travel, the automobile was now clearly America's choice.

The family retained their Model T until early 1917, at which time they traded it in for a $650 Willys-Overland Touring car from the Buick and Overland dealer in Lorraine. In 1921, Laura and Herbert added a second vehicle with their purchase of a Ford Touring car, which was basically a tricked-out Model T. In 1922, Hattie and Frank traded in the Willys-Overland for a new Buick, which set them back $935. This second-generation automobile came with a number of technological improvements, including a pedal-operated electric starter and a larger, more powerful engine. Frank stated it was a "base model" and lacking in certain "fixtures."[44] Precisely what he meant by "fixtures" is unclear. Presumably, the car came ready-equipped with things like headlights and a steering wheel. Hattie loved popcorn, so maybe he had them install a portable popping machine in the rear compartment.

Although Hattie started behind the wheel in 1914, she didn't officially obtain her driver's license until the fall of 1924. From then on, she was officially authorized to lurk about town, terrorizing her fellow motorists. Hattie had many fine qualities, but exemplary driving skills were not among them. Their diaries and letters relate a number of mishaps when our heroine was behind the wheel. Apparently, she had a knack for rearranging barn doors, fences, posts and anything else that got in her way. En route to the driving test, she relates the following misadventure: "Slept late so had to hurry to get ready to go to Watertown . . . in a hard rain I put the brakes on in the middle of a long hill, and the car turned around once and a half and landed against the bank. No harm done except a broken bumper." Oh, my!

---

44. The word Frank probably could have used was "options," which would cover both interior features and exterior trim.

EARLY AUTOMOBILES

Hattie and Frank's first automobile, the 1913 Ford Model T. This museum relic sure looks silly now, but in its day was quite the spiffy set of wheels. One driver complained these early clunkers were "rickety as hell" and scared horses with their constant backfiring. This illustration is from a period advertisement. (Public Domain)

What their Model T probably looked like after Hattie was finished wreaking her automotive havoc. For some reason, she never felt fully comfortable or confident behind the wheel, and their diaries record a number of regrettable moving mishaps. Fortunately, the only damage done was to the vehicle. What Hattie lacked in driving skills, she made up for with a kind heart. (Public Domain)

CHAPTER 28

The Economy and Retail Sales

THE disparaging terms Robber Barons and Gilded Age are frequently used in conjunction with the unprecedented growth of personal wealth and American business and industrial capacity between 1870 and 1910.[45] Robber Barons refers to the men who profited through business monopolies and accumulation of obscene amounts of wealth. In these years, their income and unscrupulous practices were wholly untaxed and unregulated and came at the expense of the vast number of Americans suffering from low wages and sub-standard working and living conditions. The term gilded refers to the glittering veneer of respectability surrounding these men and contemporary society. A sort of smoke and mirrors that effectively glossed over all the appalling greed and corruption and masked the growing poverty, inequity and mounting social issues as millions of immigrants streamed into filthy and already overcrowded cities.

It was a period of vast economic extremes. Fortunately for these New England and North Country families, the influx of "Huddled Masses" from eastern and southern Europe had only a marginal impact on life in rural America. Of more pressing concern was rapid growth in the farming and dairy sectors, which in Jefferson County alone increased from an estimated 2 million farms in 1860 to almost 6 million by 1906. Increases in population accompanied this, as the number of native and foreign-born people seeking employment in these industries more than doubled. By 1906, the total value of American farms was estimated at around 30 billion dollars, an unprecedented growth over the antebellum period. The dairy industry in New England also rose sharply during these years and remained a significant component of the agricultural sector throughout the 20th century.

It was the passage of the Sixteenth Amendment in 1913 mandating a federal income tax that finally addressed the staggering disparity between upper-class

---

45. The period derives its name from the 1873 satirical novel by Mark Twain entitled *The Gilded Age: A Tale of Today*.

wealth and the socioeconomic condition of virtually everyone else. Although a temporary income tax had appeared briefly in the 1860s in response to the burgeoning Civil War deficit, it was this Amendment that finally signaled an end to the era of unfettered riches. Payment of town and road taxes was already recorded by the Northfield family each year in central New Hampshire. Town and school taxes were always factored into the family's expenditures in Adams, in addition to Laura's tuition and the mounting cost of medical care for Frank and Flora. Curiously, their initial federal filing didn't occur until March of 1920. At that time, Frank filed a return for the tax year 1919, which listed an income from insurance sales of $1841.29, against which he paid a federal tax of $6.30 and a state tax of $1.57. Why these assessments were so low is difficult to determine. It didn't include income from Hattie's side, which was considerable, based upon her 50 percent share in the family's farming, dairy and sugar bush operations.[46] It also didn't reflect their investment income from the bonds and stocks in their portfolio.

For the tax year 1920, Frank lists a total income from the insurance trade of $2541.79, against which $29.19 was assessed in federal taxes. He also paid a "corporation tax" of $40.15 to the State of New York, presumably for his brokerage licensure. Still, the majority of their tax liabilities came from town and state assessments. In 1919, they paid a town tax of $42.42 plus an additional $39.19 in school taxes. Hattie also paid separate taxes to the towns of Worth and Lorraine for the family's farming, sugar bush and dairy operations.[47]

Overall, in the 18th and first half of the 19th centuries, commerce and trade in more isolated sections hadn't involved much in the way of cash and carry transactions. Currency as a medium of exchange was rare in rural America. Since Colonial times, British coins and small American denominations had been in circulation and were the only currency most people were familiar with half pennies, pennies, two-cent pieces, nickels and dimes. Paper money was virtually nonexistent. Regardless, most small farmers and countrymen lacked the proverbial two cents to rub together anyway. The majority of their business was conducted upon a barter economy: I need your lumber to repair my barn, and in payment, I'll swap you a cow, three chickens and four blocks of homemade cheese. When a new baby was due, the town doctor rode up in his carriage, delivered the child, and charged $10 *or* its equivalent for things like smoked

---

46. Hattie was part owner of the Lorraine Milk Company, one of the largest dairy operations in Jefferson County.

47. In his New Year's Eve entry for 1916, Frank laments their expected loss of income following the sale of D.E. Taylor's dry goods store, where he no longer worked but remained invested. For economic or other reasons, Taylor sold out to the firm of Preston & Dillabaugh, effective in January 1917.

PART III : EVERYDAY LIFE IN THE VICTORIAN ERA

ham, fresh eggs, and cider. Although most had no money, they could always rustle up something in exchange for whatever could not be produced at home.

During the early 1800s, prices of domestic goods had remained relatively stable in the countryside. By the second half of the century, the nation's overall economic outlook had vastly improved, following the extension of railroad lines and concomitant growth of the commercial infrastructure necessary to satiate an ever-increasing demand for consumer goods. By the Civil War, the families in this narrative had all been linked to various communities by railway lines. In New York, both Adams and Lorraine were connected by rail to Watertown and other destinations in Jefferson County. It is unlikely the Main Street shop of D.E. Taylor would have been viable only a generation or two earlier. By 1880, almost all mercantile activity in most communities was conducted through cash transactions. However, the vestigial bartering economy remained intact across the countryside for the reminder of the 19th century.

What most find surprising is the relatively small amounts of money required a century or more ago to purchase goods and pay bills. People made a lot less, so the cost of everything was correspondingly low. Everywhere you expect to see dollar amounts you instead find fractions of a dollar. Of course, the cost of groceries, clothing, housing and other necessities has always been determined by whatever the public is willing and able to pay. Prices for goods were always high, regardless of when or where they were purchased. Back in Bedrock, Fred and Wilma Flintstone always complained about the skyrocketing cost of brontosaur burgers (prices undoubtedly remained high until cave people stopped craving brontoburgers).

By 1900, the average annual salary in the countryside had risen to around $500. Hattie and Frank's income was significantly higher due to ownership of businesses, property and investments. The family was thus spared the subsistence level, hand-to-mouth existence that characterized so many poorer families in this period. As had been the Reverend's custom a generation earlier, Frank kept a careful record of all purchases and payments and tallied everything at the end of each month. Literally, anything they spent more than a nickel on was included, and their ledgers are an intimate snapshot of domestic expenditures in Victorian America. Modern economies of scale dwarf a sampling from 1903:

Haircut at barber: $0.30
Doctor's visit: $1
Prescription: $0.40
Clock repairs: $0.75

Shoe repairs: $0.45
50-pound bag of hen feed: $1.20
Monthly milk delivery: $1.25
Monthly P.O. Box rental: $0.25
Two dozen oysters for Christmas dinner: $0.35

Thirty cents for a haircut? Forty cents for a prescription? Of course, those halcyon, nickel-and-dime days couldn't last forever. By 1910, their monthly telephone bill had skyrocketed to between $1 and $1.50, an increase likely attributable to Frank's insurance trade.

By 1912, an additional utility bill arrived each month for electricity usage. Their home was one of the first in the neighborhood to take advantage of this new service when introduced in 1912, albeit on a part-time basis. Full-time residential service became available the following year, something they took advantage of with the installation of electric lighting fixtures throughout the house. Their first year with full-time power was 1913 when their monthly bill averaged $1.86 for approximately 14 kilowatts of usage. A small bill for an astonishingly small amount of electricity: modern residential customers in New York State average around 600 kilowatts each month. Of course, in 1913, Hattie and Frank were without such power-hogging electrical conveniences as a refrigerator, deep freezer, oven, microwave, dish washer, toaster, Cuisinart, washer and dryer, electric furnace, water heater, Jacuzzi, central air, ceiling fans, adjustable bed, big screen TV, game console, radio, multi channel stereo, vintage pinball machine, lava lamp, cordless telephone, computer, home WiFi, calculator, vacuum cleaner, rug shampooer, cell phone charger, hair dryer, curling iron, alarm clock, self cleaning litter box, electric doggie fence, security system, automatic lawn sprinkler, power tools or digital egg timer. Most everything in their home was still powered the same way as in their parent's day.

By 1919, the family income from insurance sales, businesses, property and investment had risen to around $3000, but their expenditures had skyrocketed to the following:

Haircut at barber: $0.40
Doctor's visit: $2
Prescription: $0.50
Shoe repairs: $1.50
Monthly milk delivery: $2
Monthly P.O. Box rental: $0.60

PART III : EVERYDAY LIFE IN THE VICTORIAN ERA

> Oysters for Christmas dinner: $1.20
> Monthly telephone bill: $2.20
> Monthly electric bill: $2.70

Such inflation at the onset of the roaring twenties! Their combined income and savings were nevertheless sufficient to send Laura off to college and cover expenses for her marriage to Herbert following graduation. In later life, their monthly expenditures gradually increased due to mounting medical costs for Frank and Flora.

A generation earlier, daily expenditures for Reverend Gordon and Flora were somewhat different. Monthly utility bills for electricity, telephone and gas service were nonexistent, as most homes lacked even cold, running water. They didn't have automobiles or fill-up woes at the gas pump. But they did have to budget for regular travel by stage and railway, not only for trips associated with the ministry but also for visits to family and friends in Madison and Oneida Counties. The following examples have been extracted from the Reverend's diaries during the 1870s:

> Sugar (4 lbs): $1.31
> Bread: $0.10
> Lard: $0.99
> Graham flower: $0.71
> Dentist bill: $2
> Medicine: $0.25
> Wall paper: $2
> Broom: $0.37
> Shirt collars: $0.36
> Slippers: $0.64
> Soap: $0.08
> Laundry starch: $0.14
> Writing paper: $0.22
> Two train tickets to Utica: $3
> Two coach tickets to Verona: $1.34

The Reverend's overall financial status is unclear, although the family certainly never got rich on his miserly minister's salary. His income was periodically supplemented by holiday collections taken up by the congregation. The church in the adjacent parsonage always provided housing. From time to time he receives "mortgage payments" and "interest payments" from the sale of property and other assets. Both the Reverend and Flora were descended from farming families, but the extent of their land and business holdings is unknown.

As members of the succeeding generation, Hattie and Frank could have lived a much more opulent lifestyle had they chosen to do so. But ostentatious living and extravagant spending were nowhere in their genetic structure. They were descended from frugal New England Yankee stock and, like their contemporaries in central New Hampshire, remained cost-conscious and fiscally conservative throughout their lives. Rather than spending lavishly, they invested most of their income in interest-bearing securities, including governmental and corporate bonds for utilities, railroads and real estate ventures. The exact nature of their portfolio is unknown, as information is only gleaned from sporadic references in diaries and letters.

It is known that Frank was a shareholder in the dry goods firm of D.E. Taylor in Adams, as well as in a number of local utilities and real estate developments. He makes mention of a number of stock transactions involving various companies in New York. Unfortunately, these are never referred to by name, only by their stock symbols. Their identity is further hampered by his habit of transcribing tickers in his inimical scrawl, which makes interpretation tantamount to deciphering cuneiform off 4000-year-old clay tablets. The only stock we can be certain of was mentioned by Hattie shortly after his death. At a Church Conference around 1912, Frank had been introduced to a man from Massachusetts who convinced him to invest in a cranberry harvesting and marketing operation in Cape Cod. He apparently took the advice because the year after his passing, Hattie records receipt of their first dividend check from the United Cape Cod Cranberry Company, the precursor to the Ocean Spray Cooperative.[48]

In early 1923, Hattie sat down with the family and made a careful review of their properties and assets. At this point in her life, she felt unable to maintain control over the family businesses and decided to sell their farm property to her longtime, on-site manager. She put $3500 of the proceeds into municipal bonds from the town of Lorraine. She identifies a number of additional bonds that were added to their portfolio. In total, she spent the equivalent of over $75,000 in 21st-century money on these additional investments. Even in the wake of Frank's passing, the family was far from strapped for cash.

---

48. At the time, company shareholders were sent a complimentary can of cranberry sauce each Thanksgiving.

PART III : EVERYDAY LIFE IN THE VICTORIAN ERA

What effect the stock market collapse of 1929 and the ensuing Great Depression had upon their interests is difficult to assess. Also unknown is the impact of the financial downturn upon Amanda's descendants in central New Hampshire. Hattie's diaries after 1926 are mostly lost or known only from burnt fragments in the attic on Main Street. Because the majority of their investments appear to have been in bonds, they were likely spared the colossal losses incurred by reliance upon stocks and other equity securities. But, the economic downturn undoubtedly had a significant impact on their overall financial health. Income from the nation's agricultural sector plunged almost 50 percent in this period, affecting not only large operations but also the smaller businesses that predominated in southern Jefferson County. Fortunately, it seems the family weathered the worst of the downturn and never suffered the indignity of losing their home to foreclosure, as happened to millions across the country.

CHAPTER 29

Entertainment & Recreation

IN Colonial and Victorian times, most American's spent their leisure time where they had for centuries—in the house by firelight, gas light or oil lamps. Most people in small towns and the countryside had little time or cash to devote to lavish entertainment during their long, dark evenings. Most of their time was spent at home, as there was little to do and very few options for anyone inclined to try something different. Hot tubs and Jacuzzis would certainly have livened up the festivities, but these generations were born too soon for such creature comforts. In their time, there was little ambiance associated with bath time, which was always short on privacy and long on extra work. Buckets of cold water had to be obtained from the outside well or, for homes so equipped, from the spigot at the kitchen sink. The water was then heated on the stove before being poured into a small, portable washtub, which, in most instances, was wheeled into the kitchen from storage. For a tiny degree of privacy, sheets might be suspended from hooks on the ceiling or other temporary barriers set up around the tub.

For most, the most popular pastimes were musical recitals, reading, storytelling, and parlor games, including backgammon, dominos, checkers, chess and card games. The folks in Northfield spent their leisure time visiting with neighbors and family, as well as attending the period dance in town or social functions at the Grange Hall. Card games like Flinch and Go Bang were the hot, steamy deals in Hattie and Frank's neck of the woods. Bridge is mentioned as an activity at Thousand Island Park, but no mention of this activity is recorded during their stays at the cottages. A popular pastime in the northeast was the group sing-along by the piano to the accompaniment of piano rolls or a local maestro like Hattie. When a new newspaper, periodical or almanac arrived, a literate member of the household would read aloud to others in the sitting room. For variety, stereopticon or lantern shows appeared some evenings at the school auditorium or other town venues. Churches were at the forefront of offering wholesome but rather bland entertainment, like educational lectures from ministers describing their missionary activities in exotic places like Africa, India or China. All low-tech offerings would bore the modern youngster into a catatonic stupor in a matter of minutes.

Another consideration was determining whether leisure-time activities would be acceptable to local religious censors, who were never far off and had little, if any, sense of humor.[49] In earlier years, dancing had been frowned upon by the Puritans, who considered intimacy an enticement towards lewd and lascivious behavior by otherwise God-fearing people. Nevertheless, it remained a popular pastime in all areas and across all centuries. Dances were usually held in someone's home, barn or a hall above a neighborhood store. Music was provided by player pianos or small ensembles with rudimentary expertise on the fiddle, banjo and piano. Similar to honky-tonks and juke joints in the southern states, the ambiance at these northerly sock hops was always less than ideal. Most places were cold in winter and sweltering hot in summer. Ample interior lighting was always a problem, even with gas illumination. And until around 1920, most rural places lacked electricity, so there was no way to plug anything in to help enhance the festivities.

Quilting bees and other arts and crafts activities brought local women and girls together and produced saleable articles for town and church events. The largest gatherings included regional and state fairs, which attracted crowds from surrounding communities. One of the largest in Jefferson County was the Ellisburgh Fair, which appeared each year in Belleville. Another attraction was the traveling circuses, one of which pitched its tents each summer outside of Adams. Circuses, agricultural fairs and harvest festivals provided people a brief respite from their daily labors on farms, mills and homesteads. They were one of the few opportunities to get out, have some fun, stuff their faces, buy trinkets and mementos, and perhaps purchase livestock, fresh produce and locally made goods. Frank mentions hearing John Philip Sousa on the grandstand at one event in 1911. For some reason, the sound of marching band music didn't appeal to him, although he readily acknowledged his widespread popularity. On the down side, attendees at fairgrounds were inevitably subjected to snake oil salesmen and their interminable pitches for patent medicines and other miracle cures.

---

49. A more apropos description is probably that, in this early period, most ministers had little or no sense of fun. Although exceptions undoubtedly abounded, most were hardly party animals inclined towards liquor, gambling, cavorting and unbridled merriment.

The Opera House

In the latter half of the century, opera houses began to appear in the larger towns in response to the burgeoning post-war population, the rising middle class, and the extension of railway service into more distant sections of the country. Convenient to Northfield residents was the Opera House in neighboring Franklin, an impressive multi-storied red granite and brick structure that opened in 1892. The Adams Opera House appeared in 1904 with seating for 600 patrons, making it the largest such facility in the area. This more modestly apportioned structure was made of wood rather than stone and suffered the indignity of burning to the ground a scant five decades after construction.

Although smaller and more modestly appointed than their namesakes in Europe, these facilities provided a sense of prestige and civic pride to communities hitherto off the beaten track. Contrary to what their name suggests, programs were never limited to operatic and symphonic works but included national touring troupes offering the latest in dramatic and comedic entertainment. They also hosted school and other local talent in plays, musicals and dramatic events. Around 1900, vaudeville shows were added, along with moving pictures from the evolving film industry.[50] At some theaters, minstrel and burlesque shows were offered in the evenings, mostly to adult (male) audiences. As automobile ownership increased in the 1920s, so did competition for the patron's money; as the distances people were able to travel were greatly extended. The demise of the local opera house began in the 1920s due to increasing competition from movie theaters and radios in the parlor. By the depression years, most opera houses were either converted into movie theatres or shut down entirely.

---

50. The change in nomenclature from moving pictures to movies occurred in the first decades of the 20th century. By 1916, Hattie and Frank were writing the word "movies" in quotation marks, denoting a slang expression.

PART III : EVERYDAY LIFE IN THE VICTORIAN ERA

Antique photograph of the Adams Opera House, which made its debut in February of 1904. It contained a balcony, limited electrical lighting, and seating for 600 patrons. The theater space continued into the rear section, which is partially visible at the bottom right. Ticket prices were originally 25 cents for adults and 10 cents for children. The opera house was a common venue in many towns in the post-Civil War period. Their proliferation is attributable to the rise of a middle class with a little extra cash, as well as the expansion of railway lines into distant areas previously considered off the grid.

Contrary to the name, these venues featured a variety of entertainment, including plays, musicals, vaudeville, minstrel shows, local school talent and early moving pictures. The Adams Opera House contained three floors: the lowermost for performances, the second a Masonic banquet hall, and the upper a combination of Masonic lodge and ancillary rooms. The building was constructed mostly of wood and was unfortunately destroyed during a fire in 1951. (Historical Association of South Jefferson County)

ENTERTAINMENT & RECREATION

> **"Service" Restaurant**
> REGULAR DINNERS and LUNCHES
>
> **PURITY ICE CREAM**
> CONE, DISH OR QUANTITY
>
> SCHRAFFTS CHOCOLATES
>
> C. L. SERVIS, Prop., Main St., Adams, N.Y
>
> ## TUESDAY, JUNE 10th
> At MASONIC OPERA HOUSE
>
> *Vaudeville and Photo Play*
>
> A FIVE REEL FEATURE ENTITLED
> **"BACK TO THE WOODS"**
> IT'S A GOLDWYN
>
> **EMPIRE COMEDY CO.** presents in Vaudeville
> 3 refined Acts
>
> Act I. Nurses Substitute
> Act II. Beauty, the $1000 Trick Dog. She does everything but talk
> Act III. Darktown Jubilee
>
> Admission 15-25¢. Tax included

Broadsheet advertisement for a "Vaudeville and Photo Play" at the Opera House in 1919. It is doubtful Hattie cared for vaudeville, but newlyweds Laura and Herbert probably went. The "Back To The Woods" five-reeler was an early production by Samuel Goldwyn. No doubt it was chock full and bursting at the seams with cornball and melodrama, both signature features of silent films. It featured Mabel Normand, who also starred in numerous early movies with Charlie Chaplin and Roscoe "Fatty" Arbuckle. The Empire Comedy Company toured frequently at the turn of the 20th century at Opera Houses and similar venues in the United States and Canada. Their repertoire was a combination of vaudeville, burlesque and (gasp!) minstrel acts. (author's collection)

PART III : EVERYDAY LIFE IN THE VICTORIAN ERA

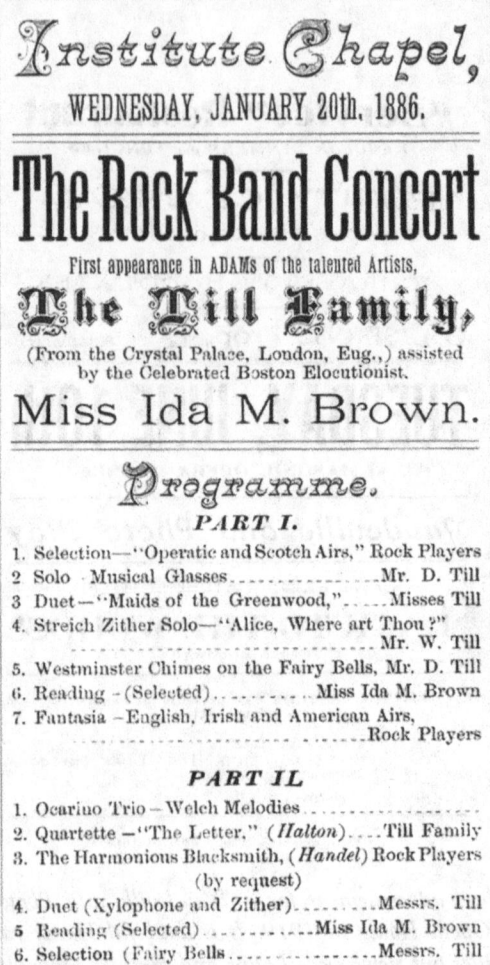

The history of rock and roll may require some serious revision. Move over, Chuck Berry and Elvis, the Till Family with celebrated elocutionist Miss Ida M. Brown was rocking the Chapel at Adams Collegiate Institute way back in 1886. Prior to the Opera House in 1904, the Chapel Auditorium at Adams Collegiate Institute was the largest venue in town for these programs, with seating for almost 300 patrons. The Till Family was a group of musicians from England who played a rock harmonicon. This rather bizarre instrument was similar to the modern xylophone but with a graduated series of tuned rocks rather than wooden bars. An elocutionist is an antiquated way of describing someone adept in the art and science of clear, correct and proper articulation. Sort of the antithesis of political speech making. Miss Ida M. Brown presumably belted out a melodic spiel in time to the rock banging. They were both popular attractions on the Chautauqua circuit in the late Victorian period. (author's collection)

Outdoor Activities

Out of doors, people's recreational opportunities were more varied, although still limited in comparison to available activities in the modern era. Then as now, the Lakes Region of central New Hampshire offered a variety of options, with excursions for swimming, boating, fishing and picnicking frequently noted by the people in Northfield. Outdoor activities in the less temperate northeastern States were wholly contingent upon variables like changing seasons and climate. Ice hockey became popular in New England after it arrived from Canada in 1875. However, no one considered the feasibility of introducing the sport into Southern Pines or Hot Springs due to the inability to manipulate temperature or create artificial ice.

Frank in Adams was no hunter, but a number of hunting and fishing clubs were active in Jefferson County. Of course, these activities had long been essential to human survival long before they were taken up for sporting or pleasure. Fishing was always high on everyone's list, as it not only permitted time away from work and chores but hopefully brought home something tasty for the dinner table. The diaries of these Victorian-age people record frequent excursions for fishing at several locations, including Thousand Island Park for the family in Jefferson County.

Economic considerations may have contributed to the scarcity of golf in the North Country, although the sport was one of many popular pastimes for snowbirds down south. Lawn tennis and badminton are frequently mentioned, although the rapid ball movement probably limited Frank's playing time at either activity. Hattie and Laura were adept at croquet but not so much out on the courts. Croquet had long been a hallowed family tradition, as evidenced by a group snapshot showing everyone out on the lawn and ready for game time. It was so popular in the northern states that one person described it as the game of choice for *gentleman farmers*, meaning anyone fully or semi-retired after decades of grueling work in barns and fields. Long experience wielding those heavy wooden *dung knockers* turned retired farmers into first-class sportsmen in later years.

PART III : EVERYDAY LIFE IN THE VICTORIAN ERA

Croquet, lawn tennis and badminton were popular pastimes in 19th century America and Great Britain. These ladies would obviously have benefited from a little tweaking to their sporting outfits. The ostentatious dress was a hallmark of affluence in times past. For the more well-to-do, the concept of dressing down for the occasion did not include backyard sporting activities or trips to the beach. Working up a sweat was certainly a problem because the only way to mask perspiration odors was by drowning them out with a liberal application of industrial-strength perfume. By the 1890s, less restrictive clothing began appearing on the market, including bloomers, two-piece outfits and sports corsets. (Public Domain)

ENTERTAINMENT & RECREATION

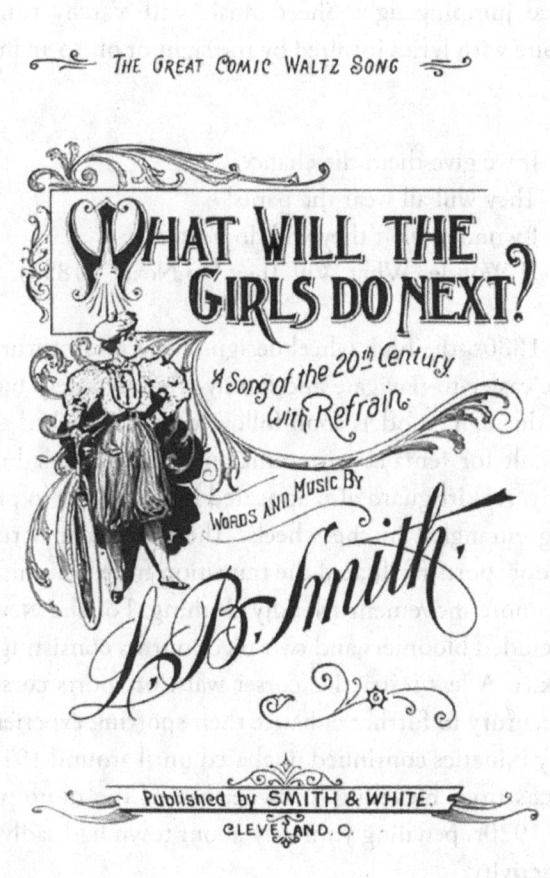

One of many similarly themed songs to appear between 1890 and 1905. The lyrics were inspired by the mass stupefaction of Victorian and Edwardian men as more and more Gibson Girls donned their un-lady-like outfits and headed out ad libitum on bicycles to God knows where. This prescient Gay 90s manifestation of women's liberation didn't go unnoticed by the gentlemen in their midst. Consternation gave way to alarm, which soon gave way to public outrage. Surely, the sky was falling on the patriarchal age of Queen Victoria. (Public Domain)

PART III : EVERYDAY LIFE IN THE VICTORIAN ERA

The 1890s were also the golden age for bicycling in America. Thanks to improvements in frame and wheel design, women could safely and comfortably ride the roads to their heart's content—or until their legs gave out or husbands started jumping ugly. Sheet music with catchy tunes entered the popular repertoire with lyrics inspired by the sight of oh-so-many modern girls pedaling away:

> If we give them the chance,
> They will all wear the pants!
> I wonder what they will do next.
> "I Wonder What Will They Do Next?" (1894)

By the late 1880s, the high wheel design of the mid-century had been superseded by the easier-to-navigate and family-friendly safety bicycle. Specially designed "step-through" models soon followed, which lacked the straight bar making it difficult for females to mount and ride in their bulky skirts and dresses discreetly. A skirt guard also appeared in the 1890s to prevent clothing from becoming entangled in the wheels. The phenomenal rise in bicycling and other outdoor sports facilitated the transition from voluminous Victorian-wear to lighter, more movement-friendly clothing. For the New Woman generation, this included bloomers and two-piece outfits consisting of a shirtwaist (blouse) and skirt. A less restrictive corset waist or sports corset appeared by the end of the century to further enhance their sporting experience. The riding craze of the Gay Nineties continued unabated until around 1910 when society changed its focus from bicycling to ownership of the more prestigious auto mobile. By the 1920s, pedaling your way about town had sadly been demoted to a children's activity.

ENTERTAINMENT & RECREATION

Advertisement for an Edwardian corset waist or sports corset. Note the elastic strips at the sides, which allowed for a greater range of motion during athletic activities. Being "formed on hygienic principles" meant that, unlike earlier corsets, the material "breathed" a bit to help inhibit perspiration buildup. By 1920, a light bulb had gone off in women's heads, and society soon dispensed with these archaic devices altogether. The heyday of the much-vaunted bulky, overdressed look of Victorian times was over. The straight up-and-down flapper look of the Jazz Age would soon replace the hourglass figure. (Public Domain)

PART III : EVERYDAY LIFE IN THE VICTORIAN ERA

Ahhhhh, a summertime jaunt to the seaside circa 1885! Nothing like going for a refreshing dip replete with woolen or mohair swimsuit, stockings and bathing slippers! It's a wonder the bulk of these outrageous getups didn't make 19th-century beachgoers sink to the bottom of Davy Jones' Locker. Commercial sunscreens weren't around back then, but they were probably unnecessary when the only body parts left exposed were the face, forearms, and maybe the tootsies. It's hard to understand the widespread Victorian prohibition against women displaying little skin while swimming or sunbathing. Even lifting the hem of her skirt when walking through a puddle could make her subject to suspicion and ridicule. In this era, the sight of bare ankles was construed by religious censors as an obscene come-on and thus verboten. (Wikimedia-public domain)

CHAPTER 30

The Farmer's Almanac

> Books to them
> Are the faint dreams of students, save that one,
> The battered Almanac - split to the core,
> Fly-blown and tattered, that above the fireplace
> Devoted sits and furnishes the fates
> And pedigrees and apogees of moons

THE regional farmers' almanacs were among the few written materials most farmers and country dwellers felt truly compelled to read. An early 20th-century study determined that, after the Christian Bible, the most widely read material in American homes was the local almanac.[51] This ubiquity is not surprising, as it was long considered an essential reference for a number of occupations, including farming, animal husbandry, dairy production and fishing. An understanding of—and adaptation to—natural cycles such as solstices, equinoxes, lunar phases, tides, weather patterns and other vagaries of nature were critical survival tools in an age with few other resources for the management of country homes and livelihoods. Many well-worn almanacs have been found with a small hole drilled in the upper left corner to hang in a home or barn for ready reference. Although the Bible was considered the sacred word of the Creator, these humble publications were a matter of life and death to people still mired in the material world.

The occupations of most readers in the 18th and 19th centuries were in the agricultural sector, which publishers and artists widely portrayed as an idyllic pastime enjoyed by those who were truly the salt of the earth. The bucolic pleasures of agrarian life are everywhere emphasized, as in this short piece which appeared in *The Farmer's Almanac for the Year of Our Lord and Savior 1837* under the heading A Farmers Life:

---

51. In the 17th and 18th centuries, the most common spelling of these publications was almanack.

> While the merchant, mechanic and the professional ma are harassed with anxiety, the farmer's life is as free and clear as the air that meets him when he goes in his field. After the labors of the day are over, the husbandman can retire to his home and enjoy the luxury of rest. Not so with the man of business . . . Farmers possess the means of living within themselves and are not under the disagreeable necessity of fawning for patronage, stooping to flattery for a livelihood, or bartering opinion, reputation and conscience for gold. Nowhere else can domestic quietness and happiness be discovered, so pure from misery, as amid the rural scenes of the farmer's happy home. If there is anywhere on earth a terrestrial Paradise, it is HERE.

It is doubtful most farmers would concur with the assessment they were enraptured within a veritable terrestrial paradise or Garden of Eden. Most were too busy scratching out a meager existence to sit back and reflect on how blessed it was to be working sixteen hours days for the privilege of breaking even.

In the past, most people had scant resources for the management of crops, livestock and households. Most information was obtained from traditional sources, including lessons passed on by older generations and the memorialization of experiences and observations in their yearly almanac. Such knowledge was essential prior to modern meteorological and agricultural studies with their effective modes of dissemination. From his trusty almanac, the farmer gained insights into crop tending, animal husbandry, barn raising, fishing and a host of other essential activities. He also obtained valuable information about the seasonal recurrence of plants and flowers, the appearance of butterflies and migratory birds, egg-laying cycles of birds and reptiles, the progress of honey bee colonies, and in autumn, when to expect the leaves to change colors before falling to the ground.

The memorialization of phenological knowledge from past experiences was the best hope for adaptation to natural cycles, including seasonal changes, variations in climate, and their effects on plant and animal life.[52] In modern times, these venerable and homey proverbs have been satirized in *Farmer Iggy's Almanac* with the saying Plant in the mornin'. Vegetables a-bornin'. Although Farmer Iggy and his down-home wisdom are wholly fictitious, genuine examples abound, including the following maxims compiled from various antique almanacs:

---

52. Phenology is the ancient practice of correlating the climate to other phenomena, including changing seasons, crop tending and animal husbandry.

Rainbow at night, Shepherd's delight. Rainbow in morning, Shepherds take warning

A coming storm, your shooting corns presage, and aches will throb, your hollow tooth will rage.

If Candlemas be fair and clear, two winters will you have this year

The chill is on from near and far in all the months that have an R

When the forest murmurs and the mountain roars, Then shut your windows and close your doors

The higher the clouds, the finer the weather

Clear moon, frost soon

Morn dry, rain nigh; Morn wet, no rain yet

Lightning in the south brings little else but drought

Rainbow in the morning gives you fair warning

Cold, wet May, barn full of hay

Moss dry, sunny sky; Moss wet, rain you'll get

If snow begins in mid of day, Expect a foot of it to lay

Sound traveling far and wide, A stormy day this does betide

When the wind is in the east, "Tis neither good for man nor beast

Ring around the moon? Rain real soon

Bees will not swarm before a storm

Go roll in the clover; the summer's near over

Red sky in the morning, Shepherd's warning. Red sky at night, Shepherd's delight.

A nearly identical rendering to this last example is "Red sky at night, sailors delight. Red sky in morning, sailors take warning." It is also probably the oldest and is based upon the New Testament Matthew XVI: 2-3: "When it is evening, ye say, It will be fair weather: for the sky is red. And in the morning, It will be foul weather today, for the sky is red and lowering." The saying refers to high or low atmospheric systems moving into the area and the associated changes in weather: A red sky in the morning means higher pressure is moving in with stormy weather. A red sky at night means lower pressure is moving in with drier and calmer air. The usefulness of these colloquialisms is belied by their homey and archaic expression.

For a number of reasons, lunar cycles, rather than solar cycles, were of especial importance to people in times past. To avoid the sun's heat, certain strenuous activities were deferred by day and performed under the light of the full moon. The waxing and waning were also believed to determine the most propitious times for a host of activities, including when to go fishing,[53] luckiest times to enter into business contracts, the luckiest times for barn raising, the best times for bloodletting to treat disease, and even when to cut your children's hair so it grows back most luxuriantly. The following recommendations were compiled from different 18th and 19th-century almanacs. Each is preceded by the month and year in which it appeared:[54]

> JULY 1774: Kill your winter pork and beef, and it will enlarge while cooking.
> APRIL 1794: A good time in the moon to sow hemp and flax if your ground be not too wet.
> JANUARY 1799: At this quarter of the moon, cut firewood to prevent its snapping.
> APRIL 1799: Wheat, sown at this quarter of the moon, is said not to be subject to smutting.
> AUGUST, 1800: MOW BUSHES! MOW BUSHES NOW! If you have any faith in the influence of the moon on them.
> SEPTEMBER 1801: Moon-arians have not neglected to haul up and destroy pernicious weeds before this day of the month.
> AUGUST 1804: Mow bushes, and kill them if you can, in the old moon, sign in heart, etc.
> JANUARY 1814: Kill your winter pork, which I presume by this time is fat and plump from good keeping.

The first almanac to appear in America was printed in Cambridge, Massachusetts, in 1639. A century later, in Philadelphia, Benjamin Franklin began the publication of *Poor Richard's Almanack* in 1732. In the years that followed, new editions appeared regularly in the Thirteen Colonies, a tradition maintained to the present today. Most people in Colonial times had limited access to printed news and other up-to-date information, aside from the one page broadsheets constituting newspapers in this period. After the venerable family Bible, the yearly almanac was often the only reading material found in the home. Literally, every topic of interest to farming and country life was found within these pages: regional and national weather forecasts, planting times for various crops, rising

---

53. As per a number of antique almanacs, fish bite best under the first quarter moon. They're also suckers for the hook whenever the barometer is rising. Go fishing with both a rising barometer and quarter moon and a veritable fish-fest will assuredly follow.

54. Noted as per pp. 305 to 307 of *The Old Farmer and his Almanack*, a 1904 treatise by George Lyman Kittredge.

and setting times for the sun and moon, tide tables, upcoming solar and lunar eclipses, reminders of dates for major religious holidays, and a wealth of other useful information.

Hundreds of new almanacs appeared over the next two centuries. The runaway success of the format translated into rapid sales increases, as more and more families eagerly awaited each yearly edition, which usually appeared in late fall. Over several days, a literate member of the household would sit by the fireplace and read everything aloud to assembled family and friends. In order to appeal to wider audiences, publishers enlivened their editions by including information well beyond their original formats. The new material included much financial, literary, medical and instructional content, along with stagecoach and railway schedules, distances from local cities to popular destinations, the location of taverns and public houses en route, postal rates for domestic and international mail, and rates of exchange for different currencies. During the Civil War years, some almanacs increased their readership by including casualty lists for residents, with names, dates, locations and whether they were killed, injured or captured while on active duty.

A number of pages were also devoted to humorous and satirical content, including jocular rhymes, puzzles, jokes, riddles, idioms and miscellaneous witticisms submitted by readers. Most of these G-rated jokes appear somewhat lame to the modern eye. Think, "Why did the rabbit (or chicken) cross the road?" and you won't be far off from this type of humor. Witticisms were elementary, reaching no further into the collective wisdom than don't set the oxen before the yolk, etc. Surprisingly, the 1863 Methodist Almanac for New York printed a relatively risqué offering in which a reader expressed his feigned surprise over the paucity of ugly women in New York. This "longtime reader" and "very eccentric gentleman" purchased a pair of "Help Wanted" advertisements in the local newspaper. The first was for an "attractive and accomplished lady of education and elegant manners," while the other was for "a woman who is quite ugly." To his astonishment, he received no end of responses for the former but not a single one for the latter. "For my part," he concludes, "I am almost to believe such a creature (an ugly woman) to be a mere chimera of the imagination and to be classed with those fictitious beings whose heads are said to grow beneath their shoulders." Racy ditties like this surely left farmers laughing uproariously on the floor and rolling dangerously close to the fireplace.

Another regular feature was the *Homo Signorum* or Man of the Signs, a diagram somewhat reminiscent of *L'uomo vitruviano* or *Vitruvian Man* by 15th century Renaissance Master Leonardo da Vinci.[55] The imagery is a man sur-

---

55. Leonardo named his 15th-century diagram after 1st-century BCE Roman architect Vitruvius Pollio.

rounded by the twelve signs of the zodiac, with indications as to which body part the individual constellations were supposed to govern. The ancient belief in beneficial and deleterious effects of heavenly bodies upon health and human affairs has been documented in medical texts dating back to the first millennium BCE, although the beliefs themselves are undoubtedly much older. Unfavorable celestial alignments were thought to result in any number of afflictions and disasters, including plague, infant mortality, insanity, famine, floods and earthquakes.

In addition to the influences of celestial alignments upon human health and welfare, the 5th century BCE Greek physician Hippocrates popularized the role of four essential *humors* within the human body in the diagnosis and treatment of disease—blood, yellow bile, black bile and phlegm. These silly notions continued to be promulgated not only in antique almanacs but also in mainstream medical texts up to the latter half of the 19th century. In the early years of the Common Era, religious authorities realized early on the utter futility of attempting to suppress these ancient superstitions. People were loathe to abandon their age-old reliance upon magic, ritual, charms, astrology and forms of divination simply due to church dogma and disapprobation. Besides, what harm could come from the simple observance of these ancient beliefs? Mainstream Christianity already offered believers the certainty of redemption and eternal life after lifetimes of suffering. A little extra help along the way is not a significant obstacle towards ultimate salvation.

As a result, the role of bodily humors, astrological calculations and the *Homo Signorum* continued as regular features in medical treatises throughout the medieval period. Well into the 19th century, there was continued debate in medical circles regarding the role of the stars and humors in the etiology and treatment of most illnesses. Obsolete procedures such as "bleeding" were prescribed to address imbalances amongst the humors and thus restore good health. What role these medical men ascribed to the zodiac for pestilence, earthquakes, famine and other disasters probably varied by individual practitioner. However, the medical profession's penchant for publishing almanacs in promotion of quack medicine cures remained an affliction well into the early 20th century.

In Colonial times, certain economic sectors began publishing dedicated almanacs with information specific to individual trades and occupations, including merchants, farmers, seamen, miners, doctors, musicians and clergymen. It also became commonplace to market a combination diary *and* almanac, with empty pages or spaces for readers to fill in personal data *ad libitum*. As early as the 1720s, one enterprising publisher offered up *The Lady's Dfiliary* or *The*

Woman's Almanack, which purported to tailor content to the female reader by "Containing many Delightful and Entertaining Particulars, Peculiarly Adapted for the Use and Diversion of the FAIR SEX." Space allotments limited diary entries to the barest essentials, vis "Morning fair. Did haying in the forenoon, then chopped wood. Agnes feeling some better today. Henry and Eliza called in the evening." The *Franklin Almanac and Diary* appeared in Cincinnati in 1857 and, similar to the modern desk calendar, included numbered squares for readers to fill in for each day of the month. Another was *Green's Diary and Almanac* from New Jersey, which included a blank, lined page aside each month's material.

Beginning in the mid-19th century, patent medicine makers sponsored their editions as convenient promotional platforms. *Hostetter's Illustrated United States Almanac*, for example, featured endless pitches for Hostetter's Stomach Bitters. Readers were assured this miracle concoction was a "celebrated and indispensable" cure for "unsettled nerves, insomnia, constipation, fever prevention, indigestion, biliousness, liver complaints, rheumatism, and as a safeguard against fever and illness while traveling." Of course, aside from the placebo effect, the only thing this fetid mixture of alcohol and putrescent plant matter was likely to do was to give users a mild booze buzz while draining money out of their purses. Still, the runaway success of the medical almanac format was a template for the creation of more and more editions across the country.

The number of new almanacs appearing in these family's lifetimes was truly astounding. Literally, hundreds of regional and national publications were in circulation, with success contingent upon individual content and the saturation of rival publications in individual areas. New England, New York and Pennsylvania were particularly well saturated, with publishers tailoring content, advertisements, weather predictions and astronomical data to specific regions of the country. The family in Northfield refers to an almanac in the house but sadly makes no mention of *which* almanac.

Beckwith's Almanac enjoyed a wide circulation in southern New England for almost a century. The *Times and Reformer Almanac* in Watertown was also widely read, with forecasts and tables of special interest to farmers, dairymen and other occupations common to Jefferson County. *The Methodist Almanac* from New York City also reached a sizeable North Country audience. The illustration that follows is from *Hostetter's Illustrated United States Almanac*, which was advertised as "Carefully calculated for such Meridians and Latitudes as are best suited for a Universal Calendar for the United States." The cover goes on to describe it as of incalculable benefit to "Merchants, Mechanics, Miners, Farmers, Planters and General Family Use."

PART III : EVERYDAY LIFE IN THE VICTORIAN ERA

The ubiquitous Homo Signorum or Man of the Signs as it appeared in Hostetter's Illustrated United States Almanac for 1878. In the latter half of the 19th century, it was commonplace for patent medicine makers to sponsor new almanacs as promotional platforms for their various products. In this example, almost half the issue was taken up by grandiose claims for Hostetter's Stomach Bitters, which, readers were assured, was the world's foremost "remedy and preventative" for everything from insomnia to malaria to a "deficiency of vital power." Yet despite all the grandiose and unsubstantiated claims, the by now standardized format of American almanacs was scrupulously followed, including the Homo Signorum and all relevant astrological, astronomical and religious holiday data for each month. These almanacs were often the only readily available source for up-to-date information on weather, farming and related activities. (author's collection)

CHAPTER 31

Beckwith's Almanac in New Haven

ONE noteworthy and venerable publication in southern New England was *Beckwith's Almanac*, which made its debut in New Haven, Connecticut, in 1848. The explanatory notice on his earlier covers read as follows: "Calculated for Connecticut and adjacent States by George Beckwith, photographer, survivor of Beers, Middlebrook & Prindle. Published to do good and make money,"[56] *Beckwith's Almanac* was noted for insightful commentaries on social topics and a wealth of useful data, including its uncannily accurate meteorological and astronomical calculations. For almost a century, if only one almanac was read in these parts, it was this one. Long after the cessation of publishing in the 1930s, previous editions could still be found hanging on hooks or tucked away in barns, homesteads and businesses throughout the northeast.

In addition to Beckwith's lengthy discourses on local and national events, each new edition included updated regional news and developments, all meticulously itemized by month and day. This included natural disasters, deaths, accidents, overdue comeuppances and other bits of information and local lore. During the Civil War years, he carefully listed names and home towns for all Connecticut casualties, including the nature of their injury, where and when it occurred, and whether the individual had survived. The regular issuance of military necrology lists affected Beckwith profoundly: just a few years earlier, many of these same young men had sat in his classroom, full of burgeoning talent and ambition. Now they were gone—victims of (he states) "institutionalized mass insanity that threatened to rend the Union forevermore into separate and unequal halves."

---

56. The term "phonographer" refers to a user of the Pitman Method, an early form of stenography used and promoted by Beckwith. Beers, Middlebrook and Prindle were three earlier defunct almanacs in southern New England. A contemporary of Elijah Middlebrook, Charles Prindle published from 1825 to 1860 and billed himself as the successor to Andrew Beers. Although publication years overlapped, in terms of bragging rights, the order of succession in the almanac racket was roughly Beers to Middlebrook to Prindle to Beckwith.

PART III : EVERYDAY LIFE IN THE VICTORIAN ERA

As was typical with most Victorian almanacs, Beckwith defrayed production costs by devoting a considerable amount of space to advertising. As his readership increased, more and more retailers sought to advertise their products in the upcoming edition. To Beckwith's credit, he never made a quick buck by promoting the quack medical cures endemic to the period. But as the years went by, he featured an ever-increasing assortment of products and services. Reading through his later editions is like thumbing through a miniature Sears Catalog. In his "Welcome to the 1870 edition" section, he states:

> In addition to the usual twelve-month almanac tables, there are many advertisements, several with full-page wood-cut illustrations. There are ads for House furnishings, clocks, agricultural implements, hardware, apothecary and druggist, musical instruments, paper hanging lace goods, diamonds and watches, mirrors, boots and shoes, savings bank, business college, books and stationery, paint and varnish, silks and dress goods, hoop skirts, church and parlor organs, and more. Also featured is a short, short story by Mark Twain, entitled Jim Wolfe and the Tom Cats.

In his lifetime (1810—1880), George Beckwith was noted as an author, publisher, social reformer, brilliant polymath and incorrigible eccentric. His peculiarities were legendary, and whenever his name came up in conversation, it evoked both an inevitable chuckle and a healthy measure of respect. His City of New Haven was home to Yale University, an institution with more than its fair share of brilliant minds. Yet whenever his former students found themselves stymied by a particularly vexing mathematical or astronomical problem, the person they turned to for answers was George Beckwith. The local *New Haven Register* once printed the following in regards to this rather peculiar habit:

> His ability as a mathematician is well known, and many a Yale Graduate has depended on Mr. Beckwith for the solution of difficult problems which they were either too lazy or too ignorant to master. Surveying and navigation he taught to many young men, and he was an expert in all the higher mathematics.

He was certainly easy enough to track down in the City: he'd be the one walking barefoot through the storm while devouring a mangy two-day-old sandwich found unexpectedly in his coat pocket. Whenever queried for answers, he would inevitably pull out a piece of chalk, bend down on the sidewalk, and work the calculation in front of an amazed assembly. There was really no one else in the City remotely like George Beckwith.

In an era of black stovepipe hats, his was always pure white, a peculiarity that made him instantly recognizable in a crowd. When he passed away, notices were posted in most Connecticut newspapers, including this recollection from one of his former students in the *Waterbury Republican*:

> The sudden demise of this eccentric gentleman will revive many reminiscences among those who were pupils of his forty years ago . . . Eccentricity with Mr. Beckwith was no assumption for the purpose of securing an ephemeral reputation for talent, but an inborn, inherent attribute of his nature. His laugh was eccentric, his language and gestures were eccentric, his pose was eccentric . . . Beckwith seldom used a word of less than four syllables . . . The members of the debating society usually put their hats under the wooden benches used as seats. On one occasion, he lost his hat . . . The writer said to him 'Beckwith, what have you lost?" (to which he replied) 'The diurnal and hebdomadal external covering that obscurates the cerebrum and cerebellum of a man's capute, vulgarly called a hat.' . . . Lean, lank, angular, lost in meditation, yet striding onward, regardless of all whom he met, straight on to his business, is our recollection of George Beckwith.

His iconoclasm was legendary, and he railed against useless convention and meaningless flattery. The custom of shaking hands he absolutely despised, believing it a ploy by unscrupulous businessmen prior to fleecing someone. In regards to this quirk, he once told a reporter:

> I dislike hand shaking; it is a hollow, useless ceremony. There are, however, four classes of men with whom I am willing to shake hands: with the old man because his habits are fixed . . . with the crazy man because it is the only way to get rid of him, with the drunken man because at such times he is generally amiable . . . lastly, with the colored man, lest he might think I felt myself as good as a negro if I behaved as well.

Although reasonably fastidious in his grooming habits, he rarely updated his wardrobe, stating the money wasted on the latest affectations would be better spent on acts of charity. He was far from rich, but whatever he did own was readily offered to anyone in need. Contemporary accounts describe him as roaming the streets at night, lending assistance to drunken men and forlorn women.

One of his peculiarities was walking through town barefoot, something he temporarily discontinued once frostbite season set in. He believed shoes were an unnecessary encumbrance upon the body, stating, "I shall not be unnecessarily restrained by the conventions of society." When inclement weather forced most others into the streetcars, Beckwith still insisted on walking back and forth from home and office. Even towards the end of his life, he would be out and about in scorching heat and freezing cold, a habit which did nothing to improve his rapidly declining health. Another of his eccentricities was to stash lunches and dinners in his pockets and eventually pull them out if and when he remembered or when queried later by his wife. In his defense, he insisted he was simply too preoccupied with work to stop and eat. Sometimes, his wife found only empty pockets, not because he had remembered but because he'd donated his lunch or dinner to some hungry stranger in the city.

In his day, George Beckwith was renowned for his progressive beliefs and social activism. His essays are liberally sprinkled with witty commentaries on contemporary issues, including the abolition of slavery, temperance and voting rights for women. His strong personal and spiritual beliefs were plainly laid out as he inveighed against the hypocrisies of Victorian society. The only legitimate acts of Christian benevolence, he insisted, were charitable donations and other tangible forms of assistance to those in need. Beckwith was the one who quite literally gave the shirt off his back to help stave off the cold. Eccentric he certainly was—but his lifelong compulsion to help alleviate the human condition was equally sincere.

He was born on July 10, 1810, at the end of the American Colonial Period, to Harvey and Martha (née Dutton) Beckwith in Berlin, Connecticut. As was typical with most people in this era, the family resided on a farmstead, which in this case was in Hartford County. Along with Litchfield County, this section of southern New England was the starting point for much immigration to the North Country. George was the sixth of ten sons. His nine brothers, two sisters (bless poor Martha) and parents made for mighty cramped living conditions during his formative years. Beckwith's father was both a farmer and a local shoemaker. And, like Reverend Gordon's dad, he had a propensity for strong drink, a habit later cited by Beckwith as his motivation for temperance meetings and anti-alcohol legislation.

His father also expected him to follow in the shoemaking trade, something he loathed but complied with to keep the old inebriate off his back. Despite his precocious intellect, his father forbade him from excessive reading or studying because such useless activities took time away from farming and shoemaking. Besides, it would be foolish to squander precious liquor money on books and school supplies. Fortunately, mother Martha had considerably more on the ball. Once the old man was dead drunk in bed, she helped George make his way surreptitiously to the barn to study by the meager light of burning pitch-pine knots. When his nightly supply of knots was exhausted, he stopped reading and went to bed.

His home situation limited formal education to a minimal number of years. Yet despite this handicap, he evinced early on a prodigious memory and intellect and matured into a knowledgeable, self-taught resource on a myriad of topics, including religion and the physical sciences. The story is told of a Sunday school assignment to take the Bible home and study certain verses from the New Testament. To the teacher's astonishment, he returned the next day and recited an entire chapter by rote from the Gospel of Matthew. As a young adult, he became infatuated with astronomy and taught himself to work out uncannily accurate charts for eclipses, lunar phases, planetary alignments and other celestial phenomena. His astronomical calculations were so precise they later became a defining feature of *Beckwith's Almanac*. He worked out his calculations so far in advance that, after his passing, his daughter and granddaughter simply inserted this existing material into each new edition.

Beckwith waited until age 30 to finally tie the knot, something unusual at a time when the average life expectancy for American males was only 45 years. Remaining steadfast in his values, his selection was made not for monetary gain or other ephemeral advantage—he married the widow Phoebe for love. She was four years his senior and already the mother of three sons and one daughter. The match proved ideal, and for forty years, she kept him more or less down to earth and anchored to married life. In December of the following year (1841) daughter Martha was born, which further inured him to the responsibilities of fatherhood. By all accounts, he matured into an adoring and attentive parent, ensuring his daughter received the best possible education for girls in mid-19th century New Haven. Beckwith took the time to personally tutor her on all important subjects, including religion, science and higher mathematics. The time was evidently well spent because Martha, in turn, passed this knowledge on to her daughter, Annie.

For nearly four decades, Beckwith made his calculations at a small office and observatory at Yale University. His aptitude for mathematics and astronomy was so extraordinary he was frequently asked to lecture at public and private schools, including the University.[57] In the 1860s, he served as County Surveyor and Assessor for the neighboring City of Bridgeport. During one civil case, it was determined his measurements for the property boundaries in question had been accurate to within half an inch. The biggest embarrassment of his life was when his design for a new bridge was off by a fraction of a degree. The miscalculation was caught in time and resulted in no damage. But if the earth had mercifully opened up and swallowed him, it would have suited him just fine. Notwithstanding the gaffe, he was appointed surveyor on a number of important projects, including Bridgeport Harbor, Seaside Park, and the city home of P.T. Barnum (Waldemere Mansion).

Beckwith described himself as a devout evangelical Baptist, a set of religious principles he inherited from his mother. Like the early Methodists, he vigorously championed social reforms and other progressive causes long before they became acceptable in the court of public opinion. He scorned discrimination or exclusivity of any sort and admonished clergymen for insisting on segregating races and genders during religious services. An active participant in abolition, temperance, women's rights and voting issues, he started a petition in 1842 to abolish the State's property qualifications for voters. Although the Whig Party to which he belonged declined to support the measure, he convinced the Democrats to bring the proposal to the State Legislature in Hartford where, after four years of haggling, it finally passed. In 1845, he took it upon himself to journey to Hartford and petitioned the Legislature to grant full voting rights to women. The following year, he returned with a similar proposal to extend these same rights to African Americans. Despite his prescience, neither measure was ever given serious consideration in the Assembly.

Beginning in 1837, his occupation was listed in the City Registry as "schoolteacher." Early on in his teaching career, he became adamant in his desire to "educate all people" and was the first educator in New Haven to open his classroom to "colored boys," something no one else was willing to do. This activism placed him at odds with the Board of Education and evoked considerable backlash within the community. One evening at a City meeting, he raised a ruckus with his insistence on integrated classrooms. When he passed away in 1880, his obituary in the New Haven Register commented on the incident with this appraisal: "This course of action generated much opposition, causing him the loss of some patronage; a circumstance which had only the

---

57. In 1926, the George Beckwith Prize for outstanding proficiency in mathematics, astronomy and related studies was established in his honor at Yale University.

effect of strengthening his resolve in the matter." Beckwith remained adamant his African American students were amongst the brightest and most eager to learn of any he'd encountered in the classroom. When he refused to relent on the segregation issue, the City promptly cut off his funding. Beckwith simply opened his school and continued as before.

His open-mindedness became the inspiration for a reappraisal and expansion of religious beliefs. One evening, he accompanied his daughter to a local séance and, despite initial skepticism, left utterly convinced of the soul's survival and the ability of sensitive individuals to establish contact under certain conditions. This was at the beginning of the 19th-century American Spiritualists Movement, during which his daughter was known in the City as a medical clairvoyant. For the remainder of his days, Beckwith periodically penned essays in various publications insisting upon the compatibility of spiritualism and his Baptist beliefs. He reasoned that, since the Bible assures us of personal immortality, why shouldn't sensitive individuals communicate with the "other side"? His daughter later republished an article in which he offered an eloquent defense of spiritualism as a legitimate religious movement:

> Investigation has resulted with me, as it has with most others, in a conviction of the verity of its facts, and a respect for its philosophy as being equally tenable, to say the least, with that of any other theory . . . It is proverbial that those who know the least about it are the most ready to condemn it; while those who will lay aside their prejudices long enough to enquire will cease their hostility, lest they should be found fighting against God.

Despite his lifelong disregard for adequate nutrition and attention to other health matters, Beckwith was always blessed with a robust constitution. His barefoot ramblings through stormy weather apparently had little effect on his overall well-being. This situation changed radically in February of 1870 after attempting to reach the basement level from his office in Bridgeport. The gas lighting was off in the hallway, and Beckwith didn't think to bring along a lantern or candle. For some godforsaken reason, he remained oblivious to the fact the stairway was under repair and missing at the moment. The only way to reach the cellar was to parachute down or take the outdoor hatchway. Down, down, down he descended—over 15 feet flat onto the packed dirt flooring. An office assistant later found him unconscious and thoroughly broken up, both externally and internally. Most of his ribs were shattered and severed from the

PART III : EVERYDAY LIFE IN THE VICTORIAN ERA

Two of several images of George Beckwith featured over the years on the cover of Beckwith's Almanac. The photoengraving at top was made in the 1840s and was in use the first few years of publication. Beckwith was always rather thin and lean, characteristics which come across in his earlier images. The engraving at bottom was made around 1879 and appeared in later editions. As he aged, he periodically updated his cover picture to illustrate the natural progression from middle to old age. Still, his final image shows a remarkably aged and bloated individual in comparison to his earlier covers. After he passed in 1880, his daughter and granddaughter continued publication until the austerity of the Great Depression finally forced a cessation after an uninterrupted run of almost a century. (author's images)

sternum. After months of convalescence and attention to broken bones and other body parts, he slowly began to recover. But it was obvious to all that he would never return to his old form. His health steadily deteriorated over the last decade of his life, and he begrudgingly acknowledged he wasn't the same man who inadvertently went skydiving one night in the office basement.

In the final year of his life, he was diagnosed with diabetes and began retaining fluid and packing on excess pounds. The final photograph and wood engraving made for the 1880 edition shows a remarkably aged, edematous and utterly transformed man compared to earlier images. On July 12, 1880, he passed away suddenly while lecturing at a temperance meeting in New Haven. Publication of his almanac continued under the editorship of his daughter and granddaughter well into the 1930s, an uninterrupted run of almost a century. A fitting tribute to his years of work was the establishment of the George Beckwith Prize at Yale University in 1926. Each year, the prize is awarded by the Department of Astronomy "to the undergraduate most proficient in some branch of astronomy or mathematics." In his lifetime, George Beckwith certainly marched to the beat of his own drum. Along the way, he left a legacy which still fascinates today.

CHAPTER 32

Death and Remembrance

THE Victorian approach towards death and bereavement can be difficult to comprehend in the modern age. In times past, everyone was surrounded by constant reminders of human mortality. People died young, and most of them died at home. The old saying was you only brought a sick person to the hospital when you wanted to get rid of them—a sure way to hasten the process. Funerals were almost always held in the home, and the families in this narrative were undoubtedly frequent attendees at services for lost family and friends. At a young age, children were confronted by the specter of sudden illness and loss of loved ones and the attitudes taken by everyone in coming to terms with this unfortunate aspect of life. Their intimate familiarity with death and dying is evident from the sheer volume of *memento mori* jewelry and portraiture these generations left behind.

Arguably, the most disconcerting aspect of life in times past was the relatively short life expectancy, irrespective of who you were, where you lived or how well you lived. Certainly people at the upper end of the social spectrum fared better than those towards the bottom. Cleaner and more adequate living conditions, enough to eat, uncontaminated drinking water and ready access to medical care obviously had certain advantages. But literally everyone—rich, poor and in the middle—could expect to stick around maybe 40 to 50 years, and that was it. Your odds of living long enough to dance at your grandchild's wedding weren't something you'd bet the farm on. And most would never see 60 or more candles on their birthday cake. Staggeringly high infant and childhood mortality rates made even the odds of a sweet 16th birthday party no better than fifty-fifty.

You'd think their dismally short life span would have made people more appreciative of what little time they did get. Whether it actually did or not varied by individual. Certainly, most were somewhat thankful. But the preponderance of outcasts and miserable wretches throughout history whose only pleasure was in screwing their neighbors and making others miserable has always cast a pall over things in general. Some Victorians took the position that, since life is for the living, a certain amount of greed and entitlement is unavoidable and thus perfectly acceptable. But even the most incorrigibly misanthropic in society surely recognize the precariousness of existence and the imminent specter of early demise. We know how cognizant they all were of the actions taken at all levels of society to accommodate the incurably ill and remember them once they were gone.

In some ways, people in America fared better than their counterparts in Victorian England. Across the pond, death and dying were fraught with peculiarities not routinely encountered in the States. In the U.K., just because someone's earthly remains had been laid to rest didn't necessarily remove them for all time from the realm of the living. The shallow depth of many graves in rural Anglican Churchyards made them extremely unpleasant places to be in summertime. Heavy storms could wash away much of the surface dirt, leaving things exposed no one wanted to see. To the horror of early morning parishioners, stray animals might complete the disinterment process by digging up freshly laid body parts, especially arms and legs, which were easy to latch onto. All this graveyard gore became a powerful disincentive against regular attendance at services. The faithful often opted to stay at home and read from the Book of Common Prayer to avoid being subjected to the freshly exposed sights and stench.

Despite the Victorian penchant for memorial jewelry and imagery, acts of veneration and propitiation of lost loved ones were hardly a 19th-century phenomenon, as antecedents are known in the mortuary practices of much earlier societies. Traditions involving ancestor worship and ancestor cults are attested in belief systems as far back as the Neolithic Period, if not earlier. It was widely believed that, for better or worse, the dead maintained a certain level of influence over the living, and thus, it was in everyone's interests to remain on the best of terms—the wellbeing of the clan depended on it. Some cultures interred the dead inside their living space to keep them at least symbolically involved in everyday affairs. After death, the corpse would be exposed out of doors until the flesh had completely decomposed. Then, the skeleton was gathered up for ritual reburial inside the home.

Sometimes, acts of veneration for a lost family member were performed for a specified length of time, followed by the ritualistic transfer of that person's individuality into the collective other side. The Minoans of early Bronze Age Crete laid the recently deceased in a separate burial space for a while, followed by permanent re-internment with the bones of others. A series of burial chambers were carved out of soft limestone or other mountainous formations indigenous to the Cretan landscape. The entryway (*dromos*) contained stone benches and ledges for grave offerings, as well as open spaces for prayer and feasting. The body of the newly deceased was laid in a small chamber towards the tomb's entrance. After some time, the bones were collected and comingled with the remains of others in the larger chamber, which served as an ossuary for family, clan or community. The deceased would no longer be venerated as individuals but as honored members of the domain of the dead.

Another historical manifestation has been the fashioning of death masks in the deceased's likeness, which people kept on display inside their dwellings. The nobility of ancient Rome crafted masks in the likeness of their illustrious ancestors, which were periodically affixed to wooden effigies and paraded about on holidays to remind everyone of their proud lineage. Religious and societal obligations in other cultures include the actual retention of skulls and other body parts, both for veneration and ritualistic/apotropaic purposes. The skull might be fancied up through the application of painted plaster to mimic the appearance of living tissue. For added effect, artificial "eyes" were sometimes inserted into the empty sockets. Some Neolithic societies used small seashells for this purpose, which made for even freakier-looking ancestors in what was already an exceedingly bizarre tradition. Thankfully, most modern practices run contrary to these arcane customs. The deceased are fully and permanently interred in extramural spaces well separated from the domestic sphere.

One curious feature regarding Colonial burial grounds is how often they are found set back a ways from the modern thoroughfare, due to factors such as town growth and roadway expansion. Conditions inside these ancient graveyards can be less than ideal, as most tombstones have undergone significant weather-related damage, with some toppled over into the thick overgrowth endemic to these unfrequented and nearly forgotten spaces. The oldest plots contain sandstone markers for the earliest settlers and are dateable to the 17th and first half of the 18th century. More prevalent are Revolutionary War period slate and sandstone markers atop the remains of local militiamen, their families and descendants.

Brownstone markers were plentiful due to their low cost and ready availability from the Connecticut River Valley and other sources. Quarried stone would be transported to various towns to be sawn, shaped and engraved by local craftsmen servicing these local communities. Behind or adjacent to the Colonial Era graves are marble and granite markers from the Civil War and late Victorian Eras. These include larger and more elaborately embellished monuments, which

Simple, unadorned brownstone marker from a 17th-century burial ground in New England. The harsh puritanical restrictions of the age prohibited the engraving of anything fancier than skull and crossbones and winged death's heads on these early tombstones. This grave is in the historic Ancient Burying Ground in Hartford, Connecticut, the location of an estimated 6,000 men, women, and children interred between 1640 and the early 19th century. Only a portion of the original graveyard remains visible today. This particular stone was erected by the parents of a child who passed from some unknown affliction in 1648. This and a number of other stones were carved by a well-known area craftsman named George Griswold. (Wikipedia- CoolGuySlate-CC BY-SA 4.0)

signify the enhanced overall prosperity of the late 19th century. The inscriptions on slate stones tend to weather time and the elements better than on the fancier white marble tombstones and are usually intelligible after the passage of more than two centuries.

The burials of settlers from the first half of the 17th century were usually made with little attention to relative placement or aesthetics. Purposefully drawn cemeteries emerged later, with individual plots laid out for each family. However, continuous burials over the years often obliterated whatever markers or boundaries were originally in place. Yet despite the remoteness, deterioration and overgrowth of these old burial grounds, it is well worth the time and effort to clear away accretions, branches, moss and other impediments that inhibit access to the evocative inscriptions and imagery on these antique gravestones. In addition to the customary listing of name, family relationship, and dates of birth and death, they typically include a biblical allusion or short rhyme to help convey the acute sense of loss experienced by these people. Most sentiments are readily identifiable from the standard repertoire found in church graveyards since the late Middle Ages:

> Tread lightly on my mortal remains,
> O' passerby
> As I am now, so you must be
> Prepare for death and follow me

Or the following rhyme from an early 19th-century tombstone in Massachusetts:

> Think, friends, when you these lines have read
> How soon we're numbered with the dead
> Our years are few and quickly fly
> O' friends, remember you must die

By the second half of the 18th century, more varied and less severe imagery begins to replace the simple, austere engravings of the Puritan Era with a number of readily identifiable funerary motifs, including the willow and urn, hourglass, hearts, Christian crosses, and vestigial icons from ancestral Europe. Grim depictions of skulls and crossbones or winged death heads gradually softened into the wide-eyed, angelic cherubs that gaze back at you during their ascent to heaven.

The stark, sinister death heads so frequently encountered on 17th-century gravestones became an inspiration for later neo-Gothic imagery in artwork, literature, film and other media. Few things are as unsettling as depictions of the death and physical decay of human remains. The eeriness inherent to the "dark and stormy night" *genre* gives rise to the same types of responses these antique burial grounds elicited from visitors during past centuries. The impact they still make is surprising, as they transcend the years to evoke the same sensations experienced by others so long ago. We read a mother's heartbreaking farewell to her twins, lost after but a few brief months of life. A father's overpowering grief after losing his wife and four daughters to a contagion is known today from text books. Memorials we can safely ponder from a distance but of unimaginable

Two gravestones from a Colonial Era burial ground in southern New England. They help illustrate the transition from the austere imagery of the 17th and early 18th centuries to the softer depictions that began appearing around 1800. The stone at left dates to the mid-1700s and incorporates a traditional funerary motif at the top. It stands about midway between the simple death's head of Puritan times and the more lifelike cherubs of the early 19th century. The soul is depicted in its ascent to heaven, courtesy of two somewhat menacing, bat-like wings. The stone at right dates to about 1790, and includes a cherub adorned with more whimsically shaped wings. Both gravestones were carved by local artisans working from sketchbooks containing variations on similar designs. (author's photographs)

hurt to those forced to inter their dead before returning to some semblance of normal life.

Beginning in the early 18th century, one of the most frequently encountered mortuary images is a funerary urn beneath a willow tree, a motif that made the transition from memento mori jewelry to the graveyard in the early 19th century. Urns are an ancient funerary device, in use as burial receptacles since prehistoric times. The Urnfield Culture of the Bronze Age derives its name from this widespread practice in central Europe. The willow is a traditional symbol of mortality and bereavement and appears in the funerary art of early Christianity as an allusion to rebirth and reunion in the afterlife. The tree is usually depicted enveloping the urn as a further indication of mortality and grief. The appellation weeping willow originated from the somber association with tears streaming down the faces of the bereaved. Urns under the willows joined a plethora of other images after the transition from unadorned death's heads to more decorative funerary elements, such as cherubs, crosses, doves, clasped hands and hourglasses.

PART III : EVERYDAY LIFE IN THE VICTORIAN ERA

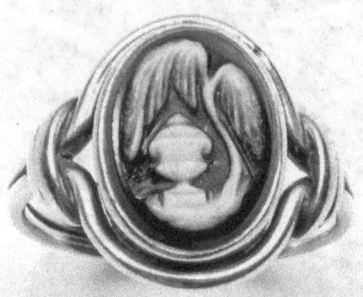

Elegant remembrance ring from the late Colonial Era, circa 1800. It features the urn and willow, one of several more decorative motifs that began replacing the morbid and austere imagery of earlier years, like death's head and skull with crossbones. Some memento mori rings include a recessed area on the band for a braided lock of the deceased's hair. Engraved on the underside of the bezel are typically the name or initials of the deceased and their date of departure. The insert on this exceptional piece is carved onyx and chalcedony within an 18k gold setting. The contrast between the ivory willow and urn and the stark black background is really striking. (courtesy Mourning Art)

Urn beneath a willow on the upper section of a gravestone in southern New England. The lower section (not shown) includes the deceased's name, date of death (1831), and relationship to others in the family plot. The urn and willow became a common funerary motif on Colonial and early Victorian gravestones around the same time as its popularity declined on memento mori jewelry. The other gravestones in this family plot date to approximately 1810 to 1870 and feature essentially this same imagery. (author's photo)

For most of the 18th and 19th centuries, the most common personal items related to death and remembrance were *memento mori* jewelry, comprised mostly of mourning lockets and finger rings. The wearing of these and other types of personal adornment became possible after the diminishment of 17th-century puritanical restrictions in the Thirteen Colonies. The term *memento mori* is a Latin expression for "remember your mortality" and is a reminder to the living that everyone must someday leave this life. When opened, the silver or gold locket revealed a small etching or photograph of the deceased on one side, with a brief memorial inscription on the other. Some examples contain a row of tiny pearls around the border to symbolize the tears of the wearer.

Finger rings were particularly favored by all levels of society and varied from simple, mass-produced copper alloy trinkets to elaborately crafted gold pieces set with precious gemstones. Lower-end varieties typically featured the skull and crossbones motif on the bezel to dispel any ambiguity as to meaning. Other common images were the willow and urn, Christian Cross, and cross with heart and anchor as symbols of faith, love and resurrection. The underside of the band is usually engraved with the name or initials of the deceased, along with their date of departure. Some rings contain a groove around the outer side of the band for a braided lock of the deceased's hair. Surviving lockets and rings are amongst the finest and most poignant examples of jewelry from the Georgian and Victorian Eras.

By far, the most striking manifestation of the Victorian preoccupation with death and remembrance is the genre of memorial portraiture or post-mortem photography. The invention of the Daguerreotype in 1839 created a near-instant demand for this type of imaging. People without the financial means to commission a memorial painting could usually afford a session with the local photographer. Studios recognized early on the lucrative potential of this bizarre new type of portraiture. Between the 1850s and early 20th century, post-mortem pictures were taken in their tens of thousands. Often, this was people's first exposure to photographic technology. And for some it was the only time the entire family would gather together for a group portrait. The first sepia-toned photographs from the 1840s were all daguerreotypes but were soon joined by ambrotype and tintype images. Most early pictures were taken in the family's home, and usually in the parlor with the body positioned *en repose* in their casket. The deceased would always be outfitted in their Sunday best, which was usually the outfit they'd soon be buried in. A judicious application of touch-up paint to the developed image brought out a healthier, more life-like hue to otherwise pallid and emaciated faces.

PART III : EVERYDAY LIFE IN THE VICTORIAN ERA

In instances when the photographer was unable to arrive soon after death, decomposition and rigor mortis inevitably set in, resulting in some rather unpleasant sessions. A mortician would need to apply thick layers of makeup over discolored or decomposed sections of the face and other exposed areas. This was also required whenever injury or a wasting disease resulted in visible levels of disfigurement. Within a few years, it became commonplace for the family to cart the corpse into the studio to have its picture taken. Regardless of the setting, the dead were now photographed in a variety of poses, including seated in a parlor chair, lying in bed, or positioned between loved ones on the sofa. Specially designed stands and braces helped keep the body in place during the long exposure times required in early photography. Sometimes, the living would move just slightly, resulting in a slightly blurred image. The dead, however, remained perfectly motionless and always came through with crystal clarity.

Certainly, the most rending examples of this genre are pictures of newly deceased newborns and young children. They are often posed in their parent's arms, as they would be in most family portraits. Other times, they're shown in their nightgowns while propped up on a chaise longue or upholstered chair. An arrangement of teddy bears, toys and flowers is seen around the body for added effect. Some images show the lifeless child lounging peaceably between their siblings on a sofa or love seat.[58] Before being photographed, the deceased's eyes were sometimes glued or stitched shut. Alternately, they might be left closed, but "eyes" would be painted on the eyelids to mimic the appearance of a child gazing out into the lens.

Imagine how grueling these sessions must have been for both family and photographer. Corpses have never been the most pleasant things to be around, regardless of the circumstances. People overcome with grief were expected to sit stoically while someone memorialized the recent loss of their loved one. Sometimes, family members are included in the picture, with their grim and forlorn expressions captured for posterity. Other times, the body was imaged by itself, with the others left mercifully on the sidelines. Alone to sit and contemplate their thoughts and feelings during a time of overwhelming tragedy and personal loss. Once the photograph was completed, the image was framed and delivered to the family for display on mantles, in parlors or sleeping chambers. The demand for these macabre pictures remained steady throughout the Victorian Era, as evidenced by the sheer volume of surviving examples.

---

58. Can you imagine a parent instructing a young child to sit quietly while some stranger takes their picture alongside a recently deceased brother or sister? Yet for over seventy years many Victorian and Edwardian moms and pops did precisely that as a matter of course. Conventions have certainly changed in the intervening years.

Death and Remembrance

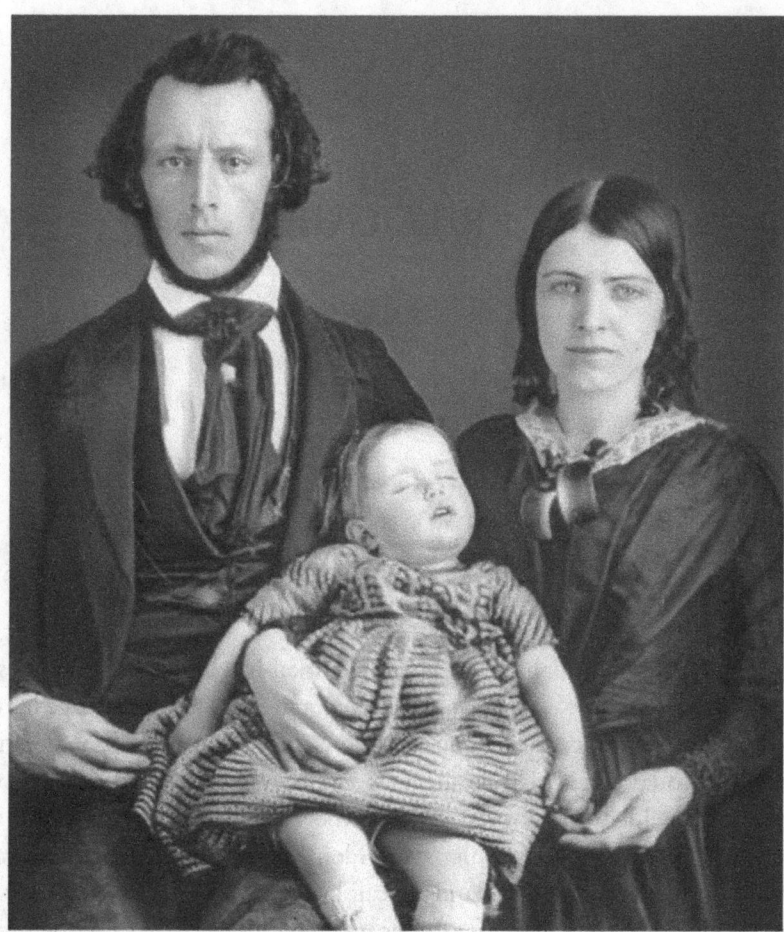

A daguerreotype from the 1850s shows a young couple with their deceased child. The youngster's reposed look makes it seem she merely nodded off for a nap. The invention of photography made it possible for people of limited means to commission portraits of those recently lost. Families unable to afford a memorial painting could usually gather sufficient funds for a session with a local photographer. By the mid-century, daguerreotypes, ambrotypes and tintypes had replaced painting and engraving as the medium of choice for memorial portraiture. Between 1850 and 1920 post mortem photographs were produced in the tens of thousands in North America and the UK. In many of these images, careful staging makes it appear the deceased are actively engaged in whatever imagery is being captured. Note the parent's appearance in their pre-war Sunday best: the father with unkempt hair and a giant bow tie, and the mother with her hair parted in the middle and a rather voluminous dress. Both seem to be holding up with a stoic grace. In some photographs, the parents are still visibly distraught over their recent loss. (Public Domain)

EPILOGUE

*One generation passeth away, and another generation cometh:
but the earth abideth forever.*

—Ecclesiastes 1:4

HUMAN nature has remained remarkably consistent, regardless of when or where we appeared. The generations that came of age in times past experienced the same sensations and dreamt the same dreams as the people of today. Their daily routines were often markedly different, as were the societies in which they moved about and eventually passed away. But their physical and psychological profiles were identical to our own, and the land beneath their feet was the same land we call home. The world of yesterday may not be visible, but it is never far off because everything that came before has been subsumed into the present. Only in liminal moments are we aware of this continuity, a realization perhaps brought about through genetic links, ancestral memory, or the collective unconscious. Everyone today is a reflection of past lives, and our recognition of these innate connections provides much meaning and context to the present.

It is said nothing in life lasts forever, and this transience makes it imperative we focus our attention on the eternal present before this temporary state of being dissolved into nothingness. Humanity is but a chimera in a much larger process that has gradually unfolded throughout incalculable eons. Even our world is but one of countless others in a virtually limitless and indefinable universe. But despite this relative insignificance, it is still seemingly mundane activities from day to day that really matter to humankind as a whole. Whatever lies beyond the mortal realm simply is and has never been contingent upon individual belief or understanding. Creation is perfectly capable of taking care of itself.

History reveals successive generations in search of answers to the same unresolved questions about life and meaning. Nor are such inquiries necessarily peculiar to our species. Chances are, in worlds billions of light-years distant, other sentient beings are seeking answers to these same fundamental questions. And perhaps all will come to the realization what really matters is not mere speculation upon what may or may not be but rather our real world thoughts and activities in the here and now. Contemplating the unknowable is of value when the knowledge gained translates into improvements in the human condition. The measure of success is the impact we make upon others and the world we leave behind. Theoretical knowledge is virtually meaningless if not transformed into purposeful action. Wisdom consists of insights shared.

Any study of the past is a hearkening to some indeterminable point of contact with things now lost—a yearning for something that was but is apparently no more. Exploration results in the accrual of disassociated bits of information regarding people, places and events that, in their totality, remain outside our grasp. This is because insights are relative, like the proverbial blind man describing an elephant. One touches the side and declares it like a wall. Another touches the trunk and declares it like a snake. A third grabs the tail and declares it like a rope. These assessments are accurate based on individual perception and experience. But the elephant is none of these things. The three wise men remain eternally insensible to the animal's true nature. Our need to know should be tempered by the realization that, as a species, maybe we were never designed to see the elephant. Thus, our understanding of life and things past remains wholly subjective and liable to much uncertainty and change. But our need to know are cultural and biological imperatives.

Our timeless inquiries into the vagaries of existence lead only to contradictions and more questions, for which there are few credible answers. Swiss psychiatrist C.G. Jung—founder of analytical psychology and an early associate of Sigmund Freud—believed there resides within the human psyche a genuine religious function compelling the individual to seek meaning and validation in life. Are we simply the random result of happenstance, or might there be some grand purpose or design about which we remain insensible? We know that everything seen and unseen was structured upon things that came before. Even the earth was born of stardust, and to the earth, we must someday return. But if energy can neither be created nor destroyed, then our essence must assuredly return to the wellspring from whence it sprang, wherever and whatever that source may be.

> From nowhere we come, into nowhere we go. What is life? It is the flash of a firefly in the night. It is the breath of a buffalo in the wintertime. It is the little shadow which runs across the grass and loses itself in the sunset. Crowfoot (1830—1890), Blackfoot Nation

Humankind seeks knowledge and inspiration through ritual, prayer, meditation and other reflective endeavors. The nature of our spiritual beliefs has, of course, varied greatly over time. But their empirical value has always been their ability to cross the threshold from the physical to the metaphysical and thus facilitate passage through life's uncertainties. But that which lies beyond is, by definition, unknowable. In our quest for certainties, we seek to determine whether the thoughts and images drifting continually in and out of our subconscious are mere illusions or genuine insights into something more substantive. Certainty on these matters seems impossible because everything is sensed but dimly, like shadows through the fog. They arise as intuition, vague sensations and impressions but inspire new artwork, ideas and cathedrals. In turn, our thoughts and activities enhance the foundation for generations yet unborn.

The laws of creation and causality operate in mysterious but purposeful ways and extend to even the smallest and most mundane matters. Seemingly minor decisions have consequences in a rippling or butterfly effect. If your fourth-great-grandfather had chosen a right turn at the fork instead of a left, he would never have met the woman who became your fourth-great-grandmother. An apparently random, meaningless, split-second decision would have altered the course of history by negating your future existence. Whatever meaning or purpose lies behind universal causality seems beyond our comprehension. But the interconnectedness of things is made manifest through apparently unrelated but meaningful coincidences.

Case in point: while at home on leave in 1863, a soldier stopped by a neighborhood store to purchase some tobacco. In payment, he used several coins, including a newly minted Indian Head penny. The merchant later gave the coin in change to another customer, who brought it home to her daughter as allowance. Later that year, the soldier died at Gettysburg. The little girl subsequently dropped and lost the coin between the floorboards in her bedroom. Four generations of the family lived and died in the house. In 2011, the family's young daughter chanced upon a reflection between the floorboards. Finagling the prize out of its hiding place, she ran downstairs and showed it to her mother. It was the same Indian Head penny lost in that bedroom a century and a half earlier. And, unbeknownst to anyone, it had belonged to the only soldier in town to die at Gettysburg: the great-great-great-great-grandfather of the little girl who found it between the floorboards. The item had been returned to the family. One of life's unperceived circles was now complete.

If physical and mental traits are passed down through generations, might there also be, at some unseen level, a retention and transmission of individual thoughts and experiences? A record of the minutiae of everyday life that naturally evanesces as things pass from living memory? Even within the familiar three-dimensional realms, there exist curvatures in space-time, which lead to breakdowns in the laws of Euclidean geometry. The standard rules no longer apply, and the shortest distance between two points is not always a straight line. And creation is a cyclical, rather than a linear, process. With our but nebulous understanding of space, time and causality, the architecture of more distant realms seems beyond conjecture. But one intriguing possibility exists: that the separation between us and all that came before has never been delineated by the simple measurement of time.

> To sleep, perchance to Dream; aye, there's the rub,
> For in that sleep of death, what dreams may come,
> When we have shuffled off this mortal coil,
> Must give us pause.
>
> —Hamlet III.1

BIBLIOGRAPHY

Beckwith's Almanac, Volumes 10–19, (Charleston: Nabu Press, 2011).
———, Volumes 33–41, (Charleston: Nabu Press, 2012).
———, Volumes 42–48, (Charleston: Nabu Press, 2011).
Beckwith—Ewell, M .L. *One True Heart - Leaves from the Life of George Beckwith* (New Haven: Henry H. Peck, 1880).
Bell, Michael M. "Did New England Go Downhill?" American Geographical Society: Geographical Review, Vol. 79, No. 4, 1989.
Bettman, Otto L. *The Good Old Days- They Were Terrible!* (New York: Random House, 1974).
"Blue Book of the Wireless Association of America" (New York: Modern Electrics Publications, 1909).
Burroughs, John. *Signs and Seasons* (Originally published in 1886) (New York: Syracuse University Press, 2006).
Cross, Lucy H. *History of Northfield New Hampshire, 1780-1905* (Concord: Rumford Printing Co, 1905).
Dickens, Charles. *American Notes for General Circulation* (Originally published in 1842) Project Gutenberg. (Public Domain).
Engels, Friedrich. *The Conditions of the Working Class in England* (Originally published in 1845) (New York: Oxford University Press, 1993).
First Annual Report of the Board of Health of the City of Manchester for the Year 1885 (Manchester: John B. Clarke, Printer, 1886).
Gordon, Linda. *The Second Coming of the KKK* (New York: Liveright Publishing Corp., 2017).
Haddock, John A. *The Growth of a Century: as illustrated in the history of Jefferson County, New York, from 1793 to 1894* (Albany: Weed-Parsons Printing Company, 1895).
———. *A Souvenir, the Thousand Islands of the St. Lawrence River* (Albany: Weed-Parsons Printing Company, 1895).
Huttenhauer, Helen G. *Young Southern Pines* (Southern Pines: Morgan/Hubbard. 1980).
Kittredge, George Lyman. *The Old Farmer and His Almanack* (Cambridge: Harvard University Press, 1920).
Lyman, Henry H. *Memories of the Old Homestead* (Oswego: R.J. Oliphant, 1900).
McDowell, Letember, et al. "Soil Survey of Jefferson County, New York" (United States Dept. of Agriculture, Cornell University Agricultural Experiment Station, 1981).

Miles, Emma Bell. *The Spirit of the Mountains* (New York: James Pott & Co., 1905).
Molloy, Barry. *Martial Minoans: War as a social process, practice and event in Bronze Age Crete* The Annual of the British School at Athens, 107, pp 87–142 doi:10.1017/S006824541200.
Moore, Donald O. *The Huddle—The Way It Was* (Watertown: Benjamin Printing, 2004).
Morley, Henry. *Memoirs of Bartholomew Fair* (London: Chatto and Windus, 1880).
Quick, Debbie. *History of the Town of Adams* Historical Association of South Jefferson (Watertown: Benjamin Printing, 2004).
———. *History of the Town of Lorraine* Historical Association of South Jefferson (Watertown: Benjamin Printing, 2004).
Randall, B., Stone, C. & Evans, D. *Around Tilton* (Charleston: Arcadia Publishing, 2012).
Riis, Jacob. *How the Other Half Lives: Studies Among the Tenements of New York* (Originally published in 1890) (New York: Penguin Random House, 1997).
Sloane, Eric. *American Barns and Covered Bridges* (New York: Dover Publications, 2002).
———. *American Yesterday* (New York: Dover Publications, 2003).
———. *Diary of an Early American Boy* (New York: Dover Publications, 2004).
———. *I Remember America* (New York: Ballantine Books, 1977).
———. *Our Vanishing Landscape* (New York: Dover Publications, 1955).
———. *The Seasons of America Past* (New York: Dover Publications, 2003).
———. *Weather Almanac* (Stillwater, MN, Voyageur Press, 2005).
Teggart, Frederick J., Ed. *Diary of Nelson Kingsley: A California Argonaut of 1849* (Berkeley: University of California Press, 1914).
Ten Cate, Adrian G., et al. *Pictorial History of the Thousand Islands* (New York: Corbin's River Heritage, 2001).
Thompson, John and Smith, Adolphe. *Victorian London Street Life in Historic Photographs* (Originally published in 1877 as *Street Life in London*) (New York: Dover Publications, 1994).
Vincent, John H. *The Chautauqua Movement* (Boston: Chautauqua Press, 1886).

ABOUT THE AUTHOR

T.N POLLIO is an historian residing along the shoreline in southern New England. Incorrigible antiquarian with insatiable interest in anything old, artsy and/or reflective of the human condition in centuries past. Strong exponent of theorem the goal of good journalism is enlightenment. Frequently spotted on soapbox pontificating how 90% of bona fide human history is rarely accounted for—let alone accurately portrayed—in most modern historical narratives. Author of two books on ancient and medieval jewelry that WorldCat lists in almost 900 academic libraries spread out over five continents. Also author of numerous articles, essays and satires on artwork, antiquities and other history related topics. Conscripted by the misguided as infallible authority [sic] on ancient and antique jewelry, and particularly finger rings. Member of the Archaeological Institute of America and administrator/moderator/contributor to sundry online history, antiquities and artwork forums. Notable life events include being stranded atop the White Mountains of New Hampshire while pushing girlfriend's dead Volvo several miles down the summit of the Kancamagus Highway. This third book (and first from Sunbury) is a lighthearted look at the lives and times of ordinary Americans between the late Colonial Period and onset of the Jazz Age around 1920.

www.ingramcontent.com/pod-product-compliance
Lightning Source LLC
Chambersburg PA
CBHW011949150426
43194CB00019B/2854